are to be returned on or before
the last date below.

KT-418-465

Children's Care,
Learning and Development

Kath Bulman

Liz Savory

Endorsed by Edexcel

www.heinemann.co.uk
✓ Free online support
✓ Useful weblinks
✓ 24 hour online ordering

01865 888058

049420

THE HENLEY COLLEGE LIBRARY

Heinemann
Inspiring generations

Heinemann Educational Publishers
Halley Court, Jordan Hill, Oxford OX2 8EJ
Part of Harcourt Education

Heinemann is the registered trademark of
Harcourt Education Limited

© Kath Townsley & Liz Savory, 2006

First published 2006

10 09 08 07 06
10 9 8 7 6 5 4 3 2 1

British Library Cataloguing in Publication Data is available
from the British Library on request.

10-digit ISBN: 0 435 499 06 8
13-digit ISBN: 978 0 435499 06 8

Copyright notice
All rights reserved. No part of this publication may be reproduced in
any form or by any means (including photocopying or storing it in
any medium by electronic means and whether or not transiently or
incidentally to some other use of this publication) without the written
permission of the copyright owner, except in accordance with the
provisions of the Copyright, Designs and Patents Act 1988 or under
the terms of a licence issued by the Copyright Licensing Agency,
90 Tottenham Court Road, London W1T 4LP. Applications for the
copyright owner's written permission should be addressed to the
publisher.

Every effort has been made to contact copyright holders of material
reproduced in this book. Any omissions will be rectified in subsequent
printings if notice is given to the publishers.

Designed by Wooden Ark Studio, Leeds
Typeset and illustrated by 🡒 Tek-Art, Surrey
Printed in the UK at CPI Bath
Original illustrations © Harcourt Education Limited, 2006
Cover photo: © Harcourt Education Ltd/Tudor Photography
Cover design by Wooden Ark Studio, Leeds
Picture research by Natalie Gray & Chrissie Martin

Websites
Please note that the examples of websites suggested in this book were
up to date at the time of writing. It is essential for tutors to preview
each site before using it to ensure that the URL is still accurate and the
content is appropriate. We suggest that tutors bookmark useful sites
and consider enabling students to access them through the school or
college intranet.

Contents

A sample *Work Experience Journal* which supports unit 5 can be downloaded from Heinemann's website: www.heinemann.co.uk/vocational

Acknowledgements

Kath would like to thank her children Joanne and Andrew, and her nieces and nephews for the many examples they have provided. Thanks to Ian for the patience and encouragement to write the book – and the endless cups of tea and glasses of wine!

The publishers would like to thank the following for their kind permission to reproduce photographs in this book.

photos.com – page 1, 245
Harcourt Education Ltd/Jules Selmes – pages 5, 6, 7, 12, 16, 31, 44, 78, 91, 92, 93,
101, 129, 137, 142, 144, 163, 197, 208, 209, 210, 211, 252, 254, 256, 266,
297, 305, 315, 324
Harcourt Education Ltd/Tudor Photography – pages 8, 105, 168, 170, 247, 274, 276
Getty Images/Photodisc – pages 49, 175, 205, 235
Dorling Kindersley – page 94
Harcourt Education Ltd/Gareth Boden – page 108
Digital Vision – page 201
Alamy Images – page 218
Corbis – pages 288, 314
Getty Images – page 308

About your course and assessment

Welcome to your BTEC First in Children's Care, Learning and Development. This book is written to support learners who are studying for the Edexcel Level 2 BTEC First Certificate and Edexcel Level 2 BTEC First Diploma in Children's Care, Learning and Development. This book can be used as a resource for any child care course of a similar level. For example, the knowledge requirements of the course are very similar to the underpinning knowledge required for successful completion of the NVQ Level 2 qualification in Children's Care, Learning and Development.

Your BTEC First Certificate or Diploma course in Children's Care, Learning and Development (CCLD) requires you to complete a number of course units, both compulsory and optional. The core units are compulsory and the specialist units are optional.

For the Certificate you must complete: Unit 1 Understanding Children's development; Unit 2 Keeping children safe; and Unit 3 Communication with Children and adults. These are the core, compulsory units. You will also need to undertake some work placements to help you with these units.

For the Diploma you must complete the three core units above plus: Unit 4 Preparing and maintaining environments for child care and Unit 5 Professional development, roles and responsibilities. These are all compulsory core units for the Diploma.

Additionally, you must complete one of the specialist or optional units: Unit 6 Supporting Children's Play and Learning; Unit 7 The Development and Care of Babies and Children Under Three Years; or Unit 8 Providing Support for a Child with Disabilities or Special Educational Needs.

Work placement is an important part of the Diploma and links with Unit 5 and the Work Experience Journal in this book.

How to use this book

You will find several activities after each section in all the units.

These activities are for you to undertake with guidance and help from your teacher or tutor. If you undertake all of the activities that cover the Pass criteria you will produce the evidence to enable you to pass your course.

The activities follow each section in the book. The sections relate to the outcomes that you have to achieve and they give you all the information you need in order to carry out the activities. You must be sure to cover all the information in each section for each activity. If you do not cover all the information needed you will not have fully met that criterion.

The activities are linked to the Pass criteria and they tell you not only what you have to do but also what the criteria are. You must be careful to describe or outline or demonstrate according to the wording of the particular criterion you are working on.

In the first year of your course you may only want to work on getting a Pass and thus meeting just the Pass criteria, but there are also activities related to the Pass criteria that enable you to meet the Merit and Distinction criteria. You can work on these higher level criteria as you undertake the activities or you can go back to them at a later time when

Diagrams and tables

Ideas and information are presented in diagrams in order to make them accessible and easy to use in class activities.

Think about it

Key issues for individual reflection.

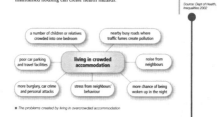

Did you know?

Introduce topical notes and points of interest.

you feel more confident and have more experience of working with children and have more overall knowledge.

Whatever you decide to do it is important to remember that you must cover all of the Pass criteria in all the units you undertake in order to get a Pass. You cannot leave out any Pass criteria and Merit or Distinction criteria will not replace them.

Getting a Pass on your course

In order to Pass your course you must meet all the Pass criteria for the core units of either the Certificate or the Diploma, the Pass criteria for the specialist unit on the Diploma and successfully undertake your work placement, which is covered by Unit 5 and the Work Experience Journal in this book.

Case studies
Links theory with actual practice to help you develop your skills in context.

Assessment Activity
Helps you develop the skills you need to achieve Pass, Merit and Distinction.

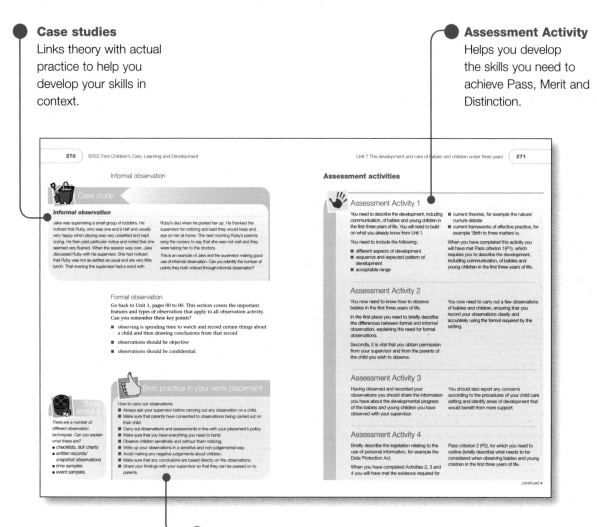

Best practice in your workplace
Indicates techniques and skills you will need in everyday childcare work.

In order to get a Pass you have to meet all the Pass criteria for these units. Usually there are six Pass criteria that you must cover.

The Pass criteria will require you to describe or outline certain things, such as outline basic hygiene principles in a child care setting in Unit 2 (Keeping children safe) and also to demonstrate certain skills such as interacting and communicating with children and adults in Unit 3 (Communicating with children and adults).

When you describe or outline something you will need to write it down. You can either write it on paper or use a computer.

Whichever it is you must produce your own work. This is your evidence for your teacher or tutor and for the External Verifier appointed by Edexcel. He or she will look at your work as well, in order to ensure that you have the evidence required for each of the Pass criteria in all the units you undertake on your course.

When you have to demonstrate something such as communication skills you will need to have a Witness statement or report from your tutor or placement supervisor as evidence that you have demonstrated these skills. Your tutor or placement supervisor will have to watch and listen to you in order to be able to say that you have demonstrated these skills.

Getting a Merit

If you want to try and get a Merit for a unit you must meet all the Pass criteria and also all of the Merit criteria for the unit.

The Merit criteria are linked to the Pass criteria and usually require you to show greater understanding and knowledge than simply describing or outlining something. You will often be asked to explain something you have described for the Pass criterion.

For example, Unit 2 (Keeping children safe) requires you to outline basic hygiene principles in a child care setting in order to meet the Pass criterion.

This is developed at Merit level where you are asked to explain the importance of ensuring that hygiene principles are carried out in a child care setting.

When you explain something you must describe in detail and write why, how and when. This means that you must show more knowledge and understanding than when you just describe or outline.

Usually there are four Merit criteria in a unit. These are always linked to one or more Pass criteria, but Pass criteria are not always developed at Merit level.

The activities in the book develop the Pass criteria activities to enable you to meet the Merit criteria. They will tell you that if you go on to do something else you will be able to meet a Merit criterion.

For instance in the first section of Unit 1, Assessment activity 4 is developed at Merit level in Assessment activity 5.

Assessment activities

Assessment Activity 4

List all the factors that affect children's growth and development.

This will be quite a long list and should include: health, genetic inheritance, gender, family background and structure, social class, cultural background, finances, poverty, environment and housing, disability, discrimination and the agencies such as health services that work for and with children and young people.

Also you need to include maturation, and how this is affected by experience and expectations.

You then need to write a few sentences about each of these factors.

When you have done this you will have met the third Pass criterion for the unit (P3)

Assessment Activity 5

Building on the work you have done for P3 you can now explain how parental income, health status and parental expectations might affect children's growth and development.

Remember that when you explain something you have to do more than just describe. You have to say how and why these factors might affect children.

When you have explained the effects of these factors you will have met the second Merit criterion (M2).

You must undertake all of the activities that relate to the Merit criteria (as well as the Pass criteria) in each unit in order to gain a Merit.

All the time you must remember that your work must be your own work.

You must not copy out of books or from the internet. This is cheating, because it is not your own work. You may, however, quote from the internet or from a book, but you must make it clear where you are getting this information from. Your teacher or tutor will explain how you should do this. It is called referencing.

Getting a Distinction

In order to get a Distinction for a unit you must meet all the Pass criteria and all the Merit criteria as well as the Distinction criteria for that unit.

As with the Merit criteria, the activities following each section in the book will give activities not only to enable you to meet the Pass and Merit criteria but also the Distinction criteria.

The activities for the Distinction criteria build on the Pass and Merit criteria and involve you in more complex activities such as evaluating or justifying. If you evaluate you must write how good something is and what the weak points are. You are weighing up its worth. For example: Evaluate the ways that policies and procedures with respect to accidents, emergencies and children's illnesses ensure the safety of children.

If you have to justify something such as 'justify the lay-out, organisation, equipment and materials in a child care setting known to you' you will have to give the reasons for or behind all of these.

Usually there are only 2 Distinction criteria for each unit and thus only two activities in each unit in the book refer to the Distinction criteria.

Your work

As already explained, your work must be your own work.

It is important that you keep it safely whether on paper or on the computer.

If you lose your work you will have no evidence that you have met the Pass, Merit and Distinction criteria in your units.

However, if you work steadily through all the assessment activities and keep your work safe you will have covered all the Pass criteria enabling you to gain your qualification. Hopefully, you will be able to get a Merit or even a Distinction for at least some of your units.

1 Understanding children's development

Introduction

To look after and work with children it is important that you understand their development. It is impossible to think about how you can meet a child's needs unless you know what to expect from him or her in terms of thinking, communication, and physical abilities for example. You will explore the principles of development and the five key stages from birth to age 16 years before looking at how physical, social and emotional, communication and intellectual skills are developed.

In this unit you will:

1 understand the growth and development of children
2 understand the role of observation of children's development in the workplace
3 learn how to observe children's development
4 understand the required planning to support children's needs and development.

1.1 Understand the growth and development of children

This section covers:

- principles of development
- stages and sequences of development
- physical development
- emotional development
- social development
- communication and speech development
- intellectual development
- maturation
- factors affecting growth and development

Growth and development

What do we mean by growth and development? **Growth** is the increase in size of the body – in height, weight and other measurable areas. **Development** is the gaining of skills in all aspects of the child's life. The different types of development are often split into four areas:

Physical development: this refers to the body increasing in skill and performance and includes:

- **gross motor development** (using large muscles), for example legs and arms
- **fine motor development** (precise use of muscles), for example hands and fingers.

Social and emotional development: this is the development of a child's identity and self-image, the development of relationships and feelings about him or herself and learning the skills to live in society with other people.

Intellectual development: this is learning the skills of understanding, memory and concentration.

Communication and speech development: this is learning to communicate with friends, family and all others.

However, it is important to realise that all the areas of development link together. Just stop and think about the changes that take place in the developing child.

At birth there have already been huge changes from two tiny cells as the egg and sperm joined at conception to a complex new baby at birth. Then from being a tiny helpless being at birth, by the age of 16 years the child changes to a highly complex young person who has all the basic skills for life, including talking, running, writing and the ability to think in abstract ways.

- Weight increases from 3–4 kg at birth to an average of 65 kg for a young man.

- From a length at birth of about 35 cm, height changes to more than 155 cm.

- From being a relatively immobile baby, the child is able to walk, run, skip and climb.

- From not being able to talk, the child becomes an able communicator.

- From being fully dependent, the child learns to dress, feed and think for him or herself.

- From wide arm movements and automatically grasping everything that is put into the hand, the child learns to pick up and use a pencil developing to pens, computers and other technical equipment.

Growth and development are connected, but are very different. Growth is the very visible increase in size of a child. It can be seen in many ways, including weight gain, increase in height and increase in head circumference. Children grow very quickly; ask your parents if they have kept a record of your weight and height gain.

Principles of development

There are three basic principles of human development that apply to everyone from birth.

1   **Development starts from the head and works down the body.**
    A new baby cannot hold up his or her head alone. Yet, within a few months, the baby will be able to sit alone. This is because control of the spine and central nervous system develops from the top of the head down to the base of the spine. You can see this control developing in a baby as he or she starts to hold the head without support. Similarly, a new-born baby waves his or her arms around vaguely, yet in nine months' time will find the tiniest crumb or piece of Lego easy to pick up with the thumb and finger. This is because the nervous system also develops from the spinal cord out to the extremities (hands and feet).

2   **All development happens in the same order, but can occur at different rates.**
    A baby has to hold his or her head up, learn to sit with support, and then without support, before he or she can stand by holding on to

furniture and then eventually walk alone. No baby can learn to walk before sitting up. But it is perfectly normal for one baby to walk at ten months and another not to learn this skill until the age of 18 months.

3 **All areas of development are linked together.**
A baby cannot start to finger feed until he or she can sit up and is developing the ability to pick things up between the fingers and thumb. The speech development of a child is affected if the child has difficulties in hearing clearly or if no one talks directly to him or her. A child who does not receive love and attention may fail to grow and develop.

Finally, remember that to develop to their best potential, children need huge amounts of support and guidance from others in their lives. Failure to meet all of the needs of a baby or child can have serious consequences on his or her development.

Milestones

Child development experts have carried out a lot of research on young children to work out what most children can do at different ages and the rate at which they grow. From this research, milestones of development have been identified. A 'milestone of development' refers to the age at which most children should have reached a certain stage of development, for example, walking alone by 18 months, or smiling at six weeks.

Many children will have reached that stage of development much earlier, but what matters is whether a child has reached it by the milestone age. You will also read about average ages for developmental stages, and these will be different. An average age is in the middle of the range of ages when all children reach a certain stage, for example, for walking the range can be from 10 months to 18 months which makes the 'average' age for walking 14 months. The important thing to remember is that all children develop at different rates and may be earlier in achieving some aspects of development and later in others.

Percentiles

Percentile charts are used to compare a child's growth and weight measurements with those of other children in the same age group. This makes it possible to track a child's growth over time and monitor how a child is growing in relation to other children. The charts can be used to recognise if there are problems with a child's height or weight, especially if the expected rate of growth is not happening. Plotting a child's growth in this way is a standard part of any visit to a clinic or developmental check-up where a baby or child is weighed and measured.

There are different charts for boys and girls because their growth rates and patterns differ and different ones again for babies who are born prematurely. The charts show the normal range of heights and weights at a certain age of thousands of children from across the country.

Did you know?

At six weeks most babies will smile socially, not because they have wind or are practising using muscles, but because they have been talked to and smiled at by parents and other carers. Sadly, not all babies have loving carers, and for all sorts of reasons may not be smiled at and talked to. These babies may not smile at six weeks. A baby who has experienced lots of talking and communication may smile much earlier than six weeks, and will vocalise with the carer.

Think about it

Ask your parents if they still have the book that your weight was marked in when you were a baby to see where you were on the percentile charts. Or ask someone, perhaps a cousin, who has a young child now if you can look at their weight records.

Stages and sequences of development

We think about growth and development in five stages:

- infancy from birth to one year
- early years from one to three years
- childhood from four to seven years
- **puberty** from 8–12 years
- **adolescence** from 13–16 years.

Birth to one year

New-born babies can:

- see faces as fuzzy shapes
- grasp an object that has touched the palm of their hand
- turn their head to look for a nipple or teat if their cheek is touched
- suck and swallow
- try to make stepping movements if they are held upright with their feet on a firm surface
- startle in response to a sudden sound or bright light
- stretch their arms suddenly and then bring them in if they feel they are falling
- recognise their mother's voice and smell
- cry when they are hungry, in pain, need feeding, changing or just cuddling.

■ *When she is born a baby can try to make stepping movements if she is held upright with her feet on a firm surface*

One to three years

By their first birthday, babies can:

- move around, either by crawling or shuffling or some may be standing with support and a small number walking alone

- sit up alone and feed themselves, at least with their fingers

■ *By his first birthday a baby can move around by crawling or shuffling*

- use their hands skilfully to move and arrange objects including dropping things on the floor and looking to see where they are

- wave 'bye bye' and point at things with their fingers

- communicate by babbling and saying two syllable words like 'dada'

- understand the world around them

- know who their main carers are and cry if they are left with someone they do not know.

Third birthday

By their third birthday, children can:

- run, climb and pedal a tricycle

- walk upstairs on alternate feet and walk on tiptoe

- use the toilet alone

- talk clearly so anyone can understand them

- tell the difference between boys and girls

- sometimes play co-operatively with other children

- build a tower of nine bricks and build a bridge with bricks

■ *By his third birthday a child can pedal a tricycle*

- undo buttons and thread beads

- enjoy playing with role play toys and dressing up

- enjoy books

- enjoy painting and may do 'pretend' writing

- have fewer temper tantrums (that started when she was about 18 months)

- enjoy copying and helping adults.

Seventh birthday

By their seventh birthday, children can:

- throw, kick and control a ball, hop and ride a bicycle
- use their hands to thread, use scissors well, build models and write clearly
- draw with meaning and detail
- take turns and play co-operatively with friends
- tell jokes and enjoy conversations
- start to understand rules
- be frightened of fictitious things like ghosts
- read and enjoy books
- dress themselves easily
- have a best friend
- worry about not being liked.

■ By her seventh birthday a child can control a ball

Twelfth birthday

By their twelfth birthday, children can:

- solve problems
- enjoy responsibility
- have a keen interest in hobbies
- use good co-ordination skills
- tell you what they are good at
- start to see physical changes in their body
- start to argue with their parents
- seem very grown up but also very childish at times.

■ By his twelfth birthday a child can have a keen interest in hobbies

Sixteenth birthday

By their sixteenth birthday a young adult can:

- have an adult body
- have high level of skills in some areas, for example drawing or computing
- enjoy their friends' company more than that of their family
- develop their own identity, tastes in music, clothes
- have mood swings
- feel very anxious at times

- be very confident with friends
- leave school and get married.

■ *By her sixteenth birthday a child can feel very anxious at times*

Physical development

Physical development covers the aspects of development that we can see happening. For example, relatives often comment on how much a child has grown. They are commenting on how a child has grown in terms of size, height and weight. With growth, there is also a dramatic change in body proportions. Look at the size of a new-born baby's head in proportion to the rest of the body. Compare this with a child of seven or eight years.

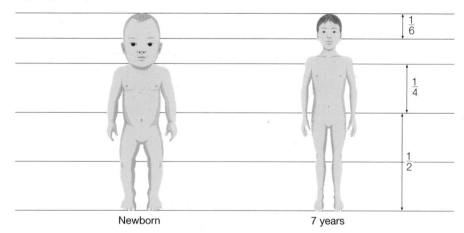

Newborn   7 years

■ *Comparison of the head in proportion to the rest of the body of a baby and a child of seven years*

Physical development also covers the important skills of using our bodies; the use of large muscles to walk, run, climb, jump and skip and the use of our smaller muscles, for example for hand co-ordination. Look at the following table to compare the gross and fine motor skills at different stages of development.

Age	Physical development (gross and fine motor)
Birth to 4 weeks	Lies on back with head to one side Head lags when pulled up to sit Primitive reflexes, i.e. rooting, sucking, stepping, grasping
1 month	Head control still unsteady Hands in tight fists Grasps objects when they touch the palm of the hand Head and eyes move together
3 months	Kicks legs and waves arms Can lift head and turn when on front Watches movements of own hands, plays with own hands Holds rattle for a few seconds if placed in hand
4 months	Uses arms for support when lying on stomach Turns from back to side Holds on to and shakes small items
6 months	Sits with support Rolls over Pushes head, neck and chest off floor with arms when on front Uses whole hand in palmar grasp, passes toy from one hand to another
9 months	Sits alone without support Reaches out for toys when sitting May crawl or shuffle Pokes at small item with index finger Uses index and middle fingers with thumb in pincer grip to pick up small items Will take and hold a small brick in each hand Lifts block but can only release by dropping
1 year	Stands alone and starts to walk holding on ('cruising') Mobile through crawling or shuffling Enjoys self-feeding and holds cup with help Picks up anything tiny from the floor using neat pincer grip Starting to show hand preference Clicks two cubes together Puts cubes in box when shown
18 months	Can walk alone Pushes and pulls toys when walking Can walk downstairs with hand held Tries to kick a ball, rolls and throws ball Squats to pick up objects from the floor Assists with dressing and undressing Can use a spoon Uses a delicate pincer grasp for tiny objects Holds a crayon in primitive tripod grasp and scribbles Turns handles Pulls off shoes

continued ▶

Age	Physical development (gross and fine motor)
2 years	Walks up and down stairs with both feet on one step. Climbs on furniture Builds a tower of six bricks Uses a spoon for self-feeding Puts shoes on Draws circles and dots Starts to use preferred hand
3 years	Stands and walks on tiptoe Can kick a ball confidently Jumps from low steps Pedals a tricycle Turns single pages in a book Can draw a face Builds bridges with blocks when shown Undoes buttons Threads large beads
4 years	Can aim and throw and catch a large ball Walks backwards and on a line Runs and hops Builds a large tower Can brush own teeth Cuts round an object with scissors and copies a square Buttons and unbuttons clothes Can do a 12-piece jigsaw
5 years	Skips Runs quickly Easily dresses and undresses Hits a ball with a bat Draws a person with a head, body and legs, and a house Can do a 20-piece jigsaw Forms letters and writes own name Accurately uses scissors
6–7 years	Enjoys hopping, bike riding, roller blading and skating Balances on a wall or beam Has finer manipulation of building bricks, jigsaws, etc Can sew simple stitches Ties and unties laces Builds intricate models Controls pencil in a small area and does detailed drawing
8–12 years	Improves physical skills that have already developed Puberty starts around 10 for girls with a growth spurt and increase in body strength
13–16 years	Brains developing with increase in reaction times and co-ordination For girls puberty is complete at about 14 and periods start For boys puberty is 13–16 and they will be stronger than girls

■ *Stages of physical development*

Social and emotional development

Learning to live with others in both our family and society generally is one of the most important parts of development – and one in which family and friends play an important part.

Socialisation is all about learning to cope in the family and society we live in. The socialisation process will by its definition vary in different societies and from family to family.

- Primary socialisation is the socialisation that takes place within the family, in the first years of a child's life. This helps children to learn how to interact with others, what is acceptable and what is not.

- Secondary socialisation starts when children come into regular contact with people and settings outside their home. This includes playgroup, nursery and school, and continues throughout life.

Secondary socialisation teaches children:

- how to interact with adults who are not family

- how to interact with friends and others

- the 'rules' of society, what is acceptable and what is not outside the home.

A number of key processes affect how well we relate to others and how well we fit into our family and social worlds. Before we look at the stages in social and emotional development we need to think about how important **bonding** and **attachment**, self-concept, personal identity and confidence are from the very beginning.

Attachment and bonding

The development of the deep feelings between parents or carers and their children comes about through a process of bonding and attachment. This attachment is helped in the early months by a number of things including:

- skin contact
- smell
- talking, and listening to parents' voices
- feeding
- bathing
- play
- eye-to-eye contact.

Multiple attachments

John Bowlby is well known for his descriptions of bonding and attachment and confirmed the idea that all children need consistent carers to allow them to develop attachments and start to form loving relationships with their carers. If the period following birth is interrupted

Did you know?

Bonding is the development of the powerful feelings between parents and carers and their children. Successful bonding is a baby's way of making sure they are well cared for and safe from abuse or being abandoned.

Attachment is the close emotional bond between a baby and its carer.

by illness in mother or baby, or is characterised by many different carers, a child may have difficulty in forming close relationships in later life.

It used to be thought that a baby could form a close attachment only to the mother, but this has been shown not to be the case. Children can and obviously do form strong bonds with a wide range of people, for example grandparents, parents, siblings, friends and others. It is regular and frequent contact that is important, and even where a child has a normal attachment to parents and family, it is important that in a nursery setting a young baby or toddler is allowed to develop an attachment to at least one regular carer.

Did you know?

It was in the 1950s that research by the Robertsons identified separation anxiety as an issue. Their research into children separated from their parents in hospital was important in developing the practice of encouraging parents to stay with their children in hospital. But until the 1970s, it was usual not to allow this as it was thought that allowing visitors would make the children too upset.

■ *A happy baby who has developed an attachment to a carer*

A child who has formed close bonds with several important people will be far more secure than a child who has not done so. Where there is a strong sense of security in a child, there is likely to be less emotional trauma caused by future separations from the main carers. Often a very clingy child will have had some difficulty in the early years in forming a close bond with carers.

However, good attachments mean that when his or her main carer is not around a baby or child will show 'separation anxiety' through crying, screaming and, if old enough, trying to follow the carer. Separation anxiety will start around six to seven months and continue until around three years when a child can understand that mummy is going to come back! Part of this is the development of a concept called 'object permanence' – that even if you cannot see something it is still there.

Think about it

Try hiding a toy under a cushion from a 12-month-old. If they see you hiding the toy they will find it. If not, they will not be able to. As a child gets older they can learn to hunt for the toy in increasingly harder places.

Self-concept and personal identity

A child's **self-concept** and **personal identity** are closely linked to the quality of parenting in their early years. Many young people and adults who harm others or carry out serious crimes have had very negative experiences as children and often have a very poor self-concept.

Many psychologists have studied how we develop socially and emotionally. Some of the key theories are described in the box below.

Think about it

1   Write down ten answers to the question 'Who am I?' (Think about your appearance, skills, personality, problems, beliefs and roles in life.)

2   Now try to identify who or what has been most important in forming those ideas of your self.

Freud

Freud identified three parts to the personality, starting with a 'symbiotic' relationship between a mother and child in the first months. Here an infant sees him or herself as part of his or her mother. This is one reason why a child of about 18 months becomes 'egocentric', or aware of himself as separate, and able to say 'no' and to be in control. As we go through childhood into adulthood we develop moral views and the 'id' (I want it now!) starts to be denied by the 'super ego' (No, it's wrong.). As the 'ego' develops it helps to deal with internal arguments to produce an acceptable result.

Skinner

Skinner believed that children learn through experience or conditioning. A child will learn if they are rewarded for their behaviour even if the 'reward' is unpleasant. Positive rewards or reinforcements for good behaviour are the basis of many behaviour management programmes.

Bandura

Bandura developed the idea of 'modelling' or social learning. Children basically copy the adults around them. Watch a tiny baby copy putting its tongue out if an adult does the same. The development of aggression was seen by Bandura as being a result of social learning. His experiment with children watching a film of adults hitting dolls was fascinating as the children copied it and saw that as acceptable behaviour. There is much evidence that a child who witnesses or experiences violence at home may develop aggressive tendencies.

Biological theory

Another theory about aggression is a biological theory. This states that humans need their own space or territory and that if that space is threatened they will react with aggression. Frustration is also seen to produce aggression; observe a small child who cannot do something he or she wants to – the result may be a tantrum or an outbreak of aggression.

Moral development

An important part of social development is moral development. Children observe other children and adults' behaviour, gradually developing a sense of right and wrong. Reinforcement is important in moral development where certain behaviours are promoted as being right or wrong – aggression is a good example of this.

Pro-social behaviour

An advanced stage of a child's moral development is when he or she is capable of **pro-social behaviour**. This refers to an act that helps or benefits others but may have some penalty to the person doing it. An extreme example of pro-social behaviour is someone rescuing a person from a burning house and suffering burns as a result. A more routine example might be a child giving their pocket money to a charitable cause instead of buying the toy they had been saving for. Can you think of other more everyday examples?

Age	Social and emotional development
Birth to 4 weeks	Responds positively to main carer Imitates facial expressions Stares at bright shiny objects
1 month	Gazes intently at carers Social smile at carers (by 6 weeks)
4 months	Smiles, engages and vocalises with carers
6 months	Starts to show interest in other babies, smiles Becomes more interested in social interaction, depending on amount of time spent with other children and his or her personality Shows fear of strangers and distress at separation from carer Interacts differently with various family members Uses comfort object, for example a blanket Seeks attention
9 months	Very interested in all around Recognises familiar and unfamiliar faces Shows stranger anxiety
1 year	More demanding and assertive, emotionally volatile Temper tantrums may start Unhappy at changes in routine Expresses rage at being told 'no' Distinguishes between self and others, but still egocentric – only concerned with his or her own view of the world. Shows definite emotions and is aware of the emotions of others Will play alone Starting to develop object permanence
18 months	Shows stranger shyness Dislikes changes in routine Starts toilet training Starts to have tantrums when upset Has separate sense of self – egocentric Little idea of sharing and strong sense of 'mine'

continued ▶

Age	Social and emotional development
2 years	Enjoys other children's company but reluctant to share toys May show concern when another child is upset Engages in parallel play (alongside others) Remains egocentric Becoming emotionally stable, but still prone to mood swings Learning to separate from carer for short periods, for example while at nursery Knows own identity
3 years	Greater social awareness Will play in twos or threes, sharing ideas May have close friends A lot of mixed play of the sexes Stable and emotionally secure Friendly to other children Increasing in **independence**, but still needs support from adults Fears loss of carers Strong sense of gender identity Less anxious about separation Plays alongside others
4 years	Enjoys co-operative and dramatic play Understands co-operation and competition Responds to reasoning Can take turns Enjoys independence but still needs comfort and reassurance
5 years	Becomes engrossed in activities Develops fears of ghosts, things under the bed Concerned about being disliked Good sense of self-awareness developed
6–7 years	Able to form firm friendships Very supportive of each other, playing complex games Plays in separate sex groups Fairly independent and confident Increasing sense of morality (right and wrong)
8–12 years	Friendships become very important – mostly same sex Concern at thoughts of others about them Often unsure about changes in settings
13–16 years	Body changes can upset self-esteem Need to resolve changes into adulthood Some are more assured about changes in settings Wants to spend more time with friends than family Peer pressure a significant influence

■ *Stages of social and emotional development*

Self-directed or imaginative play is very important in children's social and emotional development. Children will 'act out' events they have experienced in their play.

Think about it

Watch a group of children playing either in the home corner or the playground. In the home corner you may well see a child 'interacting' with a doll, or taking on the role of mum or dad.

Did you know?

There is a direct link between the rate a child's vocabulary develops and the amount the mother talked to the child in the first year. Children whose mothers talk to them a lot can be using and understanding twice as many words at 17 months than children who have had less conversation.

Source: Helen Bee: The Developing Person 1984

Think about it

Observe a group of young children playing and try to work out what is happening without listening to their speech. What were they doing apart from talking? You should have seen them using:
- *facial expressions*
- *body language*
- *listening skills*
- *different pitch intonation.*

Communication and speech development

Children communicate even before they are born. A baby in the uterus will respond to loud noises or distress by moving. A new-born baby communicates through crying and quietening with increasing sophistication. It does not take long for a carer to recognise the meanings of different cries: hungry, tired, cold, fed up, needing a cuddle, etc. Listen to a parent talking to their baby – you will probably hear them using a simple form of language that develops in complexity as the child develops language. This is called 'motherese'.

The speed of language acquisition is amazing. By eight months a child will be babbling sounds like 'dadada', by 18 months he or she will be using 30–40 words and by three years a child will be constructing complex sentences. The speed of this development depends on a number of factors, which includes some built-in ability to develop language but which is also dependent on the amount of conversation directed at a child. Naom Chomsky (a psycholinguist) was a key person in developing the idea that humans have an innate ability for language.

■ *Communication between an adult and a child*

Non-verbal communication is as important to children as it is to adults. Indeed, children probably use it more than adults do. Have a look at the section on non-verbal communication in Unit 3.

Speech is an aspect of development that can vary widely without any relationship to other developmental aspects or to the child's intelligence. Parents often become very concerned that a child is late in talking compared with an elder sibling. This can be simply because the older child is anticipating all the younger one's needs, removing any urgent need for the child to talk, or because that child is simply a later talker.

The development of language divides into two distinct stages:

- **Pre-linguistic:** the stage up to about 12 months when a child starts to say his first words.

- **Linguistic:** words now used with meaning.

Age	Language and communication skills
Pre-linguistic stage	**Birth to 12 months**
Birth to 4 weeks	Cries when basic needs require attention, for example hunger, tiredness, distress
1 month	'Freezes' when a bell is rung gently close to the ear, moves head towards the sound Stops crying at sound of human voice (unless very upset) Coos in response to carer's talk
3 months	Becomes quiet and turns head towards sound of rattle near head Vocalises when spoken to and when alone
6 months	Makes singsong vowel sounds, for example 'aah-aah', 'goo' Laughs and chuckles and squeals aloud in play Responds differently to different tones of voice Starts to respond to noises out of sight with correct visual response
9 months	Vocalises for communication, shouts for attention Babbles loudly and tunefully using dual syllables in long strings, for example 'dad-dad', 'baba', 'mam-mam' Imitates adult vocal sounds, for example coughs, smacking lips Understands 'no' and 'bye-bye' Has instant response to a hearing test conducted 1 metre behind child, out of sight
1 year	Knows own name Jargons loudly in 'conversations', includes most vowels sounds Understands about 20 words in context, for example cup, dog, dinner, and understands simple messages, for example 'clap hands', 'where are your shoes?'
Linguistic stage	**12 months onwards**
12–18 months	First words appear – uses 6–20 recognisable words, understands many more Echoes prominent or last word in sentences Tries to join in with nursery rhymes Responds to simple instructions , for example 'fetch your shoes', 'shut the door'
18–24 months	Uses two words linked together Uses more than 200 words by two years Makes simple two-word sentences Refers to own name, talks to self during play Has telegraphic speech, that is, is using key essential words and missing out connecting words

continued ▶

Age	Language and communication skills
2–3 years	Rapidly expanding vocabulary, including plurals Holds simple conversations Enjoys repetition of favourite stories Counts to ten
3–4 years	Imitates adult speech Can be understood by strangers Forms short, grammatically correct sentences Asks many questions of the type: what? why? and how? Knows parts of body, animals Still makes errors of tenses
4–8 years	Speech is fluent and correct, using descriptive language Gives full name, age, birthday and address Enjoys jokes, singing, rhymes, etc. Rapidly expanding vocabulary – 5,000 words by five years Recognises new words and asks the meaning of them Will accurately copy accents heard Produces most sounds, with some residual difficulty with some letter groups
8 years onwards	Most children are fluent speakers, readers and writers of their language Increasing use of peer influenced, coded language

■ *Development of language and communication skills*

Intellectual development

Cognitive or intellectual development is about how children learn, think and develop ideas. This is one of the areas of development that is strongly influenced by the experiences a child has. Learning the names of animals is only possible if a child has been told them. This applies to almost any knowledge or skill.

There has been a lot of research into how children develop intellectual skills. Two of the most well-known theories follow.

- **Piaget** showed that intelligence is the result of a natural sequence of stages and it develops as a result of the changing interaction of a child and its environment. A child develops 'schemas' to help him or her solve problems in their environment. For example, all dogs are thought to be black if a child's pet dog is black, seeing a white dog needs the schema to be changed.

- **Bruner** believed that as children develop they use different ways of representing the world around them. Enactive represention involves them describing their world by sensori-motor actions – that is by using their bodies – think about how you might describe a whirlpool or a spiral staircase without using your hands or body! Iconic thinking describes pictures in the mind – think about describing where you have been on holiday to a friend – often a picture or painting is the easiest way of description. The final and mature stage is the semantic, when a child can use the full range of language to describe and discuss information.

It is likely that some aspects of each theory play a part in how children develop intellectually. What is indisputable is that children develop intellectually at different rates, and some in areas that others do not. Why some children become scientists and others artists is not fully clear but it is quite reasonable to assume that experience plays a large part as well as inherited skills.

Age	Intellectual development
Birth	Blinks in reaction to bright light Turns to soft light Stares at carer Cries when basic needs require attention
1 month	Stares at soft light Gaze caught by and follows dangling ball
3 months	Follows movements of large and smaller objects
6 months	Very curious, easily distracted by movements Immediately fixes sight on small objects close by and reaches out to grasp them Puts everything in mouth Watches toys fall from hand within range of vision
9 months	Looks in correct direction for falling toys
12 months	Drops toys deliberately and watches them fall – this is called 'casting' Looks in correct place for toys that have rolled out of sight Recognises familiar people at 6 metres
18 months	Builds tower of three cubes when shown Turns pages of books, several at a time, enjoys picture books and can point to a named object Points to interesting objects outside Points to parts of the body
3 years	Copies circle and cross, draws man with head Matches two or three primary colours Paints with large brush, cuts with scissors
By 5 years	Copies square, and range of letters – some spontaneously Draws man with head, body, arms, legs and features, and will draw house Colours pictures neatly Names primary colours and matches ten or more colours Knows time of day for basic activities, for example breakfast, bedtime Matches symbols, letters and numbers Can decide on lighter and heavier objects Understands in front of, behind, next to Counts to 20 by rote
By 6 years	Ability to write developing, is able to write some words and copy others Reads simple books Increasing sophistication in drawing and painting Knows birthday Sight reads ten or more words Can predict next events Can count up to 100 Knows half and whole

Age	Intellectual development
6–8 years	Able to understand concept of conservation , for example the amount of play dough remains the same if you make a ball of dough into a long, thin snake Developing the ability to think about several things at once Enjoys games and rules Understands the use of symbols in maths, writing, etc. Great curiosity in relation to workings of his or her environment
8–12 years	Can reason and apply logic to problems Can transfer information from one situation and use in another Becoming more creative in play Reading and writing confidently Increasing preferences for subjects
13–16 years	Developing ability to think abstractly Will question sources of information Becoming more globally aware Clear preferences for arts or sciences Choices relating to future education and careers being thought about

■ Intellectual development from birth

Maturation

You may hear or read about 'maturation' in relation to growth and development. Maturity means fully grown and developed. Adults are seen to be the mature form of humans. You often hear people being accused of being 'immature'. So why are some adults more mature than others?

Look back at the theories of development, many of them are based on the idea that we for example, learn through experience. Much development also depends on our inbuilt 'programming' but needs to be further developed through our experiences. For example, we are all programmed to learn to speak, but how we speak is shaped by, for example, what we hear and how we are spoken to. It does not take much imagination to realise that the quality of, for example, what we hear can be important.

Case study

Offensive language

Lee's mum was very concerned about her son's speech. Aged four years he was using offensive language in almost every sentence. However her discussion with his nursery teacher showed the reason – every sentence she spoke contained the same language she was complaining about Lee using. Lee's teacher tried to explain that children learn to speak by example.

General behaviour is also shaped by our experiences – a child who always sees their parents behaving with care and thought for others is likely to grow up in the same way. Remember, experiences can be positive as well as negative.

An important aspect of maturation is what adults expect of children. Good support in this area is, for example, given by adults who know what is realistic to expect from a child at that age or stage of development. Conversely, if adults expect a child to do things beyond their stage of development it can have a poor effect.

We have now looked at all the key elements of development. It is worth remembering the key principles:

■ No one aspect of development occurs on its own.

■ Development is a gradual sequential process. We are programmed to learn many skills, for example to walk and talk in the same order, but not at the same speed.

■ Many things can affect the speed of development and although there are **milestones of development** it is important to remember that everyone is an individual and will mature at their own rate.

What factors can affect growth and development?

Growth and development are dependent on many factors with some affecting some children more than others. The impact can be positive as well as negative. For example, the opposite of poverty is wealth and a child growing up in a home with no financial worries may be well fed and clothed and have lots of opportunities for educational development. However, these advantages can lose their impact if the child does not have a loving and supportive family.

Poverty

People who have less than 60 per cent of the income that an average person expects may be considered to be at risk of poverty and social exclusion. In 2001 an estimated 10.7 million people (18 per cent of the population) in Britain lived on or below the 60 per cent of average earnings poverty line whereas in 1979 only 4.4 million people were estimated to live in poverty. The number of people who can be considered to be poor increased dramatically between 1985 and the early 1990s. The proportion of people with low income (18 per cent of the population) has remained the same for the last few years.

Key groups of people who have to live on very little money include one-parent families, people who are unemployed, elderly people, people who are sick or disabled, single earners and unskilled couples.

Did you know?

In 2003/04 28 per cent (3.5 million) of children in Britain were poor.

In 2004 in England only 26 per cent of children in receipt of free school meals gained five or more GCSEs at grade C or above, compared with 56 per cent of children who did not receive free meals.

Source: Child Poverty Action Group 2005

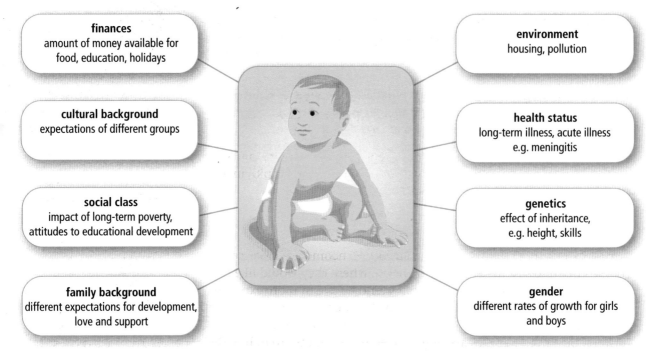

■ *Factors affecting the growth and development of a child*

Families who are poor may have enough money for food, for some clothes and for heating, but poverty means that there is little money for interesting purchases and exciting lifestyles. Families who depend on benefits have limited life choices. The latest clothes, safe reliable cars, the latest electronic equipment, holidays and so on, may not be choices for people on low incomes. Families with little money have to restrict what they can buy when they visit a supermarket or shopping centre.

In 1999 the government published a report called 'Opportunity for All' which states that the following problems prevent people (and so children) from making the most of their lives.

■ **Lack of opportunities to work**. Work is the most important route out of low income. But the consequences of being unemployed are wider than lack of money. It can contribute to ill-health and can deny future employment opportunities.

■ **Lack of opportunities to acquire education and skills**. Adults without basic skills are much more likely to spend long periods out of work.

■ **Childhood deprivation**. This has linked problems of low income, poor health, poor housing and unsafe environments.

■ **Disrupted families**. Evidence shows that children in lone-parent families are particularly likely to suffer the effects of persistently low household incomes. Stresses within families can lead to exclusion; in extreme cases to homelessness.

- **Inequalities in health**. Health can be affected by low income and a range of socio-economic factors such as access to good-quality health services and shops selling good-quality food at affordable prices.

- **Poor housing**. This directly affects people's quality of life and leads to a range of physical and mental health problems, and can cause difficulties for children trying to do homework.

- **Poor neighbourhoods**. The most deprived areas suffer from a combination of poor housing, high rates of crime, unemployment, poor health and family disruption.

Environment

Families who feel confident about their future income and finances can choose their lifestyle. They can also choose where they would like to live. Families in the higher social classes tend to live in more expensive housing areas with good facilities for travel and education. Families with lower incomes tend to live in more densely occupied housing areas. Families on lower incomes are often forced to rent rather than buy their homes. Different social class groups often live in different neighbourhoods. Marketing companies can use postcodes to work out what advertisements to send to different areas.

Does it matter what kind of location you live in? Many people would say that the important thing is to get on with the people you live with and that money, or the size of your house, does not matter. But there can be disadvantages to living in poor-quality or high-density housing. These can include noise, pollution, overcrowding, poor access to shops and other facilities, and stress from petty crime. When people are on a low income, household maintenance can become a problem. Poorly maintained housing can create health hazards.

Think about it

Can you see how being poor might lead to other problems? For example, if you have a low income, you might live in a poor neighbourhood; if you live in a poor neighbourhood you may experience more fear of crime.

Did you know?

The life expectancy of a child born to a family whose parents are professionals (for example a doctor or accountant) is seven years longer than a child born at the same time to a family who are unskilled. Children from unskilled households are five times more likely to die in an accident and 15 times more likely to die in a fire.

Source: Dept of Health, Tackling Inequalities 2002

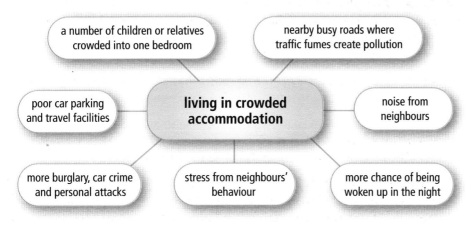

- *The problems created by living in overcrowded accommodation*

Low income and poor housing are a source of stress to many people. The table below lists the percentages of householders who said they had problems with the issues listed in the left-hand column. In general, people with money appear to have fewer problems compared with people who live in low-income areas. Living in the suburbs or in the country may also cause less stress than living 'in town'.

Problems in the area that you live	People in wealthy suburban or rural areas	People in council or low income areas	People in wealthy urban areas	Averages
Crime	49%	66%	59%	56%
Litter and rubbish	26%	58%	49%	42%
Vandalism and hooliganism	25%	58%	42%	40%
Dogs	22%	37%	25%	29%
Noise	16%	31%	35%	23%
Graffiti	11%	36%	32%	32%
Neighbours	17%	18%	17%	13%
Racial harassment	11%	18%	19%	14%

Source: Adapted from Social Trends 2002

Think about it

Think about the housing in your area. Is the housing different in different parts? You may need to walk around the streets to note what kind of housing exists. How do you think the lifestyles of families might vary between different types of housing in your area?

Family structure

People differ from one another in the kinds of families or groups that they live in. In 2001:

- 29 per cent of homes were occupied by single people
- 23 per cent of homes were occupied by couples with dependent children
- 6 per cent were occupied by single parents with children
- 29 per cent of homes were occupied by couples with no children
- 1 per cent of homes housed more than one family.

Many people do live as couples with their children, but it would be a mistake to imagine that all people are born into and grow up in small families.

A family is a social group made up of people who are 'related' to each other. This means that other people (society) recognise that this group is related. In British society, 'family' is the word used to describe groups where adults act as parents or guardians to children. Belonging to a family can have many advantages. Family relationships can provide a safe, caring setting for children. Family groups can guide and teach children, and they can provide a source of social and emotional support for adults and older family members as well as children.

Sociologists have identified four different types of family:

- extended families
- nuclear families
- reconstituted families
- one-parent families.

Extended families

An extended family is where parents, children and grandparents all live together or near each other, so that they are often together. Until the mid-1950s many families in Britain lived in this way. The extended family can have many advantages. For example, parents can work all day without having to worry about who is looking after the children – the grandparents might do this. If the grandparents need care, then the parents or even the older children can help. The extended family provides a network of people who can support each other.

Think about it

Watch the TV adverts on a typical evening. Many adverts for food products and cleaning products will show actors in a family setting. Looking at these adverts, it would seem that most houses are occupied by 30-year-old couples with two children. Is this image really how most people live?

Case study

Living with the family

Ross lives with his brother and his mother and father on the top two floors of a very large semi-detached Victorian house near the centre of a city. Ross's mother's parents live on the ground floor of the building. They have their own bathroom and kitchen, although the whole family sometimes eat together at the weekend. Ross's parents were able to buy such a large house only because the grandparents sold their home to make it possible.

Nuclear families

A nucleus is the centre of a living cell, and the nuclear family is like the centre of the extended family on its own. By the 1950s, many people in Britain no longer lived with or near grandparents. The term nuclear family was invented to describe this new, smaller family. The original nuclear family was usually a husband who would go out to work, a wife who would look after the children while they were young, and the children.

Nowadays many couples no longer fit this description. Often both parents will have full-time work and the children are cared for by **childminders**, **nannies**, or nursery services. Male and female roles have been changing for example – men and women are now usually seen as equally responsible for household tasks. However, studies suggest that women still undertake the majority of child care and housework tasks.

Case study

Grandparents

Meena lives with her sister, mother and father in a three-bedroom, semi-detached house. Meena's grandmother (her mother's mother) lives in the Caribbean and she has not seen her for two years. Meena's father's parents live about eighty miles away, and she sees these grandparents about five to eight times each year. Meena's family moved to the house they live in three years ago when her father got a better job.

Reconstituted families

Approximately one marriage in every three now ends in divorce. Many young people live together before marriage and have children, but there is evidence that a large number of these couples split up too. Over a third of marriages each year are likely to be re-marriages, and about one million children live with a step-parent. Roughly a quarter of children might experience their parents divorcing before the age of 16.

The reconstituted family is where the couple are not both the parents of each child in the family. One partner might have been divorced from an earlier marriage, and has now re-married to create a new family. Sometimes children from different relationships may be included in a new, reconstituted family. One partner may have been single but is now married to a partner who has children from a previous relationship.

Case study

Living with a step-parent

Sarosh lives with his mother and stepfather in a modern terraced house in a small town. His mother and stepfather have been married for two years. Sarosh's 'real' father calls every other Saturday to collect him for a visit. Sarosh's mother and father divorced four years ago. His new stepfather has a daughter, Zara, who lives with her mother over two miles away. Sarosh has met Zara and they like each other, but Sarosh thinks his stepfather cares more about Zara than him.

Lone-parent families

Nearly a quarter of all families with dependent children are lone-parent families. Twenty per cent of families with dependent children are lone-parent families led by a lone mother, with just 2 per cent led by a lone father.

While some lone-parent families may be well off, many are disadvantaged. A family expenditure survey in 2000 showed that twice as many lone-parent families live on low incomes compared with couples with dependent children. Many lone parents rely on benefits or receive low income wages.

Case study

Single mother

Janice is a single mother with an eight-year-old son, living in a fourth-floor flat on a large housing estate. Janice is looking for part-time work, but her son has an attention problem at school and the school often telephones her to ask her to come and collect him or to calm him. Janice depends on Income Support to get by. She doesn't have enough money for holidays or to take her son out for the day. Janice cannot afford leisure activities which cost money. At night Janice usually stays in and watches TV. There is a high drug-related crime rate on the estate and Janice worries that her flat may be broken into.

Changing families

The type of family that a child lives in can change. An extended family can turn into a nuclear family if the grandparents die or move away. Families can become 'reconstituted' if one partner leaves and is replaced by a different person. Few people can guarantee a family style for life. When people leave their partners, divorce or die, a lone-parent family may be created. If the remaining parent finds a new partner, the lone-parent family becomes a reconstituted family. The same child might live in different family structures during childhood and adolescence.

Adult expectations

Encouragement from parents is important in how well a child develops and most parents provide motivation for their children to develop to their potential. However, over-ambitious parental expectations can have a negative impact on development as well.

Case study

Skills development

John, aged six, was the youngest of three siblings. His brother and sister were both very clever and doing very well at school. John was less interested in lessons, and was slower than his brother and sister in learning to read but was very friendly with everyone and loved helping to look after the younger children. His parents were worried and employed extra help in reading for John. He started crying before school every morning, and complaining of tummy ache. Things got worse and instead of being a friendly happy little boy, John became very quiet and unhappy. Eventually John's teacher called his parents in and pointed out to them that all children develop at different rates and that too much pressure can slow down the development of skills if a child feels under pressure. Once his parents started to accept John for his own qualities and stopped the extra reading lessons and pressure, John soon started to flourish again.

Effects of disability or sensory impairment

Disability and sensory impairment, for example loss of sight or hearing, can delay development in some children. This is because an essential part of the whole picture of development may be missing. If you think about how important hearing speech is before a child can talk, it is not surprising that communication skills may be delayed. Multi-agency child development centres work with children who have some form of disability to help to promote their development.

Promoting growth and development

There has been a lot of political activity in recent years aimed at reducing the number of children living in poverty and in reducing the impact of poverty on child development and life chances. **Sure Start** is one of the best known of these and its remit is to develop children's centres in areas of poverty and deprivation. A number of services aimed at helping children – from education, health and social services – work together with families to improve children's futures.

Recent governments have finally recognised the impact of economic well-being and other factors on a child's development. There have been many programmes and developments to support families and to help children to move to a more equitable situation. For example:

- **Financial support**. Family tax credits to help families financially.
- **Family centres**. These have joint working between health, education and social care agencies.
- **Children's and Young People's Trust**. This has joint working between all agencies at local authority level.

Think about it

Are there any multi-agency organisations in your area for example? Find out what they are and what they do. You could ask your tutor to invite someone from such a multi-agency organisation to talk to your group about their work.

Assessment activities

Assessment Activity 1

Working with a partner or in a small group think about growth and development. Write down what is meant by growth and development and the principles of growth and development.

On a large sheet of paper or flipchart answer the following:

1   What does 'holistic' mean when we are thinking about children's growth and development?

2   What do we mean by the term 'interconnected? You can draw a large diagram to illustrate this.

One principle is that development is mainly in the same sequence for all babies and young children, although the rate of development may be different for different individuals. With your partner or in your group try and write a brief explanation of what this means.

There are also different stages and sequences of growth and development.

What are these different stages? For example, birth to one year.

You can now write notes to meet the first Pass criterion (P1). For this you must describe the principles, stages and sequences of growth and development in children. Remember that this must be your own work.

continued ▶

Assessment Activity 2

Produce four charts to show how children develop in different areas of development through the different stages as follows:

1   A chart to show how children develop physically in each of the different stages: 0–3 years, 4–7 years, 8–12 years and 13–16 years.
2   A chart to show how children develop socially and emotionally.
3   A chart to show how their communication and speech develops.
4   A chart to show how they develop intellectually.

This will enable you to meet the second Pass criterion for this unit (P2) for which you have to outline the physical, emotional, social, communication and intellectual development of children 0–3 years, 4–7 years, 8–12 years and 13–16 years.

Assessment Activity 3

You can now go on to look at the differences in the development of children in the different age groups.

Using the charts you produced in Assessment Activity 2 describe the differences in development of children in the different age groups. This enables you to meet a Merit criterion (M1).

Assessment Activity 4

List all the factors that affect children's growth and development.

This will be quite a long list and should include: health, genetic inheritance, gender, family background and structure, social class, cultural background, finances, poverty, environment and housing, disability, discrimination and the agencies such as health services that work for and with children and young people. You also need to include maturation, and how this is affected by experience and expectations.

Next, write a few sentences about each of these factors.

When you have done this you will have met the third Pass criterion for this unit (P3).

Assessment Activity 5

Building on the work you have done for P3 you can now explain how parental income, health status and parental expectations might affect children's growth and development. Remember that when you explain something you have to do more than just describe it. You have to say how and why these factors might affect children.

When you have explained the effects of these factors you will have met the second Merit criterion (M2).

1.2 Understand the role of observation of children's development in the workplace

This section covers:

- purpose of careful observation
- objectivity
- confidentiality
- reporting observations
- methods of recording observations.

Purpose of careful observation

Why do you think that **observation** skills are so important in a child care setting?

We have already looked at how complex and variable children's development is. It is essential that anyone working with children can identify if a child is having problems and needing extra support, or is able to assess whether work with a child is effective or not.

How do you think you could identify how advanced a child is in their development and then plan activities or work with them to support them and enhance their development further?

The answer is through observation skills.

Sometime in the future, when you are very experienced as a child care worker, you should have the skills to be in a room with children and, by watching them, be able to identify aspects of their development and progress and any issues causing concern. This is a skill that takes many years of experience, and even then experienced staff still have cause to carry out a specific observation on some children.

Observing is more than just watching – you are also **noticing** and **thinking** at the same time. You might, for example, watch a child building with bricks, but notice how the child fits them together or how he holds them and how he reacts if another child is nearby. Observation is a skill, and it is a fascinating one to have. It makes working with children more interesting, and because you are more aware of children's needs and strengths, it helps makes you a more effective worker.

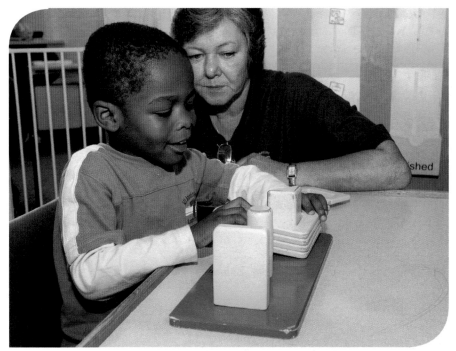

■ *Observing a child*

Objectivity

There are some important points to remember about observing.

Observation is time spent specifically to record certain things about a child, and then to draw conclusions from that record. It should be **objective**. This means you should almost imagine this is the first time you have seen the child so you are not jumping to conclusions. It is difficult to forget that a child is often very challenging but good observations can help you to work towards finding out why the child is 'naughty'. An essential part of observing is to avoid jumping to conclusions. Remember that early years' workers are not doctors, speech therapists or psychologists. To avoid wrongly assessing children, it is always a good idea to carry out several observations and also to ask someone else to watch a child in action. Observers can focus in on different things, so someone else who might have more experience may come to a different conclusion.

Confidentiality

Observations should be **confidential**. This means they should not be shared with everyone but only with the staff or other professional (for example psychologists or speech therapists) who need to know the results. Any records of observations should be kept in the child's file. Remember, the Data Protection Act and Freedom of Information legislation gives parents access to information written about their children. You should never put anything on paper or file that is untrue or not based on evidence.

Think about it

Where are observations, assessments and conclusions about children stored in your placement? Who has access to them?

Always think about the ethical considerations of an observation. Is there a valid reason for the observation? Children are not laboratory experiments; be careful about doing observations that are not necessary – especially of a child who has special needs or behaviour difficulties who may well have been observed too often already. Sometimes, knowing they are being observed can make a child's behaviour worse.

Reporting observations

Important information from an observation should be **reported** as appropriate. As a student you are only likely to be observing children in your placement to learn about development. However, if you see something that does not seem within your expectations it is important that you report this to your supervisor as soon as possible so he or she can decide if action is needed.

Case study

Maintaining confidentiality

Jason has just completed an observation on Dylan, a four year old. He is certain that Dylan is delayed in his speech development. Just as he is finishing, Dylan's mother arrives to pick him up. Jason tells her about his theory. The mother is surprised and upset and immediately sees the supervisor.

What has Jason done wrong?

Explain why it is important not to jump to premature conclusions when observing children.

What is the process in your placement for dealing with concerns about a child based on an observation?

Think about it

Find out how your placement shares information with parents and involves them in the observation and assessment process. Find out how often your placement routinely observes children and for what purpose.

In order to get an overall picture of children, observers need to talk to the children themselves and also to their **families**. When children are observed, they may be very different from usual. At home, relaxed and with family members, children can be quite different. This can mean that a child, who appears to be very quiet at school, is talkative and boisterous at home.

Any records of observations should be shared with parents and discussed with them by qualified staff. In schools this might take place during parents' evenings. In nurseries and pre-schools the findings of observations may be shared with parents when they come to collect their child.

Case study

Observing behaviour

Izzy was puzzled about Luke, aged three. He seemed to be avoiding playing outside on the big equipment which he had always enjoyed before. She spent some time observing him doing different activities and realised he didn't seem to be using his right arm very well. Izzy told her manager about this and as a result of going to the hospital with his parents, it was discovered Luke had injured his shoulder. After treatment he was soon playing out on the slide and swings again.

Methods of recording observations

Observations may be **formal** or **informal**. As the words suggest, a formal observation is one that is planned ahead and for a specific purpose. An informal one is more opportunistic; based on perhaps seeing a child engaged in an activity that shows a particular aspect of behaviour or development.

Method	How they work	Disadvantages
Checklists, tick charts	Focus the observer on one aspect of development May be used with more than one child at a time Can be repeated	Different people might produce different results The focus on skills that the child is showing might miss out how unhappy the child is Children might feel that they have failed if they cannot do a task The checklist and tick charts have to be relevant and appropriate to the child's stage of development

Child's name .... Date ....

Date of Birth .... Observer ....

Developmental checklist

By 12 months	Yes	No	Sometimes
Pick objects with finger and thumb?			
Transfer items from one hand to the other?			
Look for an object hidden under a beaker?			
Look at a person who is speaking to him or her?			
Make tuneful babbling sounds such as Da-da?			
Respond to different sounds e.g. drum, bell?			
Imitate gestures such as pat cake and bye bye?			
Hold beaker using two hands?			
Use fingers to eat finger foods such as squares of bread?			
Pick up dropped toys?			
React to the word 'No'?			
React to own name?			

■ *Example of a checklist*

Method	How they work	Disadvantages
Written records/ snapshot observations	Brief descriptions of what a child is doing in a particular time span They are popular with parents as they provide a written picture of their child Used to record any or several areas of development	Different observers might focus on different things, so can be difficult to repeat You need to be able to write quickly to capture all information It can be hard to find the right language to describe what you are seeing

Brightlands Day Nursery
107 St Georges Road
Cheltenham
Gloucestershire
GL50 3ED

Ravi is standing up in front of Michaela, who is sitting on a chair. Ravi seems to be looking down at Michaela. She is saying 'Shall we dress up?' Michaela nods and smiles, Ravi smiles too and they both walk over to the dressing-up corner.

Ravi takes a pink dress, grasping it in her right hand, and places it on the floor. She pulls the back of the dress open with both hands. She steps into the dress using her right foot first and pulls up the dress gradually to a standing position, placing her right arm into the dress and then her left.

Ravi walks over to the nursery nurse and looks up. She asks 'Can you do my buttons up? and turns around.

■ *Example of a written record of an observation*

Method	How they work	Disadvantages
Time samples	You look at what a child does at different times over a period of time, such as a morning or part of an afternoon. This means that you gain a more complete picture of the child Can be used for more than one child and one or more areas of development	A piece of significant behaviour may not be recorded if it happens outside of the time slot

Event	Activity	Social group	Comments
11.00	Snack time	Whole group	Anna is sitting with her legs swinging on a chair. She is eating an apple. She is holding it in her left hand and she is smiling. She puts up her hand when a staff member asks who wants a biscuit.
11.15	Outdoor play Climbing frame	Anna and Ben	Anna is on the top bar of the climbing frame. She is smiling at Ben. She is calling 'Come on up here!'
11.30	Taking coats off	Anna, Ben and Manjit	Anna unzips the coat and pulls out one arm. She swings around and the coat moves around. She laughs and looks at Manjit.

■ *Example of a time sample*

Method	How they work	Disadvantages
Event samples	Used to look at how often and in what circumstances a child shows a particular behaviour – as described on the sheet – filled in when seen Can be used by more than one observer Can be used to look at unwanted behaviour such as hitting Can also be used to find out about how often a child talks or plays with other children	An observer may not always be present at the time of the behaviour May forget to fill in the event sample

Event	Time	Situation	Social group	Dialogue
1	9.16 am	Curren is hovering near the painting table	Susan + 2 children	A–C 'Do you want to come and paint a picture too?' C–A nods head
2	9.27 am	Curren is finishing painting	Susan + 2 children	A–C 'Have you finished?' C smiles 'It's a lovely picture. Tell me a little bit about it.' C–A 'It's my mum. Can't take my apron off.' A–C 'Wait still, I'll do it.' Curren hands apron to Susan and runs over to sand area
3	10.12 am	Curren is waiting for his drink at snack time	Curren is sitting next to Ahmed. Jo is handing out drinks	A–C 'Milk or squash, Curren?' C–A 'Milk.' A–C 'Can you remember the magic word?' C–A 'Thank you.' A–C 'Good boy.'
4	10.19 am	Curren is putting on his coat in the cloakroom area	Jo + 5 children	C–A 'Can't put coat on.' A–C 'Keep still. There you are. You can go out now.'
5	10.36 am	Curren is waiting for his turn by the slide	Jo + 2 children	A–C 'Good boy. It's your go now.' C smiles C–A 'I go fast down now.'

■ *Example of an event sample*

Remember – observations do have limitations!

■ Observations are not perfect.

■ They tell you about the child at that particular moment and in that condition.

■ Knowing they are being watched can affect what children do.

■ Children play quite differently when they think that no one is looking at them.

■ It is hard to be absolutely accurate when you are observing as there is so much to notice. Two people watching the same child can notice quite different things about the child.

■ It is difficult to be totally objective, especially if unwanted behaviour is being seen!

Best practice in your work placement

How to carry out observations

- Always ask your supervisor before carrying out any observation on a child.
- Carry out observations and assessments in line with your placement's policy.
- Make sure that you have everything you need to hand.
- Observe children sensitively and without them noticing.
- Write up your observations in a sensitive and non-judgemental way.
- Avoid making any negative judgements about children.
- Make sure that any conclusions are based directly on your observations.
- Share your findings with your supervisor so that they can be passed on to parents.

Case study

Observing George

Jennifer wants to observe whether George, aged three, can draw a face. He has been busy playing, but she interrupts his play to ask him to come over to the table. She sits next to him and asks him to draw a picture of his little sister Ruby. George takes the pencil, looks at Jennifer and says he can't do it. He then asks if he can go back to play in the sand again. Jennifer says of course he can and then writes down on her paper that

he cannot draw a face. She is surprised later when another member of staff shows her a painting that he has done of his family with clearly marked faces.

1 Give two reasons why George may have not drawn a face.

2 How might Jennifer have done this observation in a better way?

Assessment activities

Assessment Activity 6

Think about why it is useful to observe children. Discuss this with a partner and write some notes about the reasons for observing children. Your answer should include getting to know about a child's development and identifying a child's needs, for example, the child may be tired or unwell. You should also include concerns about a child, for example, a particular child may be showing a lot of aggressive behaviour.

continued ▶

Assessment Activity 7

You need to think about the different ways in which we observe children. For instance we may observe them informally through watching and thinking or through more formal methods of observation. Discuss with a partner what time samples and event samples are and make notes of their meanings.

Now think about recording methods. Together with a partner, write a running record of each other or of somebody else in your class. Find a checklist that somebody has used and have a look at what it is like.

Assessment Activity 8

An important part of observation, if it is to be useful, is to ensure that we are not jumping to conclusions. We need to be objective.

Observe somebody else in your class and compare your observation with that of somebody else. This is part of checking your views with somebody else. Are there any differences in your observations? If there are any differences, what might the reasons be for these? Write these down. You should try and include things like looking at somebody else from your own viewpoint only instead of being objective and trying to stand outside of yourself. Another reason might be ignorance of the person being observed.

Assessment Activity 9

Another part of the role of observation of children is to report your findings to one of the workers in your placement. Discuss in a group who you report findings and concerns to. You may find that it is different from one placement to another. You should make some notes of your discussion as these will be useful for your assignment.

Also in your group you should discuss the importance of confidentiality and what the procedures are for sharing information. What about ethical considerations? Is it ethical to observe children to find out about them if you have not had their permission or the permission of the parent or placement staff? Again you should make notes to prepare for your assignment.

Assessment Activity 10

You should now put your notes together from these four activities.

You should have written why it is useful to observe children, what sorts of methods are used, the need to be objective and to report your findings and the need for confidentiality.

You have now covered P4, which requires you to outline the role of observation of children's development.

1.3 Know how to observe children's development

This section covers:

- observing and noting children's physical development
- observing and noting children's social and emotional development
- observing children's communication and intellectual development.

Observing children's development

Observation has a number of different roles in early years and children's settings. As you become more practised at using your skills you will cover most aspects of children's development.

Use this checklist, or find the one in your professional practice folder, to make sure that you see and practise the following aspects of development as you practise observation skills.

Observing children's physical development	Observing children's social and emotional development	Observing children's communication and intellectual development
Consider how children: - move about - co-ordinate their movements - use space and large equipment - manipulate and use small equipment.	Observe: - how children behave in everyday situations - how children express feelings and emotions - how children relate to each other and to adults - how confident children are and how they feel about themselves (self-concept).	Consider how children: - play - use their imagination - take on the roles of others - concentrate on activities - memorise things - solve problems - pay attention to what is around them - use their senses to gain new information.

■ Checklist of aspects of development that need to be observed

Assessment activities

Assessment Activity 11

You now need to show that you are able to observe children's development.

You should observe and record the physical, social, emotional, communication and intellectual development of children. You will probably have to observe several children over a period of time in order to achieve this.

When you have undertaken and recorded these observations you will have covered P5.

Assessment Activity 12

You now need to consider P4 as well as the observations you have undertaken. You should explain, saying how and why you undertook the steps you did to ensure the effective and appropriate observation of children. You will need to answer the following:

- What were the reasons for the observation?
- Why did you choose the methods you used?
- Whose permission did you obtain?
- How did you try to be as objective as possible and not jump to any conclusion?
- To whom did you report your findings?
- How did you maintain confidentiality?

When you have done this you will have met M3. This requires you to explain the steps undertaken to ensure the effective and appropriate observation of children.

Assessment Activity 13

You may now like to think carefully about the development of one of the children you have observed. Using the developmental charts you have already produced you should check what you would expect of a child of this age.

In order to meet Distinction criterion 1 (D1) you must compare the development of a child that you have observed with the expected development of a child of this age.

1.4 Understand the required planning to support children's needs and development

This section covers:

■ planning

■ participation

■ children's needs and development.

Planning

Children need support and help to encourage their development in all the areas we have been looking at. The role of adults is to support the children in developing skills. This support is not possible without careful planning. Good planning is based on a thorough understanding of the needs of all the children involved.

All the planning and preparation involved in an activity will be wasted if you have not thought about a vital question: have the children reached the required stage of development, and do they possess the skills necessary to take part in and enjoy the activity? A good understanding of child development and observation of children playing and working will help you to develop the knowledge you need to work out the answer to this question. Most activities are planned with the aim of extending children's skill levels, but skills cannot be extended or developed if the child is not ready for that next step.

Planning cycle

Effective planning can make all the difference to the success of an activity. You may have heard of the 'planning cycle'. The planning cycle is a very useful tool in work with children.

Planning happens at a variety of levels in a children's setting. It can be over a term, a month or a week ahead. Themes can be developed especially for younger children, for example seasons, festivals or colours.

Using observations to support planning

Within the framework of the overall plan, there will be small-scale planning of individual activities to ensure that the needs of all children are met. This will be based on observations and assessments of children with the planned activities scheduled to support their development to the next phase.

Think about it

It requires quite a high degree of manipulative skill to put jigsaw pieces together. Children need to learn to use slot-in jigsaw boards first. Next they move on to jigsaws with very large pieces, and then to harder puzzles. Giving a child a 20-piece jigsaw is of little use if all they have mastered so far are six-piece puzzles!

Planning activities

As a student you may be lucky enough to be at meetings where the overall plan and themes are being decided, at least in the department you are working in. You certainly should be able to see the plan for the coming weeks, and look at where you could plan some individual activities within that. There are different ways of planning an activity, even within the early years curriculum.

Unstructured planning for activities

Unstructured planning occurs when an adult provides an activity for children to use in their own way. The outcomes may be very different from the intention of the adult. For example, a water play activity with different containers for different volumes and density may result in the children discarding the heavier items and larger containers and using the smaller, lighter ones as boats.

Structured activities

A structured activity is planned by the adults with a specific learning outcome as the focus. For example, a cooking activity may be used to investigate ingredients, ask why things happen, aid personal, social and emotional development, and encourage working as part of a group and taking turns.

Experiential activities

An experiential activity uses the environment and expected or unexpected activities to learn from, for example the arrival of new-born lambs in the field adjoining the nursery; an adult or child going to the dentist.

Thematic activities

Thematic activities use a realistic activity relevant to a child's experience to provide opportunities to develop in several or all areas of the curriculum, for example a trip to the local park or a 'shop' inside the setting. A thematic plan is often split into the various areas of development to ensure a range of suitable activities are provided. Extension activities can then be included, for example if there are ducks on the pond in the park a suitable story and songs can be used back at the centre. Relevant creative work using images and experiences can be planned.

Supporting children's needs

The needs of children have an overall global list for different age groups but these are then made specific to each individual. Have a look at these children and their needs.

0–3 years: comfortable, safe, secure environment
              good-quality care routines
              close and loving relationships
              inclusion and equal access
              communication
              opportunity to play

4–7 years: safe, secure and encouraging environment
close and consistent relationships
age-appropriate activities, materials and experiences
assessing risk
communication
consistent response to behaviour

8–12 years: safe and secure environment
opportunities for exploration and different experiences
wide range of communication methods
allowing to take risks
praise and encouragement
sensitive answers to questions about adult issues
support when moving schools

13–16 years: support learning and development
positive communication
assess and take risks and face challenges
praise and encouragement
acceptance and love

■ *Activities for children should take account of their age and needs*

Think about it

Can you think of an activity you have prepared for which the child was not ready? What did you do in the situation?

Can you see the common issues regardless of age but also the increasing need to allow a child freedom to develop their individuality?

It is important to recognise that within each need there are many variations depending on each child. The secret of good support is in adapting the support to each individual child's needs.

That information can only be gained from detailed observation and assessments.

Participation

As a student on placement you are not likely to be involved too much in the formal planning meetings held in your placement. However, you may well attend meetings and should be discussing your progress, and how effective you are in your activities and time with the children, with your supervisor.

Although you are one of the most junior members of the team you may well be seeing behaviours or trends in a child that are not noticed by other staff. You may also have ideas for activities that others have not thought of.

It is important that you do make a contribution by making suggestions – maybe in discussions with your supervisor or other slightly more senior staff. Having the confidence to do this can take time and we will be looking at how you can develop the skills needed for this in Unit 5.

One very useful way understanding how effective planning can be is to note good practice in your placement and then talk about why it works so well with someone senior.

Cultural differences and equal opportunities

It is essential that the interests of all children are met in an activity. Careful consideration is needed to be sure that all children can join in, and that **adaptations** can be made to accommodate a child who may be shy or timid, have hearing impairments, or have poor co-ordination in his or her movements, in fact any particular need a child may have. If there are children from a range of cultural backgrounds, they should be equally considered.

Research other **cultures** in depth. Involve parents or other members of the community to help, and celebrate the **diversity** of all our cultures in a fun and interesting way. Think of ways you can promote positive images of different cultures and social classes. Think about books, posters and materials that you use. Will any child feel excluded by them? For example, a story that concentrates on a family setting with both parents at home is fine, but you need to balance this with pictures of one-parent families.

If you ask children to bring items in for a topic or the interest table, be sure it will not cost too much for the family. Be sensitive to children when talking about festivals; families who are Muslim, for example, or Jehovah's Witness do not celebrate Christmas for different reasons.

Reassessing an activity to make sure that it is suitable for all the children is often only a case of remembering the basic principles shown in the checklist below.

Think about it

Choose two activities using different skills that you have helped with in your placement. Make a chart. Show the age of the children, the skills and activities required, and notes on how the children coped.

1 Were changes made for different children?

2 Do you think there should have been?

Think about it

Observe a well-structured and organised nursery for part of a session. At the end, ask the person in charge how the session was planned and organised. Think about aspects of the adults' roles or the use of materials that impressed you, say if anything surprised you, and indicate if you feel there were areas for improvement.

Best practice in your work placement

Planning activities

Make sure you have a thorough knowledge of all the children in your group before you start planning.

- What are each child's needs?
- How are they different to the needs of another child?
- How might this activity need adapting to meet their needs?
- Is there enough room for children to move around?
- Is the equipment suitable for all children? Have you provided a range of sizes of paint brushes, for example?
- Is there special equipment for particular children?
- Can equipment be reached by all the children, to promote independence?
- Do any of the children require practical assistance, for example putting on aprons, moving to the table?
- Ask the children if they need help, rather than waiting for them to ask you.

Think about it

You have chosen the story Cinderella to read to the children and develop into an activity. As you read it, you realise that it is based on gender and appearance. The wicked stepmother is very stereotypical too. How could you adapt the story, and subsequent activities, to challenge these stereotypes?

When you are planning activities that develop a child's creative skills, do not make the mistake of basing your planning on your own cultural or gender identity. You will not meet all needs in this way. Look at the following examples.

- When baking it would be easy to limit your ideas to those you are familiar with, especially as you want to be comfortable with the activity. A simple way of broadening it is to see if an adult from a culture other than yours can be involved.

- Look for books or computer software that are in dual languages, for example English and Urdu, which will appeal to all children in your nursery or school.

- When helping to set up an interest table, use the opportunity to focus on another culture or race.

- Choose a topic that is popularly viewed as mainly female or male, and deliberately widen the appeal and interest to both genders.

How children learn

Underlying the planning of successful activities are some basic principles about how children learn.

- Children learn best when material suits the stage they have reached in their development.

- Attention needs to be given to the whole child, that is, to physical, moral and emotional needs as well as intellectual needs.

- Children learn in an integrated manner, they do not separate learning to speak from learning about numbers.

- Children learn best when they are allowed to try things out and make mistakes.

- Children need to have their efforts recognised and valued.

- You should always start with what a child can do, not what a child cannot do.

- Conditions for learning have to be positive to ensure the development of creativity and imagination; children need materials and encouragement.

- There are particular times when a child is ready to learn certain skills.

- A child's relationships with other children and adults are very important.

- Unit 4 covers all the information about a child's physical needs: toileting, feeding and **weaning** that you need to consider when planning to support a child. You should be aware of a child's needs at the age and stage they have reached. It is not much use planning a day for a baby of six months and not having suitable pureed food available, or suitable nappies!

- Likewise Unit 6 covers how to support play and learning and needs to be referred to when planning play.

- Always think about the individual needs of each child and remember that two children of the same age will be very different to each other. Can you think how they might be different? Think about:

  - stage of development

  - dietary likes and dislikes

  - cultural impact

  - personality

  - parental wishes.

Assessment activities

Assessment Activity 14

Using one of the observations you have already undertaken, write how you might use this observation to plan an activity to help the child's development. For instance, you may have observed that a child's eye–hand co-ordination was not good and that you might help the child with an activity that involves threading beads.

continued ▶

Assessment Activity 15

Planning is not usually done by one person on their own. Usually a small team of people get together to discuss plans for activities for children's development.

In a small group in your class, role play a planning meeting in an early years placement. Note how you and others contribute ideas and suggestions at this meeting. Discuss and write notes about this.

Assessment Activity 16

In your group brainstorm and draw up lists of how different materials can support children's play and how equipment can be useful to support different activities.

Assessment Activity 17

In a small group discuss and make notes about how children's needs can be supported by the way that caring routines such as toileting, feeding and weaning are planned.

Assessment Activity 18

Using your notes from the previous four activities you can now outline how to take part in planning to support children's development. This enables you to meet Pass criterion 6 (P6).

Assessment Activity 19

Using the observations you have already carried out, choose one of these and suggest a plan to support the development of one of the children you have observed.

This enables you to meet Merit criterion 4 (M4).

Assessment Activity 20

Using the plan you have suggested in Assessment Activity 19, describe the strengths and weaknesses of this plan to meet the development of the observed child. This enables you to meet Distinction criterion 2 (D2).

2 Keeping children safe

Introduction

Accidental injury is a leading cause of death and hospitalisation among children and young people in the UK. In 2003, around 300 children and young people were killed in accidents. Many children are left scarred for life or permanently disabled.

It is very important that the children you work with are safe in your care, even when you are working as a student in placement. Injuries can affect children's development and learning and in the worst situations be a cause of death. The main purpose of this unit is for you to find out what you need to know and be able to do in order to help to keep children of all ages safe both in child care settings and during outings.

In this unit you will learn:

1 how to prepare and maintain a safe and secure environment

2 how to support the protection of children from abuse

3 how to maintain the safety of children on outings

4 how to deal with accidents, emergencies and illness.

2.1 Understand how to prepare and maintain a safe and secure environment

This section covers:

- laws governing safety
- regulations
- safe use of equipment and materials
- layout and organisation
- supervision
- personal safety and safety of others
- good hygiene practice.

Laws governing safety

Luckily anyone working with children is supported by a number of laws and regulations that are designed to help to keep children and young people safe. Some of these apply to the manufacture of equipment, food and toys etc. Others affect who can look after children and yet others affect the environment that children are looked after in.

We will now look at some of these laws and regulations which help to maintain a safe and secure environment for children and that you need to be aware of.

The Health and Safety at Work Act

The Health and Safety at Work Act has clear principles to ensure health and safety at work. Employers and employees have a responsibility for the safety of a workplace. This means that when you are working in a child care setting (or anywhere else) you have the right to expect that you will not be exposed to any dangers to your health and safety. You must also make sure that you deal with or report any hazards that you see. You cannot just think that it is someone else's responsibility.

The legislation covers all of the following:

- buildings and services (design and maintenance)
- cleanliness of the environment and of food preparation areas
- safe storage and use of equipment
- working practices that promote health and safety
- provision of a safety policy.

If you notice anything that could be a source of danger you must report it immediately and/or take steps to protect other people. You must also co-operate with your employer on health and safety issues, for example by not using unsafe equipment and by taking note of warning notices. Blocking fire exits with toys or uncovering electric sockets, for example, is a very serious offence because it goes against safety regulations and can cause death or serious injury.

RIDDOR

As you can see there are a number of regulations aimed at preventing injury and illness. Sometimes, however, accidents do happen and when they do occur at a place of work they must be reported. The RIDDOR (Reporting of Injuries, Diseases and Dangerous Occurrences Regulations) 1995 require the reporting of work-related accidents, diseases and dangerous occurrences. For example all of the following have to be reported:

- deaths
- major injuries
- accidents resulting in over three days of injury
- diseases such as food poisoning
- dangerous occurrences such as a dangerous chemical being spilled
- gas leaks.

Regulations

Adult to child ratios

Day care and educational settings for children are regulated by **OFSTED**. There are 14 National Standards covering a range of important issues in relation to safe and effective child care. Although the standards for child minders and larger day care providers are slightly different, the underlying principles remain the same.

Five of the standards deal with the safety of children, as set out in the diagram below.

■ *Safety issues covered by the OFSTED National Standards*

One important standard relates to the ratio of adults to children. The registration requirements of the setting will state the number of children that are allowed to be on the premises at any one time and the ratio of adults to children. The ratio varies between age groups and settings, as set out in the table below.

Age of children	Recommended ratio of adults to children
0–2 years	one adult to three children
2–3 years	one adult to four children
3–5 years	one adult to eight children
5–7 years	one adult to eight children

■ *Recommended ratio of adults to children in a day care setting and out of school clubs for children up to seven*

At least two adults should always be present, even if there are only a few children, and two adults should be in the room during the day. At least one adult present must be a qualified first aider.

Authorised access to premises

There have been some tragic events in schools and nurseries in the past that have resulted in the improvement of security to make sure that only people who are allowed access to child care premises are admitted. A number of controls have been developed in response to the need identified in the Standards. These include:

■ controlled access by one door, often with an alert system when opened

■ a visitor book to record details

■ checking the identification of visitors

■ using visitor passes

■ accompanying visitors are not allowed to wander around alone

■ the departure of visitors is recorded in the visitor book.

Have a look at what controls there are in your placement.

COSHH Regulations

Legislation called COSHH (Control of Substances Hazardous to Health) covers substances that can cause ill-health. COSHH lays down a step-by-step approach to the precautions to prevent injury or illness from dangerous substances. Such substances must have labels on them. The examples below show that substances are dangerous and need to be kept in special containers and carefully stored.

■ *The warning signs on hazardous substances*

Thousands of people are exposed to hazardous substances at work. If the exposure is not prevented or properly controlled, it can cause serious illness and sometimes even death. This clearly is unacceptable in a child care setting. Although you may not think there are many dangerous substances in your setting, there will be some, such as cleaning products, which could be a risk of poisoning for children.

The effects of hazardous substances on children and staff include:

■ poisoning by drinking toxic liquids from bottles thought to contain water or soft drinks – sometimes with fatal results

■ cancer, which can appear many years after first exposure to carcinogenic (cancer-causing) substances at work

■ **infection** from **bacteria** and other micro-organisms ('biological agents').

Food hygiene

Think about how many times a day a child will have a drink or something to eat. When they are at nursery or school or in a holiday play scheme there will be many opportunities for them to have food or drink.

While food and drink is essential for us to live, badly prepared food and drinks can be a cause of serious illness or even death.

Food Safety (General Food Hygiene) Regulations

These regulations set out the basic hygiene principles that any food business –including all child care settings that provide food or drink – must follow in relation to staff, premises and food handling. It is important that anyone who deals with food and drink, even just serving it to adults or children, has a Food Hygiene Certificate. Ask your tutor if you can take this short course and test at college to gain a Certificate in food hygiene.

Food safety management is all about identifying how and when things could go wrong and introducing checks to stop that happening. Think about daily work with children and how you follow the principles of good hygiene. Food hygiene includes making sure that the preparation of food and drink follows the 'Four C's' highlighted in National food Safety Week 2006:

- **Cleanliness** of hands, surfaces and equipment.

- **Cooking** to the right temperature.

- **Chilling** cooked food as quickly as possible once cooked if it is not going to be eaten straight away and storing uncooked food at the right temperature.

- **Cross-contamination:** making sure that raw food does not contaminate cooked food.

Safe moving and handling

Every time you bend to pick up something reasonably heavy you are at risk of injuring your back – especially if the item is a live wriggling child or you have to twist or turn while carrying. More than one in four of all reportable injuries are caused by poor manual handling. If you are in a placement or job that involves a lot of moving and handling you should have training to make sure that you do it in the safest way possible.

Risk assessment

Accidents to children are so common that it is too easy to assume that nothing can be done to stop them happening. It would be impossible to prevent every single minor bump and graze – but it is possible to eliminate the majority of risks and protect children. Children can move onto a new stage of development before carers realise it, and can be at risk of injury.

Risk assessments have to be carried out in all public places, places of employment, care settings etc. to make sure that people are not injured unnecessarily. When a risk assessment is carried out the qualified person doing it has to think about the hazard and the risk.

- **Hazard**: something likely to cause harm.

- **Risk**: the seriousness of a hazard and its likelihood to cause harm.

For example, a child care setting on a main road could be a major risk. The hazard is the road and the traffic. However, although the risk is serious, it is unlikely to cause harm as the entrance on to the road is secure and carefully controlled and a child could not get out into the road.

Think about it

The next time you are in placement keep a tally (count) of how many times someone picks a child or object up from the floor or another surface.

Did you know?

The Manual Handling Operations (MHO) Regulations 1992 are in force to reduce the very large incidence of injury and ill-health arising from the manual handling of loads at work. As with the Health and Safety at Work Act, the MHO Regulations place duties upon employers in respect of their own employees.

Safe use of equipment and materials

Safety checks

Throughout the course of the day, checks should be made in all the following areas.

Buildings and maintenance

- Doors opening into entrances and exits from the building must not be capable of being opened by young children.

- Emergency exits must be clear and easy to open from the inside.

- Floors should not have any loose rugs or pieces of carpet.

Cleanliness of the general environment

- There should be a high standard of cleanliness throughout the building.

- Spillages should be immediately cleaned.

- Toilet areas should be regularly cleaned and checked.

Food preparation areas

- All staff dealing with food should have a Food Hygiene Certificate.

- All regulations relating to food storage should be followed.

Safe storage and use of equipment

- Cupboards at 'child level' should not contain cleaning items, knives, tools or any other potentially dangerous items.

- Toys with very small parts should be kept well away from children under three years of age.

- Children should not be able to touch heaters and radiators.

Think about it

Imagine you have been asked to help the supervisor in the toddler room with the daily safety checks. Your supervisor has asked you to write down your checklist of points for safety in the room. Make your list showing the checks you would carry out to ensure the safety of all the children in your care.

Best practice in your work placement

Being aware of potential dangers to a child's health and safety is not enough – you must plan activities and routines with safety in mind. Some of the things to think about are listed below.

- Regularly check equipment for broken parts and sharp edges.
- Make sure that large equipment and toys are arranged to allow safe use by all children.
- Check outside play areas daily for broken glass, syringes and other dangerous litter.
- Check toilet and washing facilities regularly for cleanliness and supplies of toilet paper and soap.

- Make sure that all locks, catches, etc. that stop children leaving the building alone are working.
- Do not store dangerous items, for example knives or bleach, in cupboards and shelves that are accessible to children.
- Always follow procedures for dealing with spillages of urine, faeces, blood and vomit.
- Follow the procedures for dealing with visitors to the setting, for example reporting and signing in.
- Follow good practice in the preparation of food and drink.

Outdoor areas

■ Outdoor slides, swings, etc. should have safe, impact absorbing matting provided and should be checked for safety.

■ Gates should not be able to be opened by young children.

■ Sandpits should be kept covered when not in use.

Working practices that promote health and safety

■ Adults must not leave bags or coats containing medicines within reach of children.

■ Adults must not bring hot drinks into the same room as children.

■ All stairs should have fixed guards at the top and bottom.

■ Children using baby walkers, bicycles, etc. should be supervised at all times and should wear helmets where appropriate.

Case study

Health and safety outside

Lee is working in a child care setting that also has an after-school club for older children. The older children enjoy ball games in the outdoor play area. Last night he was concerned that some of the bigger boys had been using the swings meant for younger children. When he goes outside he notices that the outside gate has been left open and there is a dog wandering around the play area, especially in the sandpit.

1 Should Lee allow the children outside to play?
2 What action should Lee take now?
3 What can the manager of the setting do to stop the events that concern Lee?

Safety equipment

Many items of equipment are used to keep children safe in early years' settings. Regular checks on all safety equipment should be carried out, and manufacturers' instructions should be closely followed, especially if items need maintaining or cleaning. In general, it is considered good practice to buy new equipment to be sure that it conforms to the latest safety regulations. Second-hand or older equipment needs to be carefully checked as some items can become less effective through wear and tear.

Type of equipment	Purpose
Bath mats	Prevent children and babies from slipping in the bath
Car seats and booster cushions	Help to protect children and babies if a car suddenly brakes or is involved in an accident Car seats have to be correctly fitted. Seats must be correct for the age of the baby or child
Cooker guards	Prevent children from tipping over pans
Electric plug socket covers	Prevent children from putting their fingers or objects into plug sockets
Fire guards	Used around heaters and radiators to prevent children from being burnt
Highchairs	Help young children to sit safely at mealtimes Include harnesses to strap children in
Reins and harnesses	Prevent children from straying into a road or dangerous area when they are outside Also used in pushchairs and highchairs to prevent children from falling out
Safety gates	Prevent babies and children from falling downstairs or from having access to certain areas
Window and cupboard door locks	Prevent children from opening cupboards and windows

■ *Safety equipment for babies and children*

Outdoor spaces

As part of the preparation for an outdoor session, you should carry out the following checks to ensure that the outdoor setting is safe.

■ **Equipment:** large apparatus such as swings and slides should be wiped down and checked for any signs of wear and tear.

■ **Access and fencing:** outdoor areas should be fenced off to prevent children from wandering away and also to make sure that strangers or animals do not have access. Fences and gates should be checked before allowing children outside.

■ **Plants and animals:** some plants are poisonous and others such as nettles and thistles can sting or scratch children. Regular checks on the plants in the area are important. You should also look out for any signs of animal droppings including cats' and dogs' faeces. Disinfect any area that has been soiled. If sandpits are contaminated, do not allow children into them until the sand has been changed.

■ **Dustbins:** some outdoor settings can be close to bins and dustbins. It is important that lids are kept on bins and wherever possible they should be moved out of reach of children. In summer there is also the added danger of wasps and other insects hovering around bins.

■ **Sun protection:** children will need adequate protection from the sun. Hats and sunscreen should always be used in sunny weather.

Safety with animals

While children can learn a lot from and enjoy contact with animals, any setting that cares for animals will have to pay particular attention to health and safety. Some diseases are associated with animals, and it is important before introducing a new pet to make sure that any risks have been thought about. For example, a risk of caring for cats and dogs is the danger that children can become infected with one of the worms that can be present in these animals' faeces.

In addition, children have to be taught that animals are not playthings. This means that an adult should closely supervise all contact between animals and children so that the animals are treated with respect. Good supervision should prevent children from being bitten or scratched by distressed or irritated pets.

Best practice in your work placement

Safety with animals

How the risk of infection can be minimised when caring for animals:

■ feeding animals away from kitchen areas
■ using separate utensils for feeding animals
■ making sure that animals are not allowed near children's food or sleeping areas

■ following recommended care routines for animals, for example vaccinations, worming, and flea control measures
■ ensuring that children wash their hands thoroughly after handling any animal
■ regularly cleaning animals' cages or areas.

Layout and organisation

The way a room is organised depends on many factors including what it is being used for, the ages of the children and the type of room. There are several basic principles that need to be thought about when planning a room. These include:

■ making sure that all the children can access everything; think about children with restricted mobility or limited vision

■ making sure that doors and fire exits are unobstructed

■ allowing sufficient space around tables for children to move around safely

■ making sure that staff have good visibility so that they can supervise children easily

- making sure that 'messy' activities are situated near washbasins and on suitable flooring

- ensuring that free-standing furniture, such as cupboards, cannot topple over onto children.

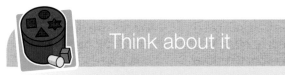

Think about it

Look at the picture below. How would you make the room safer for a young child?

- *How many dangers can you spot in this picture?*

If you are working with children who have special needs, some adaptations may be necessary to the environment so that they can safely join in with all the activities. The type of adaptations will depend on the individual needs of the children. Talking to the parents or professionals who may be working with the child to find out his or her particular needs is the best approach.

Supervision

The key factor in protecting children in your care from accidents and injury is that you understand the risks they are exposed to, especially in relation to their age and stage of development. You should then be able to help to identify risks for situations and certain groups of children.

The following table shows the common accidents that occur at different ages, why they occur and, most importantly, what you need to think about when supervising children.

Did you know?

The figures in the table below are only a part of the picture. Every year some two million children – about one in five – are seen in accident and emergency departments after an accident. Around 320 children die each year as a result of accidents and many more suffer long-term disability.

Age/stage of development	Common accidents	Reasons	Prevention
Birth to crawling Very dependent and vulnerable – but can move more than you think	Falls from raised surfaces	Even small babies can move by wriggling, the risk increases as the baby grows	Never leave a baby unattended on a raised surface or put a bouncing chair on a raised surface
	Suffocation	Babies cannot push covers or other items away from their face	Do not use duvets or pillows for babies under one year
	Choking	Young babies cannot deal with large volumes of fluid or hard objects	Never 'prop feed' Never leave a baby alone when giving solids Keep small objects away from a baby's grasp Make sure that older children do not put anything in a baby's mouth
	Strangulation	Ribbons, jewellery or wool could get caught in a cot or car seat, for example	Never put ribbons or jewellery around a baby's neck Check clothing is not too tight
	Burns and scalds	A carer has a hot drink when holding a baby Bath water is too hot because it has not been tested Feeds are heated in a microwave A baby's skin is sun burnt	Never have hot drinks near young children Test bath water carefully Never use microwaves for heating feeds Keep the baby well covered and protected from the sun
	Drowning	A baby is left alone or with other children in the bath for a few seconds	Never leave a young baby in water without an adult present
Crawling to walking, about 6–15 months Mobile at last!	Falls downstairs, from raised surfaces, highchairs, cots	As a baby starts to become mobile he or she wants to explore but has no understanding at all of danger, for example from stairs, furniture, high-chairs	Always guard stairs Use a five-point harness Never leave a baby on high surfaces

Age/stage of development	Common accidents	Reasons	Prevention
	Suffocation from bedding, plastic bags and choking by food and small objects	A baby can still get trapped in bedding A baby will explore plastic bags, which are seen as a toy A baby uses the mouth to explore, so will put anything new into the mouth – anything larger than a 2 pence piece will cause choking	Do not use a duvet on a baby under one year Keep plastic bags out of reach Always stay with a baby who is eating or drinking Keep small items out of reach Teach older children not to put anything in a baby's mouth Never allow a child under the age of six to have peanuts
	Strangulation	Clothing is still a risk Unexpected items can cause problems to a mobile baby, for example washing lines, window blind cords, belts	Never put anything around a baby's neck and always check clothing Keep blind cords, etc. short and out of reach, and never next to a cot or bed
	Burns and scalds	With increased mobility a baby can now reach things on surfaces, for example drinks, radiators and ovens, and can pull on kettle flexes and pan handles When sunny, it is difficult to keep a mobile baby in the shade A baby has no understanding of what 'hot' is and cannot learn from experience at this stage	Take the same precautions as for a young baby. Use a coiled flex on kettles and a safety gate to bar access to the kitchen when cooking, etc. Take extra care with clothes, sun creams and hats in the sun Keep out of the sun between 11am and 3pm Fit guards and keep all possible sources of burns and scalds out of reach
	Drowning	Out of curiosity a baby may peer into water containers A baby enjoys water play and being left alone in the bath	Supervise all water play very closely and empty water containers immediately when finished with. Never leave a baby alone in the bath or with older children

continued ▶

Age/stage of development	Common accidents	Reasons	Prevention
	Cuts and bruises	First mobile movements are often unsteady and poorly co-ordinated Out of curiosity a baby may grab anything that takes his or her attention, even if it is big and heavy	Carefully position furniture with hard or sharp edges so that there is less chance of injury Move dangerous and/or heavy items that are a risk
	Falls and injuries during transport	A car seat may not be correctly secured A baby may fall out of a pram or pushchair if no harness is used Baby walkers are associated with a range of injuries, especially falls and burns	Always secure a baby in the correct car seat, and use harnesses in prams, etc. Do not use baby walkers
Toddlers, about one to three years Very inquisitive and full of energy Short attention span and totally absorbed in themselves Not old enough to understand the concept of danger, and do not always learn from experience 	Falls downstairs and from windows	New found climbing skills and increased manual dexterity mean toddlers can get upstairs, onto window sills, and can open catches	Use good safety gates and window locks that cannot be opened by the toddler Teach the toddler to climb stairs but do not allow him or her to use them alone Avoid putting furniture underneath windows
	Suffocation and choking	A toddler may want to play with plastic bags A toddler may be still learning to chew and still putting things in the mouth	Keep plastic bags out of reach and preferably destroy them Take precautions as for younger children It is important to still avoid peanuts as the oil in them can cause swelling of the bronchial tubes
	Poisoning	Curiosity and increasing skills mean a toddler has access to poisonous substances even medicines (despite child resistant tops), chemicals and berries	Keep all medicines and chemicals locked away and out of reach Keep chemicals in original containers Do not keep medicines in handbags or by the bed Check gardens for poisonous plants

Age/stage of development	Common accidents	Reasons	Prevention
	Strangulation	A toddler may get his or her head into but not out of gaps Clothing may have poor necklines, loose cords, etc.	Supervise climbing games Check necklines and loose cords
	Burns and scalds	Curiosity is still an issue – pans and irons are a hazard A toddler also starts to imitate adults A toddler is more able to use matches if found A toddler's skin is still fragile and easy to burn, for example in a hot bath	Take precautions as for babies of 6–15 months, but with extra vigilance
	Drowning	A toddler has increasing mobility, independence and curiosity – especially about garden ponds Drowning is possible in very small amounts of water	Closely supervise a toddler around any water Empty water containers when they are finished with Ensure there is secure fencing around ponds Stay with a toddler in the bath
	Cuts and bruises	Fingers can easily be trapped in door jambs Toddlers may cut themselves while trying to imitate adults using scissors, knives or razors Toddlers could run into low glass in doors	Be aware of the risk of doors when little fingers are around Keep scissors, etc. out of reach Use safety glass or board up low glass doors
	Out and about	Toddlers may want to experiment with their car seat or buggy harness Toddlers may be left alone in a car Toddlers may run off when out on the street	Use the correct seat and harness, and discourage messing with fastenings Never leave toddlers alone in a car Use a harness and reins when out on the road Start simple road safety training

Age/stage of development	Common accidents	Reasons	Prevention
About three to five years Improving co-ordination and increasing understanding of action and consequence May well forget safety instructions when tired or distracted Still enjoy testing their abilities and finding unusual ways to use toys and other objects!	Falls downstairs, from windows and from play equipment	Children are attracted to stairs and windows – they use their powerful imaginations to be Superman, etc. Children test their own skills by climbing higher and so are at risk of falling further	Do not allow stairs to be used for playing Fit window locks and tell children about the dangers Choose playgrounds with impact absorbing surfaces Tell children how to use equipment properly
	Choking and suffocation	Children may want to eat on the move Ice cubes and some small sweets pose a danger Peanuts are still a risk	Encourage children to sit still while eating and not to run with sweets in their mouth Avoid peanuts with children under six
	Poisoning	Children could confuse sweets with medicines and berries Children have increased skills at overcoming locks and resistant caps	Keep medicines, etc. locked away Teach children not to eat anything they pick outside without checking with you
	Burns and scalds	When copying adults there is a danger from hot foods, liquids, taps and candles. Children understand the concept of 'hot, do not touch' but can easily forget, especially when practising their increased manual skills of turning and switching	Keep dangerous items out of reach, especially matches and candles Teach children what to do if a fire or smoke alarm goes off Use thermostatic valves on taps
	Drowning	Any open water remains a threat, especially as children become more independent A child can be left in the bath from about four years, but an adult should still be nearby	Supervise children closely near water Fence off ponds Teach children to swim
	Cuts	Children can now be taught to use scissors and knives safely There is still a risk with sharp objects if they are not used safely or in play	Keep sharp objects out of reach Teach children how to use them safely

Age/stage of development	Common accidents	Reasons	Prevention
	Out and about	Children do not have the understanding or experience to deal with traffic	Never allow children under five on the road alone – on foot or on a bike
		They may have started to ride a bicycle	Teach road safety, but be aware of children's limits of remembering and understanding
			Ensure children always use a helmet when on a bike
About five to seven years and onwards Risk assessment skills improving, but still impulsive and may overestimate ability More external influences on behaviour	Falls, choking, poisoning, burns and scalds, drowning, cuts and bruises, accidents when out and about	Injuries at this age are often due to children being keen to help and copy adults, but misjudging their abilities Boisterous play can result in accidents The increasing influence of friends persuading them to 'have a go' can increase the risk	As for ages three to five, ensure dangerous items are not easy to reach Encourage children to start taking some responsibility for their own safety, but the extent of this will vary Realise that being able to repeat a rule does not mean a child understands or will remember to follow it; this improves as the child gets older, but outside influence can 'overrule' this

■ *Common accidents, why they occur and how they can be prevented*

Did you know?

- *In 2002 more than 27,700 babies under six months were injured in accidents.*
- *In 2002 38,300 babies under a year old were taken to hospital after a fall, and 17,000 with burns and scalds.*
- *In 2002 more than 4,400 children aged between three and five years were injured in road accidents and 527 were injured in fires; two died.*
- *In 2002 falls accounted for more than 150,500 hospital attendances of five- to seven-year-olds, 13,400 going with cuts and 400 after a choking incident.*
- *Over 10,700 eight- to eleven-year-olds were injured on the roads, 12,600 in public playgrounds.*

Source: Child Accident Prevention Trust, 2003

Case study

Preventing accidents

Jasmine, aged four, has a baby brother Luke who is 15 months old. Jasmine is becoming very independent. She lives in an old house with a cellar and a front door that opens onto a busy main road. When she is outside with her carers she does not always like to have her hand held, preferring to 'do it herself'. Jasmine's brother Luke is just starting to walk and in Jasmine's words is always getting into mischief.

1 Can you think of any dangers that Jasmine and Luke might be at risk from?
2 Why do you think these are dangers to Jasmine and Luke?
3 What steps should their parents and carers be taking to protect them from possible injury?

Think about it

Consider two common and popular activities – painting and outdoor play on large equipment. What are the potential dangers to the children from each point in the list?

Painting:
■ water spilt on floor
■ children moving around with paint brushes
■ cleaning up after the activity.

Outdoor play:
■ children running around
■ height of equipment
■ recent rain.

Make a list of why children might be injured as a result of any of these points and identify what you could do to prevent injury.

It would be very easy to respond to all the risks children are exposed to by not allowing them to explore or experiment. But just think about how that would affect a child's development.

Any activity a child does has some risk attached, even something as simple as painting. If the activity is well planned and organised with thought given to possible dangers, the risk of accidents or injuries should be minimal.

The secret is to balance the risk of an activity against the benefit to and safety of the child. This is known as risk assessment.

Case study

Risk assessment for outdoor activities

Lee is planning an outing to the local park with two groups of children from his child care setting. Lee hopes that he can include some nature work, physical skill development and art work with the children. They are planning to take a group of six four-year-olds from the pre-school group and a group of eight seven- and eight-year-olds from the after-school group.

1 List the different safety risks for each of the groups.
2 What will Lee need to think about for each group?
3 How much freedom will each group be able to have when they are in the park?

Personal safety and safety of others

While you are maintaining their safety, it is important that children are given the freedom to develop their skills. They should have adult support but not too much intervention.

An important point of safety is your safety. If you make sure that you know the rules of your placement – and follow them – you should be in a safe situation. Most accidents and incidents are caused by people breaking rules.

If you are not comfortable with something you are asked to do – do not do it. Stop and tell someone in charge that you are not happy.

Best practice in your work placement

How to ensure children's safety
Equipment safety

- Always ensure that objects and equipment are regularly checked for wear and tear, such as fraying ropes and rusting joints.
- Check that equipment is clean and dry, especially slides, steps, etc.

Personal safety

- Ensure that each child has the space to move freely without bumping into other children or objects.
- Ensure that the appropriate adult to child ratio required by your social services department is maintained for adequate supervision.

- Ensure that swings and rope ladders are used by one child at a time. All other children should be discouraged from playing nearby in case they are hurt by a swing or rope.
- Ensure all children are visible.

Safety of the environment

- Check that outdoor areas are free from harmful waste such as dog faeces (which can cause eye damage to young children), broken equipment and litter.
- Ensure that surfaces are soft and safe, to encourage freedom of movement.

Good hygiene practice

All children pick up infections and become ill from time to time as their immune systems develop. However, many illnesses are caused by poor hygiene practices. The hospital superbug is mostly a result of doctors and nurses not washing their hands properly.

You do not need to know the science behind all different types of infections, but you do need to know how infection is passed on from one person to another.

The picture below shows some of the ways that bacteria and viruses can be passed on to others. Just think of all the times you may pass infection from one source to another. How can you help to protect yourself as well as the children you are working with?

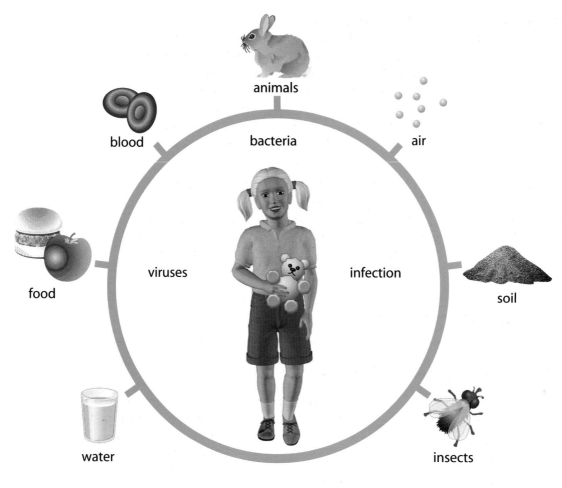

■ *The ways in which disease can be transmitted*

Did you know?

In a survey one in three men and one in five women admit they don't wash their hands after going to the loo or before preparing food. Bacteria left on a doorknob by one person can be picked up by the next 14 who touch it – then passed on to everything they touch.

Source: *Good Housekeeping, August 2004*

Best practice in your work placement

How to avoid infection

- Always wash your hands after using the toilet, changing nappies, handling animals and before handling food.
- Dispose of dirty nappies and other soiled items correctly.
- Cover coughs and sneezes and dispose of tissues correctly.
- Always cover any cuts or grazes that you may have and use plastic gloves when dealing with children with cuts or grazes.
- Follow food hygiene precautions to the letter – never use food or drink that has any risk of being contaminated.
- Take care when handling animals – make sure that children do not let them lick their faces and that they always wash their hands after handling animals.
- Take care that gardens and sandpits are not contaminated by animal faeces.

Issues concerning HIV and hepatitis

The number of people, including children, who are infected with the HIV virus or hepatitis is rising. There are many reasons why a child may be infected, but the important thing is to minimise the risk to yourself and to the children. If you follow basic good hygiene practices as outlined above, you will not be at risk from any child who is unfortunate enough to have contracted HIV or hepatitis. These infections are carried in the blood or other bodily fluids. Another person can only be infected by direct contact with that fluid or through an open wound.

HIV is not transmitted by casual physical contact, coughing, sneezing, kissing, sharing toilet and washing facilities, using eating utensils or consuming food and beverages handled by someone who has HIV; it is not spread by mosquitoes or other insect bites. If you always wear gloves when changing nappies and carrying out first aid, and always keep cuts and grazes covered you will not be at risk of infection.

Assessment activities

Assessment Activity 1

Working with a partner make a list of all the different laws and regulations governing safety.

You should include the following:

- adult to child ratios
- Health and Safety at Work Act
- COSHH regulations
- safe moving and handling
- risk assessment
- RIDDOR
- food hygiene

Assessment Activity 2

Matthew is two years old and attends nursery on a daily basis. Answer the questions that follow with reference to Matthew.

- How many other children will be cared for by an adult along with Matthew?
- Briefly describe all the ways in which Matthew will be protected by the Health and Safety at Work Act.
- How will COSHH Regulations help to protect Matthew?
- If Matthew were to have an accident what procedures would have to be followed?
- How will risk assessment help to protect Matthew?
- Matthew has at least two meals a day at nursery. How do the Food Safety Regulations ensure that his meals are safe and do not make him ill?
- One day Matthew falls over and has to be picked up by the carer looking after him. How do the regulations help to protect the carer when she picks him up?

Now think about all the other age groups from birth to seven years.

You should now make your own notes about all the relevant legislation and regulations that are in place in a child care setting.

When you have done this you will have met part of Pass criterion 1 (P1) and if you explain why these are needed you will also have met part of Merit criterion 1 (M1).

continued ▶

Assessment Activity 3

In your work placement find out what the policy is for checking the safe use of materials and equipment both inside and outside, including safety equipment such as security gates and safety with animals. Make a list of the items in your work placement's policy.

In class, discuss and record on a large sheet of paper all the safety procedures for checking equipment and materials in your placements.

This activity will provide further evidence towards meeting P1. If you explain the need for checking safety considerations you will provide further evidence towards M1.

Assessment Activity 4

Find out the manufacturer's instructions on at least three pieces of equipment and materials. In class, discuss and record these manufacturers' instructions.

Make your own notes about manufacturers' instructions.

Assessment Activity 5

At the beginning of the day check all aspects of hygiene and safety in your placement. List everything you checked.

In the middle of the day and at the end of the day, check all hygiene and safety aspects again.

Make a list of all the checks that you made at these three different times of the day. Were

there any differences in the checks you made at the different times of the day?

Assessment Activities 4 and 5 will provide further evidence towards P1 and towards M1 if you explain why these checks are needed.

Assessment Activity 6

Draw a diagram of the layout of furniture and fixtures of a nursery for children aged two to three years, thinking carefully about the basic principles that need to be considered such as access, not obstructing doors or fire exits, good visibility for staff, the situation of 'messy' activities and the stability of furniture. How does this layout help to keep children safe?

How would you change it for younger and older children or for children with disabilities?

■ Make your own notes to cover all of this. This will provide further evidence towards P1 and M1.

continued ▶

Assessment Activity 7

Briefly describe how you would supervise children at different ages, with different abilities and needs, but without overprotecting them.

You could make a chart to show this.

When you have completed Assessment Activities 1–7 you will have covered all of Pass criterion 1 (P1), which asks you to outline the safety considerations needed, including the relevant legislation, regulations to maintain a safe and secure environment in a child care setting.

If you wish to meet Merit criterion 1 (M1) you will need to explain how and why safety considerations, including legislative requirements, are needed in a child care setting with respect to equipment, materials, layout and organisation.

You can now go on to justify the layout, organisation, equipment and materials in a child care setting known to you in terms of safety considerations. This will enable you to meet Distinction criterion 1 (D1).

Assessment Activity 8

Find out from your work placement what the policy is for handling body fluids such as blood, urine and faeces and including the disposal of dirty nappies.

Make careful notes about this.

Write notes about the other steps that need to be taken to ensure good hygiene and safe food handling, and the avoidance of cross-infection.

When you have completed this activity you will have met Pass criterion 2 (P2), for which you must outline (briefly describe) the basic hygiene principles in a child care setting.

If you explain the importance of ensuring that hygiene principles are carried out in a child care setting you will also have met Merit criterion 2 (M2).

2.2 Know how to support the protection of children from abuse

This section covers:

- policies and procedures
- types, signs and symptoms of abuse
- awareness.

Policies and procedures

Most of this unit focuses on your role in protecting children and keeping them safe. Even as a student in placement you have responsibilities – make sure that you know the policies and procedures relating to safety and **abuse** in your placement. One very important part of keeping children safe is recognising when they are not safe outside the child care setting.

The National Standards for Under Eights Day Care and Childminding states that 'all registered persons comply with local **child protection** procedures that are approved by the area child protection committee (ACPC) and ensure that all adults working and looking after children in the provision are able to put the practices and procedures into place.'

It is one of the most important responsibilities of a child care worker to report suspicion of abuse to an appropriate person. Even as a student you are one of the workers in close contact with a child on a daily basis and so may be the most likely person to spot the warning signs of possible abuse. Dealing with any suspicions promptly and appropriately is vital. If you have any suspicions you must immediately report them to your supervisor who can take appropriate action. Abuse can happen as a one-off incident or can be a regular feature of a child's life. Abuse can take place anywhere and by anyone, but the majority of abuse is carried out by someone the child knows.

In 2000 the **NSPCC** published the results of a national survey of 3000 young people aged 18 to 24 about their experience of a wide range of issues and found that:

- 7 per cent had been physically abused by a carer
- 6 per cent had suffered frequent and severe emotional maltreatment as children
- 4 per cent had been sexually abused
- 80 per cent of physically abused children have also witnessed domestic violence in their homes
- a significant number of children faced repeated pathological and multiple forms of abuse at the hands of parents or carers.

Source: Cawson P., 2002, Child Maltreatment in the Family, NSPCC

Did you know?

At the end of March 2003 there were 25,700 children on child protection registers in England. The most commonly recorded risk was for neglect (39 per cent) followed by physical abuse (19 per cent) and emotional abuse (17 per cent).

Source: 12th annual report of the Chief Inspector of Social Services, Dept of Health, 2003

Types, signs and symptoms of abuse

Evidence of signs and symptoms (see below) does not necessarily mean that a child has been abused; but they can help responsible adults to recognise that something is wrong. The possibility of abuse should be investigated if a child shows a number of these symptoms, or any of them to a marked degree. It is important to realise that a child may be the victim of a combination of different kinds of abuse.

Think about a child who is neglected. The child will not be properly clothed and fed. Do you think the child will feel loved and protected? The child may well be suffering from emotional abuse as well as neglect.

It is also possible that a child may show no outward signs of abuse and may be trying to hide what is happening from everyone. If you have any suspicions about the welfare of a child in your setting, share it with your supervisor or designated person. Your fears may be unfounded, but it is better to be overcautious in passing information on than to ignore warning signs. It is very important to handle the issues in a sensitive manner and not upset the child concerned.

However, not every sign means a child is being abused. Have you cared for children who always appear a bit grubby and maybe smell a little, but are happy and loved by parents? Some physical signs such as darkened areas can be birth marks and not bruising, for example some infants of Asian or African heritage can have a dark bluish area on their lower back and/or buttocks. This is sometimes known as a Mongolian Blue Spot.

Did you know?

In 2003 the Laming Report found that far too often children are identified as causing concern, but that different agencies, for example schools or social services have not always shared information with each other. As a result children die from abuse unnecessarily. Victoria Climbie, the little girl whose death led to the Laming Report, had been seen by many different child care workers from the health, social and education services. She still died at the hands of her aunt and her aunt's boyfriend. The Children Act 2005 aims to make sure that services work together to share information to try to stop such deaths happening.

Ears
pinch marks, bruising

Mouth
torn fenulum

Shoulders
bruising, grasp marks

Arms
bruising, grasp marks, burns

Genitals
bruising

Knees
grasp marks

Eyes
bruising

Cheeks/face
bruising, finger marks

Neck
bruising, grasp marks

Chest
bruising, grasp marks

Hands
scalds, burns

Back, buttocks, thighs
linear bruising, outline of belt buckle, scalds, burns

■ *The usual position of injuries in cases of child abuse*

Think about it

Find out what is happening in your area as a result of the Children Act and the Laming Report. Does your area have a Children's Trust and a Director responsible for the protection of all children?

Physical abuse

Physical abuse is when a child is physically hurt or injured. Hitting, kicking, beating with objects, throwing and shaking are all physical abuse. They can cause pain, cuts, and bruising, broken bones and sometimes even death.

Signs and symptoms

- unexplained recurrent injuries or burns
- wearing clothes to cover injuries, even in hot weather
- refusal to undress for games
- bald patches of hair
- repeated running away
- fear of medical examination
- aggression towards self and others
- fear of physical contact – shrinking back if approached or touched.

Case study

Suspicious bruising

Hugh, aged five, has been away from school for two days due to 'being unwell' in the note from his mother. You are helping him to get changed for PE in the hall and he jumps when you are pulling his jumper off. The back of his upper arms and his back are covered in deep purple bruising. When you gently ask how they happened, he shrugs and says he fell off his bunk bed.

1 What should you do now?
2 What should you not do?
3 Who should you talk to about this?
4 Who should you **not** talk to about the incident?

Many signs of physical abuse can be confused with genuine accidental injuries. However, they are often not in the places or distribution you would expect, or the explanation does not fit, or you may see the outline of a belt buckle or cigarette burn. Suspicion should be aroused if the parents have not sought medical advice soon after the injury occurred.

Case study

Jumping to conclusions

Jane was very upset when she took Alex, her nine-month-old son, to the local hospital's accident and emergency department. She had slipped down the stairs while carrying Alex and he had obviously broken his upper leg as she fell with him. An X-ray confirmed that Alex had a fracture to his femur and would need several weeks in hospital. To Jane's horror the doctor and nurses started to suggest she had deliberately hurt her son and called in the social services department. In her distress Jane did not immediately remember that her neighbour had been in the house when the accident happened, and luckily could confirm that what she said was true.

1 Why do you think the doctor involved social services?
2 Do you think this was the right thing to do?

Emotional abuse

Emotional abuse is when a child is not given love, approval or acceptance. A child may be constantly criticised, blamed, sworn and shouted at, told that other people are better than he or she is and rejected by those the child looks to for affection.

Signs and symptoms
- delayed development
- sudden speech problems, for example stammering
- low self-esteem ('I'm stupid, ugly, worthless', etc.)
- fear of any new situation
- neurotic behaviour, for example rocking, hair twisting, self-mutilation
- extremes of withdrawal or aggression.

Neglect

Neglect, which can result in failure to thrive, is when parents or others looking after a child do not provide the child with proper food, warmth, shelter, clothing, care and protection.

Signs and symptoms
- constant hunger
- poor personal hygiene
- constant tiredness
- poor state of clothing
- unusual thinness
- untreated medical problems
- no social relationships
- stealing food
- destructive tendencies.

Case study

Possible neglect

Toby is six years old and has an older sister, Sam, who is 11. Their parents both have drinking problems. Sometimes there is nothing to eat in the house. Sam is often left alone to look after her younger brother. The school they both go to has noticed that they are always tired and appear very thin. Their clothes are often dirty and Toby is often in the same clothes for a few days.

One day when Sam comes to collect Toby from the classroom to go home, he bursts into tears and says he doesn't want to go home.

1 What do you think Toby's teacher should do?
2 What do you think should have already happened?

Sexual abuse

Sexual abuse is when a child is forced or persuaded into sexual acts or situations by others. Children might be encouraged to look at pornography, be harassed by sexual suggestions or comments, be touched sexually or forced to have sex.

Signs and symptoms

- sexual knowledge or behaviour that is inappropriate to the child's age
- medical problems such as chronic itching, pain in the genitals or venereal diseases
- depression, self-mutilation, suicide attempts, running away, overdoses or **anorexia**
- personality changes such as becoming insecure or clinging
- regressing to younger behaviour patterns such as thumb sucking or bringing out discarded cuddly toys
- sudden loss of appetite or compulsive eating
- being isolated or withdrawn
- an inability to concentrate
- lack of trust or fear of someone they know well, such as not wanting to be alone with a babysitter or child minder
- starting to wet or soil again, day or night
- become worried about clothing being removed
- suddenly drawing sexually explicit pictures
- trying to be 'ultra-good' or perfect; overreacting to criticism.

Bullying and harassment

This is also a form of abuse that affects older children particularly. It can continue for a long time and can include one or more of the following:

- emotional bullying – the most common type – including not speaking and excluding (sending to Coventry), tormenting, ridicule, humiliation
- physical bullying including pushing, kicking, hitting, pinching and other forms of violence or threats
- verbal bullying including name-calling, sarcasm, spreading rumours, persistent teasing
- racist bullying involving racial taunts, writing graffiti, gestures
- sexual bullying involving unwanted physical contact or abusive comments
- homophobic bullying including hostile or offensive action against lesbians, gay males or bisexuals, or those thought to be lesbian, gay or bisexual.

Bullying can be carried out by one person against another, or by groups of people 'ganging up' on a person. Bullying is not always delivered as a personal, face-to-face attack, but can also be delivered through technology, such as mobile phones and the internet. This is known as cyber-bullying.

Persistent bullying can result in:

- depression
- low self-esteem
- shyness
- poor academic achievement
- isolation
- threatened or attempted suicide
- running away.

Did you know?

An estimated 77,000 under-16s run away from home each year putting themselves in considerable danger of physical or sexual assault. Some 80 per cent of runaways say it is due to family problems. More than 20,000 of the runaways are under 11 years. Runaways under 11 are more likely to have experienced physical abuse at home.

Case study

Dealing with children who have been bullied

Aysha, aged 13, contacted a telephone support service after years of constantly being bullied at school. She often had things stolen from her, especially new school bags or trainers. The two girls who were bullying her had started at primary school by calling her names and following her home. More recently they had started to push her over if she walked past them and were spreading unpleasant rumours about her father. Aysha has started to miss going to school to avoid meeting the bullies. The telephone counsellor explained to Aysha that it was her right to be educated without fear and encouraged Aysha to ask a friend to go with her to talk to the head of her year.

1 Why do you think it has taken so long for her to tell someone?
2 How do you think this has made Aysha feel about herself?
3 What do you think you could have done if you were working at Aysha's school?

Awareness

It is essential to encourage children to be aware of their own bodies and to understand their rights not to be abused according to their age, needs and abilities.

The United Nations Convention on the Rights of the Child, signed by the UK, aims to make sure that all children are treated equally and fairly. It is an undeniable right that all children are fairly treated, loved, protected and helped to develop to the best of their ability.

■ *A happy and well-nurtured child*

These rights include:

- the right to life and the best chance to develop fully
- the right to enjoy a decent standard of living
- the right to a free education
- the right to be as healthy as possible
- the right to live in a safe, healthy, unpolluted environment and the right to safe, nutritious food and water.

The Government **must** protect children from:

- doing work which could be dangerous or which could harm their health
- doing work which interferes with their education
- dangerous drugs
- being abducted or sold
- sexual abuse.

Children may be separated from parents or carers **only** if it is in the child's best interests. If separated, for example in care (being looked after by someone else), the child has the right to keep in regular touch with his or her parents and siblings unless it would be harmful to do so.

If you are aware of the rights of children, you will be able to think about how you can help to protect children and also help them to protect themselves.

Best practice in your work placement

How your placement should be helping to keep children safe

- Teaching children how to keep themselves safe.
- Encouraging them to share worries about abuse with their friends and to tell a trusted adult.
- Making sure they know that being abused is never their fault and that abuse is never right.
- Promoting services such as Childline or the NSPCC Child Protection Helpline to older children.

Did you know?

In July 2004 the Children's Rights Director for England produced a report about keeping children safe. The Director asked children of all ages for their views about this important aspect of their lives. The children identified many different risks they felt exposed to. The commonest were bullying, illness and accidents. Many children felt that the risk of abuse was greatest when they were being looked after by people they did not know (although this is not the case).

The children in the report all felt good about being asked for their views. These are some of their statements.

- *Pay attention and talk seriously to children.*
- *Don't patronise us – explain so we can understand – don't talk complex.*
- *Don't always believe an adult over a child.*
- *We want to be looked after by adults we can trust.*
- *Treat us individually – children are not all the same.*

Source: Morgan, R. (2004) 'Safe From Harm: Children's Views' report, CSCI

Helping to protect children

Very young children and babies need protecting by adults, and when abuse happens the carers responsible need a lot of support and help. Abuse happens for all sorts of reasons. One of the best ways of preventing abuse is to ensure that all parents feel good about themselves and have the support they need when things go wrong for them. This is the role of more senior workers but it is important to be aware of this issue.

You can help by knowing that to feel safe and protected, children need to feel good about themselves. They need to have a good level of self-esteem and helping a child to develop this is an important skill of a child care worker. A child who has high self-esteem will do better in many aspects of development. Self-esteem can be helped by:

- giving lots of praise and encouragement
- encouraging independence with lots of opportunities to try things out

Think about it

How could the Keepsafe Code be used in your placement?

Could you put it into a picture format with titles?

How could you get the children to practise actions for the Keepsafe Code?

What else might you need to do with the children so that they understand about hugs and touching that they are not comfortable with?

- teaching children how to be assertive – that means having their own needs met but still respecting those of others
- encouraging co-operation, respect and tolerance between children, and giving a positive example yourself.

It is important to be available to talk with children about any concerns they may have. If they are upset by a reported case of abuse, be as reassuring as possible. These cases are very rare, even though it is hard to believe when they are constantly in the media. Stress that almost all children lead safe and happy lives and only a very tiny percentage of adults want to hurt children in any way.

The right not to be abused

To be able to tell someone that they are unhappy with someone else's behaviour, children need help to use the right language, to draw pictures or show an adult on a doll, for example.

Using correct anatomical language, at a level appropriate to the child, is important when you are talking about bodies. However, you also need to be aware of the many different terms used by people for a part of the body such as the genitalia or for functions such as passing urine. Simple, age-appropriate sessions, linked to other activities, on how the human body works help children to understand what their bodies can do and raise awareness of what is normal and what is not. You need to help children to understand that they have a right to be safe, and to have people they can tell if they are not feeling safe.

What is safe however? What is OK and what is not OK? Child care settings – along with agencies such as the NSPCC, Childline and Kidscape – are very important in educating children about looking after themselves. The important fact for all children is that they should never feel uncomfortable about someone they are with or about something being done to them.

Have a look at this code for safety from Kidscape. Do you think it can be useful for all children?

The Keepsafe Code

1 Hugs
Hugs and kisses are nice, especially from people we like. Even hugs and kisses that feel good and that you like should never be kept secret.

2 Body
Your body belongs to you and not to anyone else. This means all of your body. If anyone harms you or tries to touch your body in a way which confuses or frightens you, say *no*, if possible, and tell.

3 No
If anyone older than you, even someone you know, tries to touch you in a way you don't like or that confuses you, or which they say is supposed to be a secret, say *no* in a very loud voice.

4 Run or Get Away
Don't talk to anyone you don't know when you are alone, or just with other children. You don't have to be rude, just pretend you didn't hear and

keep going. If a stranger, or a bully, or even someone you know tries to harm you, get away and get help. Make sure you always go towards other people or to a shop, if you can.

5 Yell
Wherever you are, it is all right to yell if someone is trying to hurt you. Practise yelling as loud as you can in a big, deep voice by taking a deep breath and letting the yell come from your stomach, not from your throat.

6 Tell
Tell a grown-up you trust if you are worried or frightened. If the first grown-up you tell doesn't believe or help you, keep telling until someone does. It might not be easy, but even if something has already happened that you have never told before, try to tell now. Who could you tell?

7 Secrets
Secrets such as surprise birthday parties are fun. But some secrets are not good and should never be kept. No bully should ever make you keep the bullying a secret and no one should ask you to keep a kiss, hug or touch secret. If anyone does, even if you know that person, tell a grown-up you trust.

8 Bribes
Don't accept money or sweets or a gift from anyone without first checking with your parents. Most of the time it will be all right, like when you get a present for your birthday from your grandma. But some people try to trick children into doing something by giving them sweets or money. This is called a bribe – don't ever take one! Remember, it is possible that you might have to do what a bully or older person tells you, so that you can keep yourself safe. Don't feel bad if that happens because the most important thing is for you to be safe.

9 Code
Have a code word or sign with your parents or guardians, which only you and they know. If they need to send someone to collect you, they can give that person the code. Don't tell the code to anyone else.

Source: Kidscape

Best practice in your work placement

How to respond to a child's disclosure of possible abuse

- Find out to whom you should report any concern you may have about the safety of a child in your setting.
- Make sure you understand your setting's child protection policy and procedure.
- Always pass on any information that may be related to possible abuse to the correct person.
- Never promise to keep a child's disclosure a secret. Explain that you may have to share the secret.

Think about it

Find out the procedures that are followed in your placement when there is suspicion of abuse of a child. Make sure you have a copy in your file and that you have read it and asked your supervisor if you are not sure about anything in it.

Assessment activities

Assessment Activity 9

Write down the different types of abuse.

You should include physical, emotional, neglect, sexual, bullying and harassment.

When you have done this you will have partly met Pass criterion 3 (P3).

Assessment Activity 10

You must now write down the signs and symptoms of each type of abuse.

This will also partly cover P3.

Assessment Activity 11

Your work placement will have a policy and procedures to follow should anybody suspect that child is being abused. You must find out what these are and record them. You should also find out and record the procedures for responding to disclosure by a child.

Discuss with a partner or in a small group why it is important to follow the policies and procedures of the work setting. Make your own notes from this.

This will also lead to meeting P3.

Assessment Activity 12

As part of their policies many work placements may encourage children to be aware of their own bodies and understand their rights not to be abused according to their age, needs and abilities.

Write what your placement does to help protect children in this way. This may include ensuring a high level of self-esteem in children, teaching them how to keep themselves safe, for example the Keepsafe Code, encouraging them to share worries, reassuring them that being abused is never their fault and promoting services such as Childline and the NSPCC.

After completing Assessment Activity 12 you will have met Pass criterion 3 (P3), which requires you to state the possible types, signs and symptoms of child abuse and why it is important to follow the policies and procedures of the work setting.

2.3 Understand how to maintain the safety of children on outings

This section covers:

■ laws governing safety

■ support planning and preparation

■ accompanying children on outings

■ help undertake regular safety checks

■ help implement emergency arrangements as required.

Support planning and preparation

When you are planning outings, safety is as important as the value the children will get out of the activity. Safety depends on:

■ appropriate staffing levels for the number and ages of the children

■ where you are going

■ how you will get there

■ what you intend to do once there.

A risk assessment should be carried out by the person arranging the outing. This should identify any potential hazards on the journey or at the location as well as considering the risks involved in taking the particular group of children.

Just imagine taking a group of children out together without any planning, preparation or thought for safety. Would it be possible for you and your colleagues or the children to enjoy the outing?

Outings can vary from a walk in the park to feed the ducks with nursery age children, to a visit to a living museum with primary school children, through to an outing to a theme park or even an overnight stay with young people. The arrangements and issues will be different for each of these, but whatever the scale of the outing, you need to think about the following:

■ choosing a suitable venue, which will depend on the planned outcomes

■ risk assessment of the outing

■ consulting with staff and children if old enough

■ informing parents and having consent forms signed if needed

■ arranging transport if needed

■ lists of children and adults on the outing and the ratios

■ information about the venue

■ travel and insurance details

Think about it

Find out what is included in the planning of outings in your setting. Does it differ for different age groups?

- first aid cover
- appropriate clothing
- food and equipment
- contingency plans – the 'what if' plans.

Think about the different issues for each of the following cases:

- a group of six three-year-olds on a walk to the park
- a group of 25 seven- and eight-year-olds on a visit to an outdoor farm
- a group of 20 13- and 14-year-olds going to a theme park.

Case study

Organising an outing to the park

A new countryside park area has been opened near to the Blue Jays child care centre. It boasts of lots of items of interest for children to enjoy including a wildlife observation area, pond dipping, an interactive information centre and picnic area.

The manager decides it would be a good idea to take a group of children aged 4–12 years during the holiday club scheme period. You go along with her and have a look at the area to see what the safety issues might be of the planned outing.

The park is very large, with all the areas of interest spread around an eight square kilometre space. Apart from the main entrance, there are two other exits out of the wire perimeter fence. The pond dipping looks very interesting – the pond is large and has a steep bank on one side and a shallow approach on the other. There are two wooden jetty areas to walk on to look into the pond more easily.

The information centre has a lot of computers set up with interactive quizzes on wildlife and a film show on the facilities. All the activities are placed around a maze arrangement with the exhibits in separate areas.

The picnic area looks over a lake with lots of bird life. It is on a raised platform with a railing around and 15 wooden steps down to the lake.

You agree that the children will enjoy the outing and that there is plenty to keep all of them occupied. Your supervisor asks you to think about the following safety aspects.

1 Make a list of the possible safety hazards at the park.
2 Group the risks according to the ages of the children in the group.
3 Are there some risks that are more of a problem to the younger children or the older children? Which ones?
4 What plans will have to be made to protect the children?
5 How do you think you will be able to work with colleagues to make sure the children all have a safe and enjoyable day?

Accompanying children on outings

Going on an outing with a group of children is great fun. You should enjoy the day and be amazed at how children learn in new environments. However it is important to be constantly aware of the children and their needs throughout the outing – even if it is only a walk to the local park.

Think about why it is important to be alert to the children on the outing – think about their needs. Are you listening to them and thinking about them? Are you watching what is going on and not just enjoying the day out yourself?

Think about why someone has to make sure that spare clothes are being carried, or that all the children have sun hats and long sleeves on if the weather is sunny.

Also, why is it important that a first aid kit is carried, and everyone knows how to look after the other children if an accident occurs?

Think about why you need to always be aware of where all of the children are at any time. It is very easy outside your usual placement where everyone is conscious of safety for a child to wander off in a strange place. How will you help to make sure this doesn't happen?

Think about:

- being observant at all times

- making sure all children are linked to an adult

- buddying children in threesomes so they are each looking out for someone else

- checking all children are present – head-counts on a regular basis

- checking for toilet needs so that no one goes wandering off in search of a toilet.

Case study

Organising an outing

It was the end of the play scheme summer outing to a well known theme park, which also had an animal sanctuary area.

Jo had really enjoyed her time in the placement, which was in the middle of a large town, and was looking forward to the trip. Most of the children had never been to the park before and many had never been outside the town very much.

Six staff were on the trip along with 24 children aged six to eleven years – the staff were looking forward to going as well, as the theme park had just got an exciting new ride.

At the end of the day though, the staff were all saying they would never organise such a trip again.

- Two children had been lost (but luckily turned up after over an hour).
- One little boy was bitten by one of the animals in the sanctuary.
- Another caused quite a panic as he had an asthma attack and at first no one knew where his inhaler was.
- One girl had spent most of the day back in the coach wrapped in a blanket as she had fallen into the lake and hadn't any spare clothes.
- The picnic was a disaster – four of the children were vegetarian and there wasn't much food for them.
- Three children were sick on one of the rides early in the afternoon.

1 Why do you think the day was such a disaster?

2 How could a lot of these problems have been avoided?

Assessment activities

Assessment Activity 13

Your work placement is going on an outing to see some ducks on a nearby pond as they have just had some babies and the theme of the Nursery is currently 'young animals'.

The suggestion to do this was made by one of the staff in a team meeting in your placement and this was considered to be a good choice for an outing.

Although, as a learner, you cannot be expected to choose a venue for an outing, you are expected to be involved, to support and to be involved in outings.

Sylvie, the early years worker, whose idea this was, asks you to help her with the planning and preparation.

Briefly describe the procedures and practices that need to be adhered to when preparing to take children on an outing.

You should include:

- consent and involvement of families
- adult to child ratios
- lists of children and other adults
- travel and insurance details
- first aid cover
- appropriateness of clothing, footwear and protection from the sun
- food and equipment
- contingency plans
- contacts.

Assessment Activity 14

Outline your role on an outing:

- wearing suitable clothing and footwear
- being aware of children's needs including talking and listening, toilet needs, cover in the sun
- helping to undertake regular safety checks for example being observant, constant vigilance, head counts to check all children are present
- helping to implement emergency procedures if required, location of first aid box, giving assistance in supportive role.

You have now covered Pass criterion 4 (P4) by outlining the procedures and practices that need to be adhered to when taking children on an outing.

You can now explain – by describing why – the reasons underlying the procedures to be undertaken when taking children on an outing in order to meet Merit criterion 3 (M3).

2.4 Know how to deal with accidents, emergencies and illness

This section covers:

■ policies and procedures
■ basic first aid
■ first aid box
■ illness.

Accidents and emergencies

Young children tend to have accidents and injure themselves. Even a simple banging of heads when two children run into each other could be serious if the carer failed to notice symptoms that something was wrong. Sadly some children have died because the people caring for them have not known what to do.

Preventing accidents and incidents is the best way of dealing with such situations. It is very important that everyone in a child care setting knows if a child is allergic to something for example. Children have died because they have been given food that they are allergic to by someone who did not know, or worse still, who thought it would not matter for once.

When an accident happens, children who are not involved need looking after as they will be frightened and upset and could be at risk if all attention is on the injured child.

A key incident management technique is to be aware of the safety of others at all times during an incident.

First aid

All child care settings must have at least one person qualified in first aid. Child care workers have a responsibility to take a first aid course that specialises in first aid for children. You should also keep your first aid knowledge up to date. If you have not done a first aid course there are some basic procedures you must know about.

■ If a child is injured, you must tell someone in charge immediately.
■ If you are at all worried about a child after an accident, you should ring for an ambulance.

Dealing with accidents

In the case of an accident, in addition to taking action to help the casualty, you or someone else needs to:

- send for a qualified first aider
- call for your supervisor
- calm the other children
- inform the child's parents
- record the incident in the accident book.

Ambulances

When dialling 999, always have ready:

- the details of the accident and injury
- the age of the child
- where the injured child is.

In serious incidents involving breathing difficulties or severe bleeding, an ambulance should be summoned as soon as possible – preferably while first aid is being given.

Emergency contact numbers

The child should have a record card with the emergency contact numbers of parents, grandparents or other relatives. They should be people who are usually easy to contact, and who in turn can contact the parents if necessary.

The person in charge must get in touch with the emergency contact as soon as possible and tell that person about the incident, and where the child is being taken. If the child has to go to hospital before the parents arrive, someone the child knows well should go to the hospital with them.

Accident book

Even a minor accident should be entered in the accident book. The accident may need to be reported to the Health and Safety Executive. A full report is needed. In any incident the person in charge should look at what happened to see what could be done to prevent a similar incident happening again.

Case study

A child is injured

You are working with a small group of children in an after school club. During a game with a ball, Ainsley aged six trips and falls heavily on his left leg. You see that his leg is swollen and it looks a strange shape.

1 What do you do immediately?
2 What, if anything, do you do with Ainsley's leg?
3 What else do you do with Ainsley?
4 What do you do with the other children?
5 Who do you contact first and how?
6 What do you think will need recording?

What is an emergency?

An emergency is whenever someone is injured or seriously ill, or is in danger of being so. Examples include:

- choking
- swallowed poisons
- severe bleeding
- allergic reactions
- **convulsions**
- head injuries
- broken bones
- unconsciousness
- difficulty breathing
- uncontrolled, unusual crying in a baby.

Emergency procedures

As part of the Health and Safety at Work Act 1974 and its Regulations, your setting will have a safety policy if it employs five or more staff. The policy will cover emergency procedures in the event of a fire, accident or other emergency. There are many different types of emergency and it is important to know what the different procedures are, especially for fires, a security incident or if a child goes missing.

Evacuation procedures

A building may need to be evacuated in the event of a fire, gas leak or bomb scare. All adults need to know what to do. In most settings, one member of staff is responsible for these procedures and will need to make sure that all staff are aware of the evacuation procedures. Evacuation practices need to be held regularly and relevant signs and notices must be kept in place. Drills and practices should always be taken seriously so that any difficulties can be reviewed.

When did your placement have a practice evacuation? Find out if there is an evacuation practice every three months and whether the following things happen during a practice evaluation:

- If there are problems with the procedures is it repeated or advice sought from a fire officer?

- Are children reassured during the practice by the adults staying calm and explaining what is happening?

- Are the children praised and thanked for their help in carrying out the evacuation?

- Is an absorbing activity, such as reading a story or playing a game, provided afterwards to help the children to settle down quickly after the practice?

Think about it

Find out what the emergency procedure is at your placement.

- *How is the alarm raised?*
- *Who contacts the emergency services?*
- *Who takes out the registers and checks them?*
- *What are the safest exit points?*
- *Where is the assembly point?*

- *How often is there an emergency practice?*
- *How are visitors to the setting made aware of evacuation procedures?*
- *How are children reassured during evacuation practices?*
- *Is there a notice like the one below in view?*

IN CASE OF FIRE

- Close doors and windows and try to get the children out of the premises by the normal routes.

- Do not leave the children unattended.

- Do not stop to put out the fire (unless very small).

- Call the fire brigade by telephone as soon as possible as follows:

  - Lift the receiver and dial 999.

  - Give the operator your telephone number and ask for FIRE.

  - When the brigade replies give the information clearly, e.g. 'fire at the Tall Trees Nursery,
    223 Southfield Rd,
    Anytown, XY5 3ZA,
    situated between the Police Station and
    Indian restaurant'.

  - Do not replace the receiver until the address has been repeated by the fire operator.

Basic first aid

Always remember to keep calm.

1 Assess the casualty
   Danger – are you or the casualty in danger?
   Response – is the casualty conscious?
   Airway – is the airway open?
   Breathing – is the casualty breathing?
   If not, get someone to dial 999.

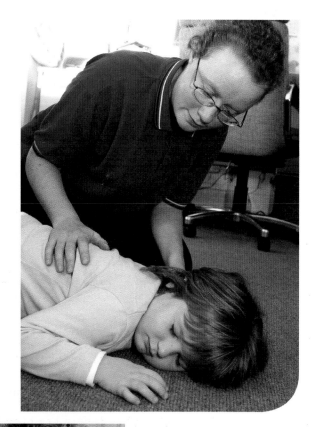

2 Act on your findings and call for help!
   Casualty conscious, breathing present:
   Treat any injuries.
   Call for help if needed.
   Casualty unconscious, breathing present:
   Treat any life-threatening injuries.
   Place in the recovery position.
   Call for help.
   Casualty unconscious and not breathing:
   Open the airway and call for help.

Recovery position

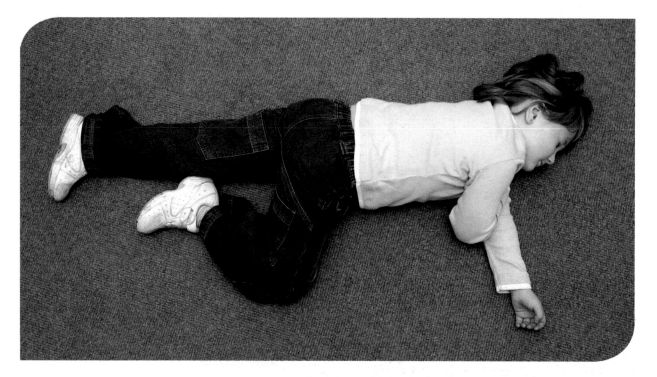

An unconscious casualty who is breathing and has no other life-threatening conditions should be placed in the recovery position.

- Turn the casualty onto his or her side.

- Lift the chin forward in open airway position and adjust the hand under the cheek as necessary.

- Check the casualty cannot roll forwards or backwards.

- Check the casualty's breathing and pulse continuously.

Note: if you suspect an injury to the back or neck, place your hands on either side of the casualty's face. With your fingertips gently lift the jaw to open the airway. Take care not to tilt the casualty's neck.

If the casualty is a baby less than a year old, hold the baby in your arms. Make sure the head is tilted downwards to prevent the baby from choking on the tongue or inhaling vomit. Keep checking for breathing and call for help. Take the baby with you if you need to go into another room for the telephone.

Opening the airway

- Open the airway by tilting the head, removing any obvious obstructions in the mouth and lifting the chin.

- Look, listen and feel for breathing.

- Keep the chin held up and put the casualty in the recovery position.
- Call for help.

Opening the airway is the single most important first aid action for anyone who is unconscious, whether it is an adult or child. It is a simple action that can and does save lives.

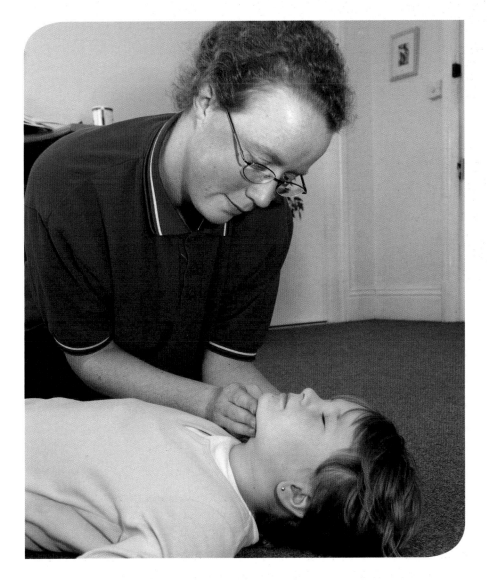

Bleeding

Bleeding from wounds should be controlled as follows.

- **Elevate** the wound.
- **Press** on the wound (over clean material if at hand).
- Apply a **dressing**.

- If there is a foreign body in the wound, leave it and press around the wound to stop the bleeding. Do not try to remove it as this may make the wound worse.

- Treat the casualty for **shock**, reassure the casualty and keep him or her warm.

- Lay the casualty down, lower the head, raise the feet and loosen tight clothing.

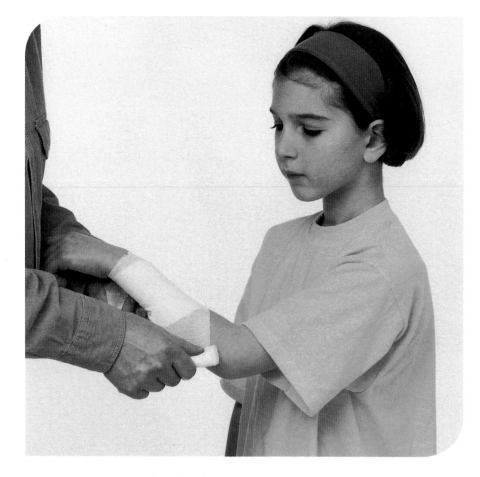

When a child is bleeding, make sure you:

- **reassure** the child and encourage the child to relax

- **do not** move the child unnecessarily

- **do not** give food or drink

- retain normal body heat by covering the child with a blanket or coat

- if serious, or there is doubt, call an ambulance.

Responding to emergencies

The following table shows some other common illnesses and emergencies that may affect children in your care and how to deal with them. However, this is not a substitute for attending a first aid course.

Emergency	Treatment
Cuts and grazes	For minor cuts and grazes wash with clean water to remove any dirt Cover with an appropriate dressing – check your settings policies on this
Head injury	Control any bleeding by applying pressure with a pad Lay the casualty down Take or send the casualty to hospital Monitor the level of consciousness, vomiting, etc.
Convulsions Often the result of a high temperature in a child	If the child is hot, help to cool the child by removing clothing Protect the child from injury – clear surrounding objects Sponge the child with tepid water Place the child in the recovery position Dial 999 for an ambulance
Back injury Always suspect after a fall from a swing, slide, tree, etc.	Do not move or attempt to move the child Steady and support the neck and head Dial 999 for an ambulance
Allergic reaction to stings, medicines or irritants – red blotchy skin, swelling of face and neck, problems with breathing leading to anaphylactic shock	Dial 999 for an ambulance Put the child into a comfortable position Monitor the airway, breathing and pulse
Choking in young children – may go very quiet and blue around lips. May be very noisy breathing and coughing	Lean an older child forward or put a baby over your knee, face downwards, and give five back slaps between the shoulders Remove any obvious obstruction from the mouth Next, give five chest thrusts: stand behind the child, make a fist against the lower breast bone, grasp the fist with the other hand and press it sharply into the chest For a baby, press two fingertips on the lower half of the breast bone Check ABC (airway, breathing and circulation). Dial 999 for an ambulance
Asthma attack or breathing difficulties	Make the child comfortable. The child should be seated in the position most comfortable for the child away from other children in a quiet area. Let the child use an inhaler if he or she has one – usually a blue reliever Encourage the child to breathe slowly If the attack does not subside, call for medical help
Suspected broken bones or sprains	Support the affected limb with a sling (if an arm) or padding Take the child to hospital or call an ambulance
Burns and scalds	Cool the burn with cold water for at least ten minutes Remove any clothing that is not stuck to the burn Cover the burn with a sterile or clean dressing or even a clean plastic bag For any burn or scald on a young child call an ambulance or take the child to hospital
Poisoning from drugs, plants, etc.	Dial 999 for an ambulance Try to find out what has been taken and keep the evidence If unconscious, check the airway and put the child in the recovery position

■ *Common emergencies and how to treat them*

First aid box

Always make sure you know where the first aid box is kept and what is in it.

A good first aid box should contain the following items:

a range of plasters in different sizes

FIRST AID KIT

crepe bandages

disposable gloves

safety pins

tweezers

triangular bandages (slings)

sterile eye pads

gauze pads

ANTISEPTIC WIPE

non-alcoholic cleansing wipes

medium and large sterile dressings

scissors

cotton wool

Think about it

Find out where the first aid kit is at work. Is it easy to find?
Do the contents match the list above? Is anything missing? Are there any extra items, and if so what are they for?

Childhood illnesses

You should be familiar with the signs and symptoms of childhood illnesses in order to know when to suggest that a child should seek medical help. As a student in placement you should, of course, refer the parents or the child to a supervisor. It is useful to know the basic treatments for a sick child and how to protect other children.

It is important to ensure that a child who has any of the following is seen by a doctor as soon as possible:

- continuing high temperature
- severe headache
- persistent or strange crying
- breathlessness
- very pale and lifeless
- rash that does not disappear when pressed with a glass
- persistent vomiting and/or diarrhoea.

The following chart shows some of the common signs and symptoms, treatment needed and the incubation period (the time before the child shows signs of the illness after catching it).

Illness	Signs and symptoms	Treatment	Incubation period
Common cold	Sneezing, sore throat, runny nose, headache, temperature.	Treat symptoms with rest, plenty of fluids. Encourage child to blow nose.	1–3 days
Gastro-enteritis	Vomiting, diarrhoea, dehydration.	Replace fluids (encourage child to drink water), seek medical help	1–36 hours
Tonsillitis	Very sore throat, fever, headache, aches and pains.	Rest, fluids, medical attention as antibiotics may be needed.	Varies
Scarlet fever	Fever, loss of appetite, sore throat, pale around the mouth, 'strawberry tongue', bright pinpoint rash over face and body.	Rest, fluids and observe for complications.	2–4 days
Dysentery	Vomiting, diarrhoea with blood and mucus, abdominal pain, fever and headache.	Medical attention, rest, fluids. Strict hygiene measures for example careful hand washing.	1–7 days

continued ▶

Illness	Signs and symptoms	Treatment	Incubation period
Chicken-pox	Fever, very itchy rash with blister-type appearance.	Tepid bath with sodium bicarbonate, and calamine applied to skin to stop itching. Try to stop child scratching to avoid scarring.	10–14 days
Measles	High fever, runny nose and eyes, later cough, white spots in mouth, blotchy red rash on body and face.	Rest, fluids, tepid sponging. Medical attention to check for complications.	7–15 days
Mumps	Pain and swelling of jaw, painful swallowing, fever. May be swollen testes in boys.	Fluids, may need a straw to drink, warmth to swelling, pain relief.	14–21 days
Rubella (German measles)	Slight cold, sore throat, swollen glands behind ears, slight pink rash.	Rest, treat symptoms. Avoid contact with pregnant women.	7– 21 days
Pertussis (whooping cough)	Snuffly cold, spasmodic cough with whooping sound and vomiting.	Medical attention. Rest, fluids, feed after a coughing attack.	7–21 days
Meningitis	Fever, headache, drowsiness, confusion, dislike of light, very stiff neck. May be small red spots on the body.	Immediate urgent medical attention. Take child to hospital.	2–10 days

■ *Signs, symptoms and treatment for common illnesses*

In nearly all cases a child is most infectious to others before the symptoms appear. Many illnesses have a cold or fever as their first signs; it would not be possible to exclude all children with these symptoms from nursery, nor would it have much effect on the spread of a disease. Different settings have different rules about excluding children with common illnesses, ranging from excluding all children with symptoms, to exclusion only while the child feels unwell.

You should always make sure that you follow the routines that help to protect children from illness, for example careful hand washing and cleanliness of toilet areas.

When a child is taken ill in your care, the parents or guardians must be informed. As a student or junior worker you should always tell your supervisor if a child is ill and they will make the decision about contacting medical services and parents. You can provide support to a child who is ill while his or her parents are coming by sitting quietly with the child, perhaps reading a story.

Often after an illness a child may need to take medicine while at nursery or school. Most settings have a policy that parents must give written consent for their child to have medicines administered by the nursery nurse or teacher. Child care workers are not allowed to give medicines to children without this written permission under any circumstances.

Think about it

Find out the polices about children being ill in your placement. What advice is given to parents?

Assessment activities

Assessment Activity 14

Find out the policies and procedures relating to accidents and emergencies in your work placement.

Write out these policies and procedures step-by-step.

You need to make sure that you include:

- fire
- evacuation
- first aiders
- missing children
- remaining calm
- calling for assistance
- informing the supervisor/manager

- allergic responses (and why it is important to follow instructions about children's diets and allergies)
- maintaining the safety of others
- providing reassurance and comfort
- carrying out reporting and recording procedures correctly.

This will enable you to provide evidence towards Pass criterion 5 (P5).

You now need to say why your placement has these policies and procedures with respect to accidents and emergencies. This will provide evidence towards meeting Merit criterion 4 (M4).

Assessment Activity 15

You need to be able to recognise signs of illness to include:

- fever
- vomiting
- diarrhoea
- dehydration
- crying

- loss of appetite
- rash
- headache
- breathlessness
- pallor.

Briefly describe these signs of illness.

continued ▶

THE HENLEY COLLEGE LIBRARY

Assessment Activity 16

You must now find out the policies and procedures in your placement with respect to children's illnesses and record these.

You should include:

- the giving of medicines to children
- informing your supervisor/manager
- contacting parents.

Explain how the policies and procedures help to keep children safe.

You have now covered the evidence required to meet P5, for which you must outline the policies and procedures related to accidents, emergencies and children's illness in a setting known to you.

Also you have covered M4, for which you have to explain and describe how policies and procedures, with respect to accidents, emergencies and children's illnesses, help to keep children safe.

You may now evaluate – give the good and bad points, and weigh them up – the ways that policies and procedures, with respect to accidents, emergencies and children's illnesses, ensure the safety of children. This will enable you to meet Distinction criterion 2 (D2).

Assessment Activity 17

You must now undertake basic first aid procedures and be observed by your tutor or trainer, who will fill in a check list of competences.

You need to know the location and content of the First Aid box.

You also need to recognise and carry out the correct responses to:

- choking
- unconsciousness
- breathing difficulties
- bleeding
- anaphylactic shock
- burns
- minor injuries, for example bumps, grazes.

You have now met the requirements of Pass criterion 6 (P6).

3 Communication with children and adults

Introduction

Try to imagine a whole day without communicating with others. What would that feel like? Do you think you would achieve very much? Communication skills are a central point of all work with children. You will need to communicate with children, other workers, families and other adults.

It is important to remember that when you communicate with children you must communicate at the age and stage of development of the child.

The material in this unit is important to all aspects of your life as good communication skills are an essential life skill. To work in any care or education setting it is even more important. If you are taking the Diploma course you will need to have evidence of your good communication skills for Unit 5, Professional development, roles and responsibilities.

In this unit you will learn:

1 about the key features of effective interpersonal communication

2 how to interact and communicate with children

3 how to interact and communicate with adults.

3.1 Understand the key features of effective interpersonal communication

This section covers:

- verbal and non-verbal behaviour
- listening skills
- communication difficulties
- overcoming barriers
- promotion of self-esteem.

Verbal and non-verbal behaviour

It is very unusual for anyone to communicate with another person only using one limited form. Even on the telephone we can express far more than just words by the way our voice sounds. In person, everything about us passes on messages to those we are communicating with.

Just sit back for a few moments and think about your own communication skills. Have you ever been in a situation where you have thought that your 'message' has not got through to the person you were talking to? This could be family, friends, teachers or indeed anyone.

If this has happened to you, write down what happened and as you work through this unit try to see if you can identify what went wrong and how you would approach the situation differently.

Think about it

How does your family communicate with each other?

Even coming into the house people sound different from each other:

- one closes the door very quietly, another lets it slam
- one shouts through to announce their arrival, another slips into the room quietly.

Does this sound familiar?

Try listening and watching how different people do the same everyday actions and think about what they are 'saying' in their actions.

Think about it

Have you ever tried to pass on some important information to a friend when you have not been able to talk to them? Or have you ever played the game 'charades' where you try to explain the title of a book or film without using words? If you have done either of these things you will have been using 'non-verbal' communication skills – getting your message over to others without using words.

Whenever you use 'verbal' communication you are also using non-verbal skills. Try to tell a friend about something you are really pleased about, but use your body gestures to look really annoyed. How difficult is it to do this?

You may remember a very clever advert on television of a man asking a hairdresser to tidy his niece's hair up after he had made a mess of cutting it. As the girl's mother was watching he tried to make it seem through his body language as if he was very annoyed with the hairdresser for cutting the hair badly. In fact, he was asking her to help!

Communication in child care settings

Communicating with adults and children in child care settings is very different to the way you communicate with your friends, although the principles are the same. You use all the various techniques shown in the table below. It is very important to be aware of cultural differences when working with children and their carers. Take your cue from staff in your placement and ask what the differences are if you are not sure.

In any interactions it is important to be sure that the person on the receiving end gets the right message. Working with children and young people and their carers is even more important. You are quite likely to be working with children and adults from a number of different backgrounds and cultures. Almost every culture and area in a country has slightly different ways of communicating apart from any language differences.

Styles of communication

We pick up the full message a person is trying to give through some or all of these aspects of communication.

Style of communication	What does this mean?	Examples
Form	Speech can be formal for public use or informal – possibly using special language known to those listening	Formal, as you might use in an interview for an important job or to read the news! Informal, as you would use with friends
Pitch	Whether your voice sounds high or low	Some voices are quite high and squeaky, others very low and deep
Tone	Expression of feeling in your voice	As in expression of anger or comfort You may have heard some one say 'Don't use that tone of voice with me!'
Volume	How loud your voice is	Quiet whispers if you are trying not to disturb someone Very loud if you are shouting in an argument or to stop someone getting into danger
Turn-taking	Waiting for the other person to finish before you speak shows respect for them and what they are saying	When having a conversation about your holidays with a friend you allow each other to tell your stories
Questioning skills	Knowing what are good questions to ask	'Closed questions' only produce a 'yes' or 'no' answer 'Open questions' encourage ideas to flow
Reflective listening	Listening and responding with thought to another person's, often distressing, conversation and testing your understanding of their message	A friend telling you that they are upset that their grandmother is dying. Your response may be 'You must be very sad that she is so ill'

continued ▶

Style of communication	What does this mean?	Examples
Pausing	A short gap in the conversation – allowing time for the message to be recognised, or to decide what to say next	
Silence	Saying absolutely nothing can say as much as many words	Supporting silence when someone is very upset and you are there in person or refusing to speak because you are too upset or angry with someone
Eye contact	Looking at someone when you are talking to them. Direct eye contact varies between cultures. Find out how this may affect people you are talking to	Some cultures see not looking at someone in the eye as evidence they are lying, others as a sign of disrespect
Facial expression	How your facial muscles react to the conversation you are having	Try to tell someone you are very sad but look very happy and smile!
Posture and body movement	How you stand or sit can show a lot about how you are feeling	Sitting perched on the edge of a chair says something very different to lounging in a laid back style on a sofa Arms folded across the chest can be very negative
Gesture	How you use your hands in conversation	Jabbing your finger at someone while talking is usually seen as aggressive, while opening your arms to welcome someone is much friendlier! Gestures are very variable in different cultures, for example a thumbs up sign is an insult in some countries
Muscle tension	How you hold your body can be a response to how you are feeling	If you are very nervous in an interview you may be very stiff and not relaxed. Your voice may even sound different as your vocal chords tense as well
Touch	Physical contact is usually by hand – beware cultural differences!	Putting your arm round someone's shoulders or just touching their forearm to show concern
Proximity	How near you stand to someone – acceptable distances vary between cultures	When you are talking to someone you know well you will stand much nearer to them than when you are talking to a teacher at school or college
Mirroring	Copying the other person's postures and movements, often subconsciously	Sitting opposite someone and resting your chin on your hand as they are doing

■ Different styles of communication

■ *Folding your arms could be seen as a negative gesture*

Think about it

With a friend, role play:
- *listening to some bad news*
- *telling a friend some good news*
- *sharing some gossip.*

Ask someone else to make a note of how you use your bodies, voices and facial expressions. Then think about how you approached each situation and why.

Did you know?

Most people only remember one of every 2,000 things that they hear in a day!

Listening skills

Being a good listener is as important as being a good talker. Do you know someone who is a good listener or maybe you are one! Why are they seen as being a good listener?

Listening means hearing the other person's words, thinking about what they mean and planning what to say back in reply. To be a good listener you have to hear what is said and then understand and remember the meaning.

Real or active listening can be hard work, especially if you are busy and want to rush off to do something else. It is important in any sort of caring work to be alert to someone who may be trying to tell you something that is very important to him or her. The best way to avoid missing something important is to learn to be a good listener nearly all the time.

Sometimes it can be hard to remember everything someone says to you. In this case, it can be very useful to stop the person who is talking by using a pause in the conversation and summarising what has been said. This is called reflecting and paraphrasing. Try this when you are having a conversation with a friend about an important topic – how you are coping with this course maybe! You could set up a conversation about your last holiday and talk about what was good and bad about it, with the other person reflecting and paraphrasing what is being said.

Think about it

When you are in placement, watch how the staff communicate with different people such as other staff, parents and children. How do their styles of communication vary between each encounter?

TV soaps are excellent examples of people using different communication skills. Record an episode, watch it with the volume down and decide what the tone of the conversation is by watching faces, bodies and other non-verbal skills. Then rewind and see if you were right.

Communication difficulties

Those who can communicate well and are communicating with people who speak the same language do not give much thought to the skills they use. If they wish to say something, they open their mouths and say it. For some people this is not always easy. For a range of reasons, they may have problems in communicating or there may be barriers preventing them from being understood.

Think about it

Imagine going into a very dark room with a loud radio on. You cannot find where to sit. Someone is trying to tell you something important but they are shouting at you in a language you do not understand. List all the barriers to communication.

Did you include:

- *sensory difficulties: not being able to see may induce panic*
- *barriers in the environment: room layout, noise, lighting*
- *barriers to understanding: not being able to understand the language and shouting.*

For anyone who has any degree of communication difficulty, these feelings will be familiar. In these cases, it is very easy to become quite angry and aggressive with the whole situation and make communication even harder.

Many people have some form of barrier to successful communication. These may be internal – part of the person – or external – the problem of the person trying to communicate with them, for example through misunderstanding or stereotyping.

Some barriers to communication include:

- **physical barriers:** there may be damage to the parts of the body involved in speech production, for example the ears, vocal chords or parts of the brain

- **emotional barriers:** shyness, fear or lack of confidence may prevent communication skills from developing

- **cultural barriers:** different languages, accents or backgrounds or being the child of deaf parents can cause problems

- **communication problems:** stammering may hamper the development of speech.

Different physical environments can make a difference to effective communication. Think about a time you have been trying to listen to something in a large room that has a pillar in the way, for example in a concert or lecture. Physical barriers can make a big impact on how sounds are transmitted. Very large rooms with high ceilings can 'eat' noise and make it difficult for people to hear. If someone uses a hearing aid, background noise can make it very difficult to pick up the sounds a person wants to hear.

One of the biggest communication barriers can be nothing to do with the actual process of hearing, but one of attitudes. Assuming that someone of a different background to yours may not understand your communication is a common mistake that stems from making stereotyped conclusions. Always start communication on a simple level to check understanding with anyone you do not know. Then check that you have a shared understanding of the communication and be prepared to adjust if necessary.

Overcoming barriers

Having English as a second language, having a hearing impairment or being deaf, has no relation at all to someone's intellectual abilities or any other ability. What it does for a child is to make their need for support in developing appropriate communication skills for his or her education a high priority. If we cannot hear and communicate effectively we may find it difficult to learn. It is important not to underestimate the skills of a child who has learned a second language. Think about the complexity of learning one language, now double that, and think of how rarely multilingual speakers mix their languages up.

An ideal way of realising just how difficult it can be to make sense of the world when you cannot understand what is being said is to put yourself in that situation. Exercises have been carried out by inviting someone into a classroom and asking them to give some information and instructions in a language that is not known by anyone in the group. Imagine being confronted on your first day at college by a Russian-speaking tutor who gets very frustrated when you are not filling in your college enrolment forms, also in Russian. How do you think you would feel? Now transfer those feelings to a child who understands very little English or who is deaf. What can you do to help them?

It is important to become skilled at recognising that someone is having problems communicating, and know how to help to improve the situation. Here are some suggestions:

- communication aids, for example hearing aids, hearing loops and electronic speech synthesisers for people with little speech
- interpreting non-verbal behaviour
- using clear speech and plain language
- adapting the environment, for example reducing background noise, eliminating distractions such as people passing through rooms
- understanding cultural differences, for example accepted gender relationships
- checking understanding
- using skilled communicators
- interpreters or signers for deaf people, Makaton for people with learning difficulties.

Think about it

Watch someone who is elderly and maybe slightly deaf being spoken to by a shop assistant or carer. It is quite likely that the shop assistant will be shouting, in the mistaken belief that it helps with hearing, when in reality clear, well pronounced speech is much easier to hear.

Best practice in your work placement

A significant number of children experience barriers to communication in many forms. Think about the following suggestions to help them overcome them:

- one-to-one attention
- reading stories
- talking clearly to the child
- encouraging communication by asking open-ended questions about things the child understands
- responding to the child as an individual
- finding out how you can get help from others, for example the speech therapist
- learning how to use alternative methods of communication, for example Makaton, electronic speech synthesisers.

Case study

Communication barriers

Liam, aged four, is a very shy child who lives in an isolated village with his single mother. His contact with other children has been limited and he seems to have a serious degree of speech delay. He often seems to have difficulty in hearing what you say to him.

Zak is also four and is the eldest of three children. His parents came to England from Pakistan just before he

was born. Although his parents do speak some English, they speak in their mother tongue of Urdu at home.

Think about these two boys.

1 Which other professionals do you think might be involved with the children?
2 How could you help these two boys to overcome their barriers to communication?

Promotion of self-esteem

It is very easy to build anyone's self-esteem, or sense of value and worth, but even easier to totally destroy it. Both verbal language and non-verbal language is a powerful weapon in building or destroying self-esteem.

Promoting self-esteem	Destroying self-esteem
Open, welcoming **body language**	Closed, rejecting body language
Smiling warm facial expressions	Unpleasant, sneering expressions
Language is full of praise, for example: 'Well done!' 'Excellent!' 'How wonderful!', 'You were great!'	Language full of put downs, for example: 'That was dreadful!', 'How awful!', You were terrible!'
Tone of voice is warm and positive	Neutral words, for example 'That was all right' but in a negative tone

■ *Promoting or destroying self-esteem*

Communication is vital in conveying respect and value for people. Think about these points that show you value and respect the other person:

- remembering the person's name
- introducing yourself
- giving time to listen to them
- paying attention
- active listening
- asking questions
- not interrupting
- checking your understanding
- mirroring (for example, smiling back, physical gestures matching theirs).

Think about it

Think about a time when someone has been pleased with you. What did they do to make you know how pleased they were?

Now think about a situation when someone has made you feel worthless. What did they do to make you know how they felt?

Case study

Promoting self-esteem

Two children, aged five, run to meet their parent collecting them from school. Both are carrying the craft work completed that day.

One child runs to their parent waving their work to be greeted by an excited parent, claiming how good the work is and saying: 'We must put that on the table when we get home so everyone can see it.'

The other child drags the work down near the floor as they meet their parent, who glances down and says: 'Oh no! Not more rubbish, what on earth is it? That can go in the bin when we get home.'

What effect will these reactions have had on the children's self-esteem?

Assessment activities

Assessment Activity 1

You need to describe the key features of verbal and non-verbal communication when communicating with another person or people.

Describe these features and their importance when communicating with other people (interpersonal communication):

- form
- pitch
- volume
- tone
- turn-taking
- questioning skills
- reflective listening
- pausing
- silence

- eye contact
- facial expression
- 'conversations' with babies
- posture
- body movement
- gesture
- muscle tension
- touch
- proximity
- orientation
- mirroring
- cultural differences.

When you have done this you will have part of the evidence towards meeting Pass criterion 1 (P1).

Assessment Activity 2

If you now explain these features (by describing how and why) you will have produced some of the evidence for Merit criterion 1 (M1).

Assessment Activity 3

Listening skills are also an important feature of interpersonal communication.

Describe what is meant by active listening.

Describe the following features of listening:

- giving attention

- reflecting
- paraphrasing.

When you have done this you will have covered the evidence for P1 and if you explain these listening skills you will have more evidence for M1.

continued ▶

Assessment Activity 4

Part of effective interpersonal communication is showing people that you value them as individuals as well as promoting their self-esteem, which is helping people to feel good about themselves.

Describe how value and self-esteem can be developed in both children and in adults through your verbal and non-verbal behaviour as well as your listening skills.

You will need to include:

- body language
- facial expression
- positive comments
- tone of voice
- giving attention
- active listening
- checking understanding
- mirroring.

When you have completed this activity you will have met Pass criterion 5 (P5).

Assessment Activity 5

You now need to outline (briefly describe) the difficulties that may arise in communication.

These should include the following:

- language differences, including signing
- sensory difficulties, for example hearing
- emotional distress

- environmental barriers, for example noise
- cultural differences and belief systems
- stereotypes and assumptions.

This will provide some of the evidence towards Pass criterion 2 (P2).

Assessment Activity 6

You should now outline (briefly describe) the ways in which barriers may be overcome.

You should include the following:

- use of communication aids, for example hearing aids
- interpreting non-verbal behaviour
- use of clear speech and plain language
- adapting or changing the environment
- understanding cultural differences
- using skilled communicators, for example interpreters, signers

- awareness of own attitudes and beliefs and differences between these and those of others.

When you have completed this activity as well as Assessment Activity 5 you will have met Pass criterion 2 (P2).

If you explain (describe how and why) how verbal and non-verbal behaviour assists in overcoming difficulties in communication and have completed Assessment Activities 2 and 3 you will have met Merit criterion 1 (M1).

3.2 Understand how to interact and communicate with children

This section covers:

- giving attention
- activities to encourage communication and language
- communicating clearly
- enabling children to express themselves.

Did you know?

In the early weeks of life, babies develop the skills to respond to verbal and non-verbal language as they interact with their carers through crying, blinking and smiling.

Source: National Literacy Trust 2005.

Giving attention and communicating clearly

The principles of good communication with children are just the same as those with adults. One of the most important points is to give your full attention to children during communication with them. Watch someone who is good at communicating with children – how do they act?

Valuing a child is essential for their self-esteem – you do this by listening to them and responding appropriately, using body language, expression and the tone of your voice.

Children need you to be a good communicator. Remember children learn from those around them and so you are a role model for them. Always think about the way you communicate with other adults when you are around children. Bellowing across the room to attract attention will be picked up by children observing as being acceptable. A polite approach to your colleague is a much better example to set!

Even very small babies respond to expressions in voices and on people's faces. If you talk to a baby of only a few weeks old and then pause, they will 'talk' back in gurgles and coos.

Think about it

Which of these examples do you think a child will respond to best?

Spot the difference! Try to list at least five key differences in communication skills between the two adults. What else will help a child to have confidence in you as a good communicator?

Case study

Using communication skills

Liza, aged nine, came into the after school club and sat quietly in a corner near the drinks counter. Jez, one of the workers, brought a pile of empty cups back and said 'Hello!' to Liza, adding 'How are you doing?' Instead of then just carrying on, expecting the usual bright 'OK', Jez stopped when Liza paused before saying, 'Not bad, but…'.

Jez sat down with Liza and discovered she was very unhappy because a girl at school had been saying unkind things about Liza's mum.

How did Jez find out that Liza was unhappy through using his communication skills?

Best practice in your work placement

Think about the importance of verbal and non-verbal communication skills. These apply to all types of communication in the child care field. Remember the important points:

- Always talk to children at their level – crouch or sit down.
- Maintain appropriate eye contact.
- Show you are listening by nods and smiles and asking questions to check your understanding.
- Show that you value the child's views, feelings and opinions.
- Actively listen, do not interrupt.
- Think about your body language. Do not stand talking with folded arms or appear distracted by other activities.

- Be sensitive to communication barriers, for example an accent that is difficult to understand or someone with poor hearing. Have an interpreter present if needed or use pictures and visual aids.
- Never belittle the other person.
- Never shout back if a child starts to shout at you. Talk quietly and calmly and encourage them to express their needs.
- Use different methods of communicating, especially for different needs and ages.
- Be a listening ear when needed.
- Be available to support children when needed.

Activities to encourage communication and language

Communication is the area of development that most dramatically shows the effects of input by carers. A baby as young as two or three months who is regularly talked to, sung to and experiences general communication will vocalise far more than a baby who has little one-to-one communication. From birth, babies learn patterns of speech and are absorbing them ready for when they start to reproduce all the sounds. The vocalisations of babies and toddlers are part of the pre-language skills that prepare a child for speaking fluently.

Repetition is involved in learning a language. This is clearly demonstrated in children with 'glue ear' (a blockage of the tubes in the inner ear which stops sounds travelling to the auditory nerve). They cannot hear consonants at the beginning of words, so they hear 'bus' as 'us', 'car' as 'ar', and they repeat them as they hear them.

Direct one-to-one contact is more important than 'group' interactions in learning language. Studies of young children who have spent a lot of time watching TV show their language development is behind that of children who spend more direct one-to-one time with carers talking with them.

We all continue to improve our communication skills throughout life – the first part of this chapter was about you improving yours!

In placement you may well work with older children who need support in communication. Even teenagers may need support in developing their skills. Some teenagers have problems with self-confidence as they are growing and developing and this may show in communication problems. Some children may need support in developing English as a second language, although remember that learning a second or third language is a demonstration of advanced communication skills, not of a problem. Many children have developed **bilingual** skills from birth and can switch between the languages with ease.

Think about how you could use the following ideas to promote communication skills with children, adding to the ideas as a child grows:

Birth–twelve months
- respond to cries promptly and identify the meaning of the baby's sounds and actions
- model and repeat sounds, be consistent in feedback to these sounds
- enter into conversations with babies
- demonstrate pleasure at a baby's response and maintain eye contact
- use songs and rhymes with accompanying actions
- limit the amount of exposure to noise from the TV and radio

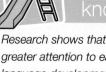

Did you know?

Research shows that greater attention to early language development by parents and carers encourages the development of later literacy and communication skills.

Source: Literacy trust 2005

- talk to the baby at mealtimes, bath times, and about everything that is happening

- play animated games such as 'Pat-a-cake'

- tell the baby the names of objects they see.

1–2 years
As above, plus:

- speak slowly in simple sentences

- praise the child for words used correctly

- encourage play and real telephone talking

- do not rush a child who is talking and maintain eye contact

- do not correct the child if the wrong word is used, but extend first words

- encourage the child to speak to other adults and children directly and translate for them if their language is unclear

- encourage them to talk about daily events

- ask purposeful questions and repeat instructions such as 'wave bye bye'

- sing with children and listen to music with them

- provide opportunities for children to start conversations

- respond to their verbal and non-verbal communications.

2–3 years
As above, plus:

- extend and demonstrate new sentences

- have fun with language

- encourage children to talk about their experiences, present, past and future

- answer children's questions patiently and fully, do not talk down to them but give positive feedback

- find opportunities to expand the child's vocabulary and to explain new words.

One of the easiest ways to encourage the development of communication skills in a child is simply to listen to and talk with them and explore different sounds and experiences. Show that you enjoy listening to the child's view of the world and ask questions about things. Use open questions that need more than a simple 'yes' or 'no' response. For example, 'Tell me about your painting' instead of 'Is that a painting of your little sister?'

You can engage a child in a wealth of activities to encourage language development. Any activity a child takes part in involves language and can be explored with them.

Think about it

Josh is four years old and seems very shy. He has never been to any pre-school group before, and his health visitor and family are concerned about his lack of speech. Think of some activities you could do with him to help his communication.

These principles apply to any child, but are particularly important for children who find communication challenging, for example children who may have hearing impairments, speech difficulties, a second language or emotional problems. Very often a child who seems delayed in language development will make rapid progress after starting nursery or playgroup because the constant contact with other children and adults helps to stimulate speech. A child may, of course, require professional intervention to help him or her to make progress and this is explored further below.

Songs, music and rhymes

From birth, many children hear a carer singing lullabies and rocking songs. As children grow they delight in songs and rhymes; the constant repetition makes it possible for them to join in these familiar, sing-song types of communication. New songs and rhymes introduce new words and phrases which are quickly learned. Once a child is attending any sort of group, from toddlers to school, songs are an important activity. Used with actions or puppets, group songs allow a child to try joining in without being singled out. Songs and rhymes can fit very easily into themes and topics in the nursery or school.

Music is a medium to which most children respond. A piece of music can serve many functions including soothing children, allowing them to express themselves in movement, promoting dance and providing inspiration for a painting. All these are forms of communication, and are especially important when a child has difficulties in verbal communication. Apart from listening to music, children love to make music and again this can be used for communicating. Clapping hands is the simplest form of music making.

Have a look at the range of musical instruments in your placement. Do they include any of those shown below? Try them out to see what type of noise they make.

xylophone

glockenspiel

tambourine

cymbals

sleigh bells

maracas

chime bars

drums

shakers with rice

shakers with pasta

bottles with water

You could develop your own collection of songs, music, rhymes and stories that encourage communication and language development. Every time you hear or see a new example in a book or in your placement, etc. write down or copy the details. Create a resource file with various headings. Choose a theme, for example autumn or animals; an ideal theme would be one that is in current use at your placement. Collect as many relevant songs, rhymes and examples of music as possible and file them in your resource file. Choose one of each and try them out with a few children in your placement, making notes on the success of the activities.

Books

As with music, you should look at the range of books available to seek out ones suitable for helping language and development. Reading stories to children is an important part of communicating. Very few children, if any, do not enjoy hearing a story, either as part of a group or on a one-to-one basis. Reading promotes all of the aspects of intellectual and language development.

Choosing the right book is important. The choice of book has to be related to the child's:

- age
- stage of development
- ability to understand the story
- interests and cultural background.

The same book can serve different age groups. A storybook with bright, attractive pictures will provide stimulation to a toddler who enjoys the pictures and an older child who enjoys the story. Books that open up discussion are an excellent medium for promoting language development. Examples include books that show familiar scenes, for example a street with shops. Such a book will help you encourage children to talk about their local shops and the goods inside or about lorries or vans.

Books can be a good basis for developing a theme for further activities. *The Very Hungry Caterpillar* is an excellent example. This book describes the growth of a caterpillar into a butterfly, showing what the caterpillar ate on its way to forming a chrysalis. Work on food, growth, change, insects, numbers and colours can all develop from reading this one book. It is a book with a story that is easy to remember, so it can help in memory development with children.

Having heard a story from a book, children can be stimulated to produce paintings, models and collages. Older children might develop their own related story. Children will enjoy verbally extending the story they have heard, or 'writing' their own story in pictures. These activities all help in the development of communication.

Think about it

Choose at least two different books and briefly describe them. Make a list of all the extra activities that can be linked to the books and how the book and the activities will help to promote language and intellectual development.

Think about it

Observe parents and carers with young children. Many 'conversations' tend to be the adult talking at the child, sometimes not giving him or her the chance to say anything. Busy parents can sometimes find themselves just giving instructions and not taking time to sit and listen to their children.

Enabling children to express themselves

An important part of communicating with children is giving them the chance to express themselves in their own way.

Think about it

Imagine what it would be like if you were not allowed to have your say about something important to you. All your thoughts and reactions would be bursting to get out. How would you get rid of that frustration? What if you were two years old and unable to express yourself?

Circle time in primary schools is an excellent example of how children can be encouraged to express themselves in groups. In circle time children have to indicate when they want to say something, sometimes by having possession of an object. They also help children learn to allow other children the chance to have their say as well. They are times when often quite sensitive issues can be discussed in a secure situation.

Assessment activities

In this part of the unit you have to show that you know and understand about communication and you also have to demonstrate that you can communicate.

In this next part of the unit you have to show that you can interact and communicate with children. You will probably have to do this in your work placement and you will need to ask either your tutor or your supervisor to observe you communicating with the children and take notes as this will be the evidence you need for both P3 and P4.

Assessment Activity 7

You need to show the importance of giving attention to children by showing that full attention is being given through the following:

- body language, for example at the child's level

- facial expression, for example eye contact
- speech and gesture
- active listening
- a considerate and sympathetic approach
- asking questions to check understanding.

continued ▶

Assessment Activity 8

You need to show that you can communicate clearly by doing the following:

- communicate at the child's own level
- be a good model of communication
- check understanding
- convey value of feelings, views and opinions

- encourage the expression of needs
- use different methods of communication as required
- be a listening ear when needed
- be available to support, listen and encourage with children of all ages.

Assessment Activity 9

You need to take part in activities to encourage communication and language, for example take time to communicate with children in everyday activities.

Other activities include the following:

- music, movement, rhythm, rhymes, games and stories

- effective use of eye contact, body movement, voice and appropriate language
- ensure suitability to children's age, needs and abilities
- use every opportunity to encourage children's communication and language development.

Assessment Activity 10

You need to enable children to express themselves and show the importance of enabling children to express themselves and to be heard whether as individuals or in groups.

You should do this by means of the following:

- give children time to express themselves in their own manner, words and time

- acknowledge children's expression including expression of feeling
- enable expression of feeling by children in groups and acknowledge this.

When you have completed these three activities you will have met Pass criterion 3 (P3).

Assessment Activity 11

You should now justify the ways in which children were given encouragement to express themselves in the interactions

undertaken. This will enable you to meet Distinction criterion 2 (D2).

3.3 Understand how to interact and communicate with adults

This section covers:

- principles of good communication
- communication methods
- confidentiality.

Principles of good communication

The basic principles of good communication apply to any age group. The following basic good practice principles should be used to communicate with anyone.

■ *Principles of good communication*

Think about it

Can you think of a time when you met someone and did not get off to a good start with them? Think about why this was the case. Did you say the wrong thing or seem over familiar? How did you cope with the situation and did you manage to change the relationship?

It is likely that you already think about these issues when you have conversations and interactions. Friendships are built on respect for each other, valuing people and respecting each other's views and opinions. You do this without needing to think about it.

When you are in a working environment in placement you need to start almost from scratch with staff, parents and other adults because you are at the start of new relationships with different people. It is very easy to start on the wrong foot by saying the wrong thing or being insensitive to others.

Communication methods

The communication methods you need to use with adults are the same as for children, except that your approach will need adapting. The key principles are:

- think about the age of the person you are talking to – are they older or younger than you?
- think about their relationship to you, for example placement supervisor, other student, and parent
- use different ways of communicating if there are difficulties
- pay full attention to the conversation, do not be tempted to look out of the window
- show that you understand what is being said, for example nods, repeating words
- show that you respect their views
- check out any potential misunderstandings by summarising what you think has been said
- make suggestions and give information when requested.

Sometimes you may not agree with something an adult wants you to do. You may already have experience of this at home but how you react to arguments at home is very different to what is acceptable in placement or any other work situation. Slamming doors and sulking is not an acceptable way to deal with a disagreement in placement.

 Case study

Placement

Mo was late for his day in placement again. For the last three times the bus had been late and he had made an effort to catch an early one. This time the bus had not turned up at all. When he arrived his supervisor called him into her office and explained that it was not acceptable and did not seem to want to listen to Mo's excuse. Mo kept trying to interrupt her but without success. She announced that she was going to have to discuss his placement with his college tutor. Mo was very angry and upset and stormed out the office slamming the door behind him.

1 Why do you think Mo reacted like this?
2 What do you think he should have done?
3 What do you think he should do now?

Confidentiality

Confidentiality is essential in any care setting. Your placement will have a policy about confidentiality and the exchange of information. Sometimes information about a child may need to be shared with other professionals, for example **health visitors**, schools or the police or social services if a child's safety is at risk. This should be clear in the confidentiality statement.

As a student, your rule should always be 'if in doubt …ask'. This applies to many aspects of your experience as a student, but especially in relation to confidentiality. When parents are in a school or nursery, they may confide personal information to staff. It is advisable for you to ask parents to talk to a member of the staff when you are a student but if you are given confidential information by a parent you should make it clear you will have to pass it on.

Personal information about parents should not be the topic of gossip in the staff room and should never be repeated to other parents. In an early years setting you have to exchange information with other members of staff to help each other operate effectively. As life is busy in a nursery or school, this exchange of information may take place in the room with children. Ensure that parents are not able to overhear such conversations or you will be guilty of breaching confidentiality.

Information that is divulged by parents is confidential to those who need to know, for example care staff caring for the child. You need to be aware of the pressures many parents are under in bringing up their children; these pressures can affect how they view the early years setting and indeed which they choose. Life events such as illness, moving house, divorce, death or redundancy can have a profound impact on parents and their children. Having to work very long hours to support yourself and your children may not be the choice of a single parent, but he or she needs support from you, not silent criticism because he or she leaves the children so late at the nursery.

Workers with children will often receive very personal information from parents. Some information has to be shared with others, even if the parent has indicated that he or she does not want the information to be passed on.

Most child care settings hold a lot of personal information about their charges. It is important that everyone concerned is aware of the requirements of the Data Protection and the Freedom of Information Acts. These allow people to view the information that is held on file about them or their children. Remember this when you are committing your thoughts to paper or computer; you must report facts and events objectively, factually and accurately. Parents should be made aware that they have rights under the legislation and be reassured that all files are kept in a secure environment.

Think about it

What should you do in these scenarios?

- *A parent confides that her new partner is hitting her children, who are already on the child protection list.*
- *A grandparent says that a child has developed asthma, but the parents have not mentioned anything.*
- *You are told about changes in the child's circumstances that may affect his or her behaviour, for example a parent losing a job.*

Best practice in your work placement

- Parents need to feel that confidentiality is respected when they are working in close partnership with carers.
- Everyone concerned must be aware of the rules of 'professional confidentiality', including which information must be shared with a line manager, such as issues relating to child protection.
- Let parents know that you may have to share some information with your line manager, before they start to talk about confidential issues.
- Never gossip about parents, children or other members of staff.
- Never discuss one parent with another parent.
- Do not make value judgements about a child or a family, but always respect a person's culture and identity.

Remember to share information about a child's dietary needs, allergies, who collects the child and any concerns with the rest of the care team.

Respecting confidentiality and trust

In any area of care, you will hear and see a lot of confidential information about children and their parents. Remember that confidential information is not to be discussed with your friend on the bus or told to your family at home. It could be that the person sitting behind you on the bus is linked to the family concerned.

Sometimes, however, you have to share information with colleagues. As a student or a junior worker remember: 'If in doubt, shout!' but rather than shouting, have a quiet discussion with your supervisor. This is called 'professional confidentiality', sharing information for the good of the children in your care.

■ Confidentiality is very important

Think about it

Ahmed, aged seven, tells you he and his parents are going on holiday to Pakistan next summer, but that it has to be kept a secret in the meantime from his little brother, aged four.

Jane, aged six, tells you her uncle has been showing her his penis, but it is a secret and no one has to know.

Do you think you should keep both of these secrets to yourself or should you share either of them with your supervisor?

You do not need to share Ahmed's secret with anyone, but clearly Jane could be in need of protection, and it is your responsibility to share that secret. You should always tell a child that you cannot promise to keep everything he or she tells you a secret; if you do not say so, you may lose a child's trust.

Assessment activities

You now need to show your ability to communicate with adults as well as with children. Some learners find this more difficult than communicating with children.

It is a good idea to role play the ability to interact and communicate with adults. You can do this in class with guidance from your tutor. Your tutor may feel that this enables you to demonstrate your ability to interact and communicate with adults but he or she will still want to observe you demonstrating these skills in your placement.

Your supervisor in placement will also be able to observe you demonstrating your ability to interact and communicate with adults in a number of different situations.

Assessment Activity 12

You must show that you can take the right approach when interacting and communicating with adults. You can do this by:

- showing courtesy
- showing respect
- valuing adults' needs, preferences, views and opinions
- developing positive relationships.

continued ▶

Assessment Activity 13

Show that you can use the right communication methods with adults. You can do this by:

- using methods appropriate to adults, who are older than you are with a different relationship to you
- using different methods of communicating where there are difficulties
- giving full attention and not looking out of the window
- showing understanding of what is being said to you and clarifying uncertainties
- responding positively and showing respect for the views of others
- making suggestions and giving information when requested
- coping with a disagreement with an adult.

Assessment Activity 14

Show that you understand the need for confidentiality when interacting and communicating with adults.

Show that you can reassure adults of the confidentiality of shared information.

When you have completed Assessment Activities 12, 13 and 14 you will have met Pass criterion 4 (P4) which requires you to demonstrate the ability to interact and communicate with adults.

Assessment Activity 15

You should now go on to explain (describe what, how and why) the differences and similarities between interacting and communicating with children and adults in the demonstrations undertaken. When you have done this you will have met Merit criterion 2 (M2).

Assessment Activity 16

Having completed your work for M2 you can go on to meet Distinction criterion 1 (D1) which requires you to evaluate (give the good points and the points that need improvement) the interactions and communications carried out with children and adults.

Assessment Activity 17

You will need to put together the notes and descriptions in your work for P5 with your work for P3 and P5 here.

In order to meet Merit criterion 3 (M3) you must explain (describe) how value and self-esteem were communicated and promoted in the interactions and communications with adults and children.

continued ▶

Assessment Activity 18

You need to show your understanding of the need for an organisational policy with respect to confidentiality and the exchange of information. There should be such a policy in your placement.

You need to describe a policy in a child care setting concerning confidentiality and the sharing of information. This enables you to meet Pass criterion 6 (P6).

Assessment Activity 19

Building on your work for P6 you must now explain why it is important to have a policy with respect to confidentiality and the sharing of information in a child care setting. This enables you to meet Merit criterion 4 (M4) which requires you to explain why it is important to have a policy with respect to confidentiality and the sharing of information in a child care setting.

4 Preparing and maintaining environments for child care

Introduction

The environment of the setting is very important to a child. All children must feel comfortable and secure there, so that they can learn and develop to their potential. Parents must also feel comfortable. A positive environment should be warm, safe, secure and encouraging. Everyday care routines and activities should be used to support development and the environment and activities must be arranged so that all children can take part equally. Time should be arranged to make sure that children have quiet periods as well as play and learning and support must be given for all aspects of development, from toilet training to helping children to cope with their feelings and giving support when they change setting, for example primary to secondary school.

In this unit you will learn:

1 how to prepare and maintain the physical and play environment

2 how to prepare and maintain a stimulating environment

3 how to maintain an environment that builds children's confidence and resilience

4 how to support routines for children and integrate play.

4.1 How to prepare and maintain the physical and play environment

This section covers:

- ensure health and safety
- use of space
- meeting children's needs.

Ensure health and safety

Unit 2 covered a lot of the information that you need to think about generally in relation to health and safety issues in placement. Just to recap, you should remember that to make an environment a safe place to work in, there is a number of legal health and safety requirements. Your placement will have a list of policies and procedures that guide the working practice of the staff and ensure the legal requirements are met.

All settings that have under-16-year-olds on site for more than two hours a day are likely to be inspected by your country's inspectorate or regulator, for example OFSTED in England, and will have to meet certain requirements. These can be found in detail in your national standards. There are slightly different requirements for different kinds of child care settings, for example the ratios of staff to children vary; a good rule of thumb is that the younger the children, the more staff are required.

There are several important basic health and safety issues to think about in the preparation of a good and safe environment for children.

Policies and procedures of the setting

The diagram which follows outlines the physical requirements of health and safety. It should also be obvious that your placement has policies and procedures that ensure:

- a welcoming clean and well-maintained environment
- safe and appropriate toys and play equipment
- appropriate indoor and outdoor space with suitable equipment
  - outdoor areas should be checked each time they are used. The RoSPA (The Royal Society for the Prevention of Accidents) guidelines are a source of useful advice with regards to the security of boundaries
- appropriate toilet, kitchen and laundry facilities

Heating
Temperature at 15–18°C, or 20–22°C for babies
Fireguards in front of fire
Radiators and pipes covered
Smoke alarms and emergency equipment available

Lighting and electricity
All areas well lit so that there is full visibility
Current breakers for all electrical equipment
Plug sockets covered

Ventilation
Window open when necessary to circulate air
No draughts
Locks and toughened glass on windows

Doors and gates
All the external gates and doors locked and coded as appropriate
Handles and locks out of reach of children
Safety gates to BSI standard
Toughened glass where necessary

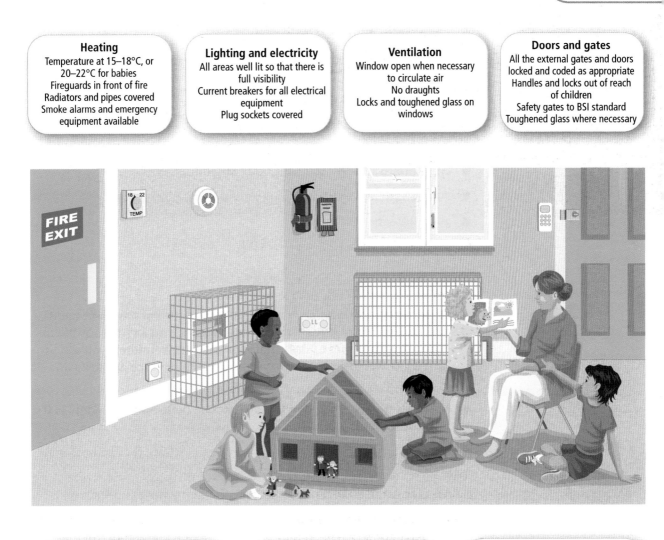

Access points
These must be kept clear, unlocked and made known to all children and adults, including visitors, in the case of an emergency evacuation

Outdoor and indoor surfaces
Stable
Non-slippery
Soft under climbing equipment
Easily cleanable

Risk assessments
All required risk assessments have been done
Identified issues have been addressed

■ *The physical requirements of health and safety*

- meeting minimum requirements for type of setting
- adequate storage for equipment
  - □ including play equipment, safe storage of cleaning and other fluids
- safe supply of hot, cold and drinking water
- safe supply of gas and/or electricity
- appropriate supervision for the children in all situations

- safe outings and use of transport
- good telephone communication with emergency numbers available for services and the children
- good levels of security
  - access to premises by adults
  - ensuring children cannot leave the setting alone
- appropriate arrangements for first aid requirements
- good awareness by all of arrangements in an emergency
- good fire safety awareness
- adequate insurance.

Assessing risks

As a student you will not be responsible for the formal risk assessments that are carried out in your placement. However, you are responsible for being aware at all times of risks that may affect the children you are working with. Whenever you are working you should be aware of the following points:

- Is there a suitable space for this activity? Is there enough room? Is the surface safe, for example for water or sand play?
- Is all the appropriate safety equipment in position, for example mats under large play equipment and guards on the cooker?
- Are all materials used safe, especially for very young children, for example paint or dough?
- Are there too many children? There should be maximum numbers in force for using the sand tray or running around outside.
- Is another activity going on that will clash with it? There may be another class in the playground at the same time.
- Are there enough adults to ensure adequate supervision? If scissors or some other potentially dangerous equipment or tools are being used, the number of adults may need to be increased.
- Can you make sure that the children will not be harmed by equipment being used, for example a cooker when baking?
- Is help available if a child is harmed by the activity? A child may get paint in his or her eyes or fall off outdoor equipment.

Think about it

Think about three different types of activity that you have helped with in your placement.

1. *Make a safety checklist for each activity.*
2. *What risks were there for each activity?*
3. *Were there any actions that should have been taken to minimise them?*

Use of space

The layout of a room is important for ensuring the success of activities. There must be enough space for all activities that may happen and be appropriate for the type of setting and ages of the children who will use it. Certain points need to be checked regardless of the activities that are planned; others are more specific to particular activities.

General checks that must be made at the start and finish of every session in a setting include:

- fire exits kept clear and easy to exit from
- flooring sound with no tears or lumps on the floor
- no spillages on the floor
- safety gates and door locks (where appropriate) in use and working
- warning alarms on entry doors working
- rooms heated to appropriate temperature
- toilets and washing facilities working
- tables, chairs, large toys and equipment are all sound and in good condition
- all equipment not in use is stored away.

Even a small room can support a number of children and allow a range of varied activities. Well-designed and well-planned storage is the first priority. Storage boxes should be clearly labelled and easily accessible so that children can help in the setting out and clearing away. In a small room it may only be possible to have one or two activities going on at the same time.

A larger room needs just as much organising as a small one. Lack of planning and organisation will result in disorganisation and lack of progress. Again, storage and clear labelling are essential. In any setting a clear plan for the day, of which all staff are aware, is a necessity. Staff who know the routine and the position of all equipment will ensure the smooth running of a nursery or classroom. Careful organisation and structure can give the impression that the children have control over their own activities and support them in becoming more independent.

Think about it

Have a look at the plan of the room in a nursery below.

How does it compare with the room in your placement?

If it is very different can you suggest why that might be?

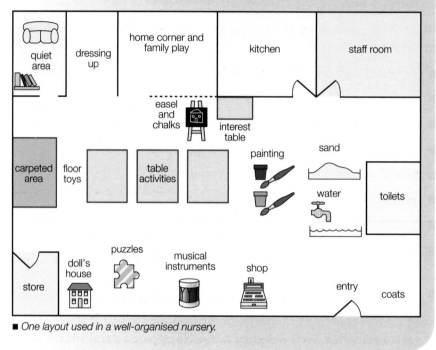

■ *One layout used in a well-organised nursery.*

Even though a setting for children needs to have an overall structure, smaller areas for specific activities may need adjustment depending on the activity planned. This applies to outdoor areas as well as indoor. For example:

■ using an outdoor area for a game of football instead of playing on outdoor equipment

■ using an indoor space for dancing instead of large scale junk modelling.

Checking the layout and equipment for an activity

Whenever an activity is planned and being prepared for it is important that the layout and equipment is suitable, safe and ready for use.

Suitable layout

When you are helping with an activity look at the area being used and think about the following points:

■ Is the area big enough for the planned activity (think about floor space, table space, sand or water tray if used)?

- Are chairs, tables or any other equipment arranged to encourage children to work together or alone, depending on the intended aim?

- Is there enough space for children to move about safely?

- Are support facilities nearby if needed, for example sinks?

Suitable equipment
- Is the equipment suitable for the activity?

- Is the equipment suitable for the stage of development of the children?

- Is the equipment safe and clean (no breakages, tears, incomplete equipment)?

- Is there enough equipment for the children involved? Think about aprons, cloths, brushes for cleaning up, protective coverings for floor, etc.

Preparation
- Make sure all the necessary equipment is put out or readily available.

- Can the children reach everything they need?

- Does the area look exciting and inviting to the children?

- Is everything on hand for adults to support the children, for example drying lines for paintings?

- Are there plans to follow on after the activity, for example does it lead into snack time? If so, has time been allowed for hand-washing?

- Does everyone involved know what is happening and what they need to do?

- Do other staff know of the plans and when the activity will finish?

- Are there 'back up' plans, for example if one child cannot do the activity how will it be adapted? If some children finish early is there an extension planned?

Meeting children's needs

All the planning and preparation involved in a successful activity will be wasted if a vital question has not been asked: have the children reached the required stage of development and do they possess the skills necessary to take part in and enjoy the activity?

A good understanding of child development and observation of children playing and working while you are in placement will help you to develop the knowledge you need to work out the answer to this question. Most activities are planned with the aim of extending children's skill levels, but skills cannot be extended or developed if the child is not ready for that next step. One example is the use of jigsaws. It requires quite a high degree of manipulative skill to put jigsaw pieces together and children need to learn to use slot-in jigsaw boards first, where they can match the picture underneath. Next they move on to jigsaws with very large pieces and gradually move to harder puzzles.

Think about it

Can you think of an activity you have been involved with for which the child was not ready? What happened?

Age	Play needs of the child	Indoor equipment	Outdoor equipment
0–2 years	The child is mobile and gaining gross motor and fine manipulative skills. The child needs plenty of opportunities to strengthen muscles and develop co-ordination.	Push and pull toys Toys that make music Dolls Trolleys Building bricks Posting toys Bright simple books	Paddling pool Baby swing Small slide
2–3 years	Children are starting to notice and play with other children. Language is increasing and much of their play is pretend play. Children are gaining confidence in physical movements and enjoy playing outside. Children of this age can be easily frustrated and have a short concentration span – less than 10 minutes – so they need opportunities to be independent in their play and range of activities. There should be plenty of equipment as children find it difficult to share with each other.	Dressing-up clothes Home corner equipment, for example tea sets, prams, cooking utensils, pretend telephones Building blocks Toy cars and garages Dolls and cuddly toys Dough Paint Jigsaw puzzles Musical instruments	Paddling pool Sand and water tray Slide Climbing frame Swings Sit and ride toys Tricycles
3–4 years	Children are starting to co-operate with each other and enjoy playing together. Most of their play is pretend play. Pieces of dough become cakes; tricycles become cars! Children enjoy physical activity, gaining confidence in being able to use large equipment such as climbing frames. They are also developing fine manipulative skills and beginning to represent their world in picture form.	'Small world' play, for example playmobil, Duplo figures Dressing-up clothes Home corner and equipment Dough and other malleable materials Water and sand Construction toys such as train tracks, building bricks Jigsaw puzzles	Climbing frame Slide Balls and bean bags Bicycles with stabilisers Tricycles Paddling pool
4–6 years	Children are more interested in creating things, for example making a cake, drawing cards and planting seeds. Children enjoy being with other children although they may play in pairs. Children are beginning to express themselves through painting and drawing as well as through play. Children are enjoying using their physical skills in games and are confident when running and climbing.	Materials for junk modelling Cooking activities Dough and other malleable materials Jigsaws Home corner Construction toys Small world play, for example Duplo people Simple board games	Mini gardening tools Skipping ropes Hoops Climbing frame Slide Tricycles Different-sized balls

continued ▶

Age	Play needs of the child	Indoor equipment	Outdoor equipment
6–8 years	Children are confident and can play well with other children. Children are starting to have particular play friends and are able to share ideas about their play. Games that involve rules are played and rules are added and changed as necessary! Most children enjoy physical activity and play organised games. Sometimes this age can be very competitive. Children are also keen on making things – either of their own design or by following instructions.	Creative materials, for example junk modelling, crayons, pieces of card and paper Board games Jigsaw puzzles Complex construction toys Books Collections, for example stamps and stickers	Balls Hoops Bicycles Roller-skates Skipping ropes Climbing frames Slides Swings
8–12 years	Self-led displays. Development from 6–8 years. Increasing independence.	IT equipment Resource areas Quiet areas	As above plus skateboards Formal games Large spaces
13–16 years	Ongoing development. Approaching independence.	As 8–12 years Areas for meetings Socialising area	As 8–12 years Outdoor expeditions

■ Chart showing play needs linked to age

Promoting inclusivity

The Disability Discrimination Act 1995 requires the provision of access for all children to educational facilities, indeed to all facilities for all in society. The Act requires **'reasonable' adjustments** to be made to allow access. Clearly a very old building with narrow stairs to the main services could be very difficult to change to give access for a wheelchair user. Buildings and services like this are in the minority, and changes such as wider doors, lifts, ramps, suitable toilet facilities, etc. must be provided in public places. Society has moved a long way from the dark ages when a child with a disability would be kept out of sight and often placed in institutional care. However, it is still very difficult for disabled people to access some facilities and to avoid the pointing and staring of some people.

All child care workers have a responsibility to promote the rights of all children, especially those who may experience difficulty in taking part in activities. It is important for child care workers to ensure that a child is not discriminated against in terms of the opportunity to reach his or her full potential. Look at these three examples.

■ Jodi has hearing difficulties and as a result her speech has been delayed. She experiences communication difficulties unless alternative methods of communication are considered. When her group at nursery has story time, the nursery nurse always makes sure that Jodi sits at the front and that the story has a lot of visual appeal, using puppets, pictures and miming.

■ Samir has **cerebral palsy**, which means he has difficulty in controlling his movements without shaking. Playing in the home corner was difficult because it was a small area, and Samir tended to knock things over. His teacher has relocated the home corner so that it is in a bigger area and Samir can now play safely in it.

■ Joel has difficulty getting into the playground as access is up two small steps. However, he can move very quickly once in the playground in his lightweight wheelchair. With the help of one of the staff, Joel's friends have invented a new form of football that allows him to use his arms instead of his feet.

There are many other ways to overcome barriers to inclusion. It is essential that activities and opportunities are planned for the entire group of children in your care, taking all needs into account. All children are individuals and need consideration for their individuality when working with them. Some children require more thought because of additional needs beyond those of most children. All children can benefit when activities are adapted, such as making story time a wider experience, and learning new ways of playing traditional games.

Special equipment

Sometimes special equipment may be needed to allow children with special needs to practise and develop all their skills.

■ A child who has poor fine motor skills and difficulty with fine hand and eye co-ordination may benefit from the use of thicker pencils and other tools.

■ Children with delays in developing gross motor skills (large body movements such as walking or running), or sensory problems (vision, hearing, etc.) may enjoy large-scale toys such as ball pools and soft foam cushions.

■ A child with a visual impairment may be able to read large-print books or books written in Braille and will enjoy listening to stories recorded on tape.

Some centres are equipped with multi-sensory rooms that provide opportunities for children with a wide range of specific needs. These rooms feature a range of lights, sounds, smells and touch sensations that stimulate (or in some cases soothe) the senses. Any activity, game or toy designed to develop an aspect of a child's skill should aim to allow the child to use the skills that already exist and encourage him or her to extend them. For example, when a child reaches the stage of being able to turn the pages of a book, make sure the child has books with thick pages, showing pictures of interesting objects.

■ *Sensory rooms provide many opportunities*

Sometimes there is no need to adapt equipment, but the methods of promoting an activity may need changing. A child who has difficulty sitting still for long will struggle to take part in a modelling activity lasting 15 minutes. How could this modelling activity be adapted? Someone could sit with the child and keep up the encouragement or ask to look at progress at frequent intervals. The child could be given some responsibility for drawing all the children's efforts together, say for a display. This may help to prevent the child's behaviour becoming unacceptable.

Through imagination and consideration of safety issues, most children can enjoy most activities and equipment. They can usually be adapted to suit all children without losing the aim of the exercise. Careful thought has to be given to making sure that no one is discriminated against in play and exercise.

There are many ways to include a child who is disabled. Many manufacturers make suitably adapted play equipment, for example tricycles with bucket seats. Equipment specifically designed for children with disabilities can usually be used by all children. The manufacturers of 'ball pools' and huge foam wedges in different shapes originally designed them for children with disabilities but they now feature in most adventure playgrounds for younger children. Careful use of foam mats can take much of the risk out of physical exercise for all children, so that falls do not have hard landings.

Think about it

Create or adapt an activity or toy to meet the requirements of a child with a specific need (ideally a child you have met).

Think about it

Choose a popular game. If you had a child with visual impairment and another child with difficulties in gross motor skills, how would you adapt the activity to meet the needs of both?

Although the safety of all children in your care is of paramount importance, you also need to strike a balance so that children are allowed the freedom to enjoy their activities. Occasionally it may be necessary to support a child in play if he or she cannot play alone. In this situation you should respond to the child's wishes as far as is practical, and not stop the child exploring and developing his or her skills.

Best practice in your work placement

Maintaining safety

- Avoid leaving items lying around on the floor.
- Make sure equipment is kept in its proper place.
- Use large foam pads and cushions around a slide, or provide a play area made up of shaped foam blocks to allow a child to roll, jump and fall in safety.
- Make sure special adaptations are in place on equipment such as slides, climbing frames and bicycles. Usually when a child has a special need of some type he or she will have had an assessment by an occupational therapist and equipment adaptations provided.
- Make sure children who have them, wear their protection to allow them free access to indoor and outdoor play space, for example helmets, knee and elbow pads.

Think about it

You are helping with a group of eight energetic five-year-olds, five girls and three boys. Samir is slower than the others in walking, due to a condition affecting his muscles. Paul does not like rough games and is reluctant to join in groups. Lucy likes any game that is noisy and rough, but she broke her arm last week and has it in plaster. The weather was wet and windy all morning and now the sun has started to shine. The class teacher asks you to help the assistant to take this group outside and organise some exercise for them in the grounds of the school for half an hour.

1 How do you think the time could be planned to include all of the children?
2 What checks would need to be in place to ensure the environment was safe for all the children?

Assessment activities

Assessment Activity 1

When preparing and maintaining the physical and play environment for children the primary consideration must always be that they are kept safe and healthy.

When Sahinda's mother comes to look around the nursery for the first time she asks you how you ensure the children's health and safety.

You have to describe for her how all aspects of health and safety are ensured in the children's environments.

You tell her about the health and safety requirements which are inspected by OFSTED such as the ratio of staff to children, heating, lighting and electricity, ventilation, doors and glass, access points, outdoor and indoor surfaces and the risk assessments that must be carried out.

You then tell her about the need for cleanliness with safe and appropriate play equipment inside and outside, meeting RoSPA guidelines, appropriate toilet, kitchen and laundry facilities, storage for equipment and materials, safe supplies of water, and power as well as the telephone, supervision at all times including on outings, security for children and families, adequate insurance and good arrangements and awareness with respect to first aid and emergencies.

You also tell her that risk assessments are carried out by staff on a regular basis and that you have to be aware of these and of the results of these assessments. Your role, however, covers risks and you have to make a number of checks both before the children arrive and during the day to ensure safety. These include space, the positioning of safety equipment, safety of materials, the number of children in any one area, the number of adults in any one area and ensuring that help is available.

When you have completed this description you will have met Pass criterion 1 (P1) which requires you to describe how all aspects of health and safety are ensured in children's environments.

Assessment Activity 2

An important part of preparing and maintaining the physical and play environment is how space is used and the room inside and area outside laid out.

Draw a plan to show the layout of a nursery area both indoors and outdoors.

Along with the plan, give your reasons for this layout to include consideration of doors and fire exits, how furniture and materials are set out, storage facilities and labelling, positioning of 'messy' areas, quiet areas and book corners.

Assessment Activity 3

Describe the checks that need to be made before, during and after a session.

continued ▶

Assessment Activity 4

However well you have planned the environment to be safe, it is also important that the environment is suited to the needs of the children. Describe how play materials, equipment and the environment need to be linked to children's ages.

Some children's abilities may not be so well developed as those of other children of their age. Describe the main requirements of the Disability Discrimination Act as it applies to children and how you can plan to enable access for all children as well as including them in all activities.

How could equipment, the use of space and activities be adapted to ensure the inclusion of all children?

When you have completed Activities 2, 3 and 4 you will have met Pass criterion 2 (P2), which requires you to outline (briefly describe) the steps needed in preparing and maintaining the physical and play environment.

If you explain (describe how and why) how all aspects of the physical and play environment should be prepared and maintained you will have met Merit criterion 1 (M1).

4.2 Understand how to prepare and maintain a stimulating environment

This section covers:

■ displays

■ use of senses

■ nature of environment

Think about the children's settings you have seen, even if only on a video or TV. Can you think of one that was particularly vibrant and exciting for the children? Can you think why it had that sense of being stimulating for the children there?

Displays

A very important contribution to the atmosphere of a setting is the quality and effectiveness of the displays. The displays should be colourful and interesting and be varied in their content.

The following material should be displayed in a child care environment:

■ information for parents/carers

■ information for children

■ timetables, programmes and plans

■ menus if meals are served

■ age-related displays on various topics by staff

■ work by the children or young people.

Whatever the type of material on display there are a number of important rules to consider:

■ What is the condition of the material? There should not be any tears or marks.

■ Is it age appropriate to the setting?

■ Are appropriate formats such as language and symbols used?

■ Can the intended audience see it? For example, is information for parents near the entrance, are posters at the right height for small children?

■ Is it inclusive? Does it apply to a range of cultures and backgrounds without stereotyping?

Think about it

What is displayed on the walls of your placement? How is the children's work displayed?

■ What will the method of display be? For example, on walls, tables or folders.

■ Think about safety when displaying, including the staff mounting the display and the children and staff in the setting.

■ Consider the length of time material will be displayed.

Range of displays

Displays can be used to inform and raise awareness of issues to help children learn about the world around them, for example different forms of transport, jobs helping people, animals. They can also be used as reminders for their learning, for example timetables or number squares in school. Above all, displays are the ideal way to allow a child to show off their work to parents and carers with associated benefits for a child's self-esteem.

Displays can range from being mounted on the wall to look at through to a low level display full of different textures to encourage children to feel the display, or to a whole section of a room. Of course, a display can also involve several senses and have sound included and maybe use ICT through a computer interactive display.

Involving children in the display of work is vital as it helps them to take responsibility and be part of the work of the setting. Even the background of a display can involve children, for example orange and brown handprints on a roll of backing paper for a display on Autumn.

■ *Displaying children's work*

Case study

Themed displays

Year 2 of Roshtown Primary School had been spending time on the theme of 'the jungle'. Miss Darzy, the class teacher, and Al the nursery nurse have spent a lot of time making the reading corner into a mini jungle. Children's paintings of jungles and animals line the wall. A line strung up around the area has dyed green sheets hanging with crepe paper leaves and creepers. Papier mâché models of animals and birds done by the children are suspended from the ceiling. The book corner is full of books on the theme and Miss Darzy has a tape recording of croaking frogs and other jungle noises for occasional use.

Think about how this theme corner display could be used.

Whatever or whoever the display is for it should always:

- be professional in appearance
- be labelled to a high standard, meeting any specific printing policy of the setting
- be safe
- appeal to, and where possible promote, a variety of cultural backgrounds.

Interest tables

Interest tables usually have a theme, for example colours, toys, a country or holidays. It is possible to create a 'growing' table by planting bulbs, seeds or plants that can be observed in progress. Objects for interest tables can be collected on walks or outings from the placement so that children feel a sense of ownership. Even older children can enjoy interest tables, perhaps based round a popular activity, for example a recent film or skateboarding.

Once constructed, the interest table is a focus of attention and can be used to:

- stimulate discussion about the objects – what they are, where they are from, what they are used for, etc.
- stimulate creative activities – paintings, stories, model-making
- promote learning in areas of science, literacy and numeracy, and interest in the world at large.

Think about it

Spend some time in your placement looking at the displays and observing and perhaps helping with the mounting of a display. Make notes on the following:

- *What sort of background materials are used?*
- *What materials are used in the display work?*
- *What type of writing has been used in the labelling?*
- *How are the artefacts displayed?*

How have the children been involved?

Think about it

With a partner, list as many themes for an interest table you can think of to appeal to different ages of children.

Think about it

Ask if you can plan and prepare an interest table in your placement. Write about your experience, including details of the items shown, the use made of the table and any problems encountered. If possible, include a photograph of the finished display.

Best practice in your work placement

- On a table, display items to their advantage to help to stimulate discussion.
- Cover the table with a plain cloth or fabric. Choose a colour that complements the objects to be placed on it.
- Use boxes and books under the cover to raise certain items above the level of the table.
- Do not include precious objects that could be lost or spoiled.
- Arrange objects so that children can see and touch them.
- Label objects neatly and make sure the names of their providers are on them.
- Encourage the inclusion of everyday objects from home; contributions do not have to be exotic.
- Beware of inadvertently encouraging the picking of wild flowers or plants from gardens.
- Try to add additional material such as books or pictures relevant to the theme.
- Take a photograph of the finished table.
- Watch the pride and raised self-esteem of even the shyest child proudly showing off their exhibit to parents or carers!

Use of senses

We all have five senses through which we learn and experience the world:

■ The five senses

Even children with reduced vision or hearing will have some level of light or sound perception but will need help to experience the world through their other senses.

Some settings have multi-sensory rooms that are full of opportunities for children to spend time in and experience different sounds, sights, textures and smells. Some of these are specialised for children with learning difficulties and/or disabilities to stimulate their development. Children's hospitals often have them to provide a soothing comforting environment away from the clinical and perhaps upsetting aspects of the wards.

You do not need a multi-sensory room however to encourage children to develop their senses. The jungle theme discussed on page 143 challenges children's senses of sight, sound and touch. Can you think how taste and smell might have been used?

A walk in the park can use every sense except taste and a shopping outing can use all the senses if something immediately edible is bought!

Activities within the setting can and should be thought about to include several of the senses. Have a look around your setting at the huge range of tactile materials, for example:

- sand
- water
- fabric
- floor surfaces
- chairs
- dough
- paint
- doors
- different toys
- paper.

Now do the same with another sense and just look at how many opportunities there are to help children explore their senses!

Nature of environment

Depending on the age of a child, their attention span will be short, relative to that of an adult. An activity that absorbs a three-year-old for 10 minutes will not maintain that same level of interest for 30 minutes. It is essential that children have the opportunity to change their immediate environment and activity to keep them stimulated, even though they may come back to an earlier activity.

Good planning in a children's setting takes this into account to make sure that there is sufficient flexibility, variety and choice of resources for play according to children's ages, need and abilities.

Think about it

Watch the children in your placement as part of an observation, timing how long they stay engaged in different activities. Are there differences with different activities and different aged children?

Wherever possible children should be actively involved in decisions about their environment. This can be as elaborate as the design of an entirely new or refurbished setting or as simple as a choice in the toys that will be set out that day. All opportunities to involve children and to respect and work with their views are excellent ways of helping them to develop their sense of worth and self-esteem. Older children will also be able to review how effective their ideas were.

Case study

Encouraging children's involvement

Every week, Southfield after school club staff sit down with the children to talk about what they would like to do the following week and month. They also look back over the previous week to talk about how enjoyable the activities have been. In the weeks that this has been happening the activities have changed and some of the older children are now helping the younger ones. The behaviour of the older children, which was causing concern, has also improved.

Why do you think the children are enjoying their club more now?

Assessment activities

Assessment Activity 5

Maggie, the early years worker who supervises you, asks you to help her with a display about Spring as this is the theme for the next three weeks. This is going to be a visual wall display with an interest table that goes with it so that children can touch and feel objects as well as looking at them.

Describe the following considerations that must be taken into account:

- position of display and interest table
- suitability for the children's ages
- materials and methods to be used
- height/level
- labelling and lettering
- safety
- inclusivity, for example cultures, disabilities
- promotion of positive values
- involvement of the children and their families
- display of children's own work in a way that encourages and promotes self-esteem
- types of objects for the interest table
- use of objects and materials to promote discussion
- links with IT, science, numeracy and literacy.

continued ▶

Assessment Activity 6

Check out your work placement and describe how it helps to stimulate the different senses. Take into account the following:

- Are there plenty of colours of different shades and hues and interesting things for children to look at?
- In what ways is sound used to interest children, for example musical instruments, headphones for listening to tapes?

- What are the different feelings of touch, from rough to smooth, in the materials and equipment in the placement?
- Does your work placement use mealtimes to encourage different smells and tastes? How else could this be done?
- Some work placements have a multi-sensory room. Describe what these are like.

Assessment Activity 7

Describe how the environment of a child care setting could be changed on a regular basis to stimulate and maintain children's interests.

You should include the following:

- layout of the setting
- changes in activities, materials and equipment
- making sure there is something for all children of all ages and abilities

- involving children in decision making regarding changes to their environment
- finding out what children want in the play environments.

When you have completed these three activities you will have met Pass criterion 3 (P3), which requires you to describe how to prepare and maintain a stimulating environment.

Assessment Activity 8

You can now go on to explain (describe in detail) how to ensure that the environment is stimulating for children. This will enable you to meet Merit criterion 2 (M2).

Assessment Activity 9

You should now think about the senses and give reasons for using the senses in stimulating children's interest and involvement.

This will enable you to meet Distinction criterion 1 (D1) which requires you to justify the use of the senses in stimulating children's interest and involvement.

4.3 Understand how to maintain an environment that builds children's confidence and resilience

This section covers:

- achievements
- change and consistency
- socialising
- backgrounds.

Adults involved in caring for children sometimes forget that children need to make mistakes in their drive for independence. All children are working towards the ultimate goal of full independence in all areas of life and having a clear view of the answer to 'Who am I?'. Child care and development workers play an important role in supporting children to reach this.

Praise and acknowledgement of achievements

If children are cared for in an environment where they are praised and made to feel worthwhile, they will gain the confidence to become independent and cope with things such as unforeseeable changes or criticism. You can encourage children to cope with change by ensuring that they are confident.

Self-esteem

Think about it

How do you think constantly being told you are useless will affect a child's self-esteem?

Self-esteem is when a child or adult feels good about him or herself. If a person feels that he or she is not worth spending time with, this shows that the person has 'low self-esteem'. The opposite is 'high self-esteem' when a child or adult feels that he or she is worth spending time with. Self-esteem is important for children in middle childhood, from about the age of seven or eight, but the foundations are laid from birth from the responses of other people to them.

You must never forget the importance of maintaining a child's self-esteem. Offering a child an activity usually aimed at much younger children could make the child feel inadequate and frustrated. The best person to consult is very often the child involved. For example, a child who has some delay in development of fine motor skills may have difficulty with small Lego bricks. Using larger bricks may be easier, but ask the child first and let him or her make the choice. This will help to maintain the child's self-esteem.

The opposite is also true as asking a child to attempt something that is clearly too advanced is damaging. It is important to offer challenge but not impossibility!

Good knowledge of a child's development and setting targets that are appropriate for them is an important part of planning activities.

Self-confidence

Self-confidence is linked to self-esteem. How can we be confident about ourselves and happy to engage with others, if we have a low self-esteem? It is easier for a child with high self-esteem to try new things out, make friends and find out about the world. Promoting self-confidence is an important part of caring for young children.

Turn-taking is important in promoting self-confidence. A shy child may need a gentle helping hand to go first for once and not be overwhelmed by a more assertive child.

Self-reliance

By encouraging independence, we automatically encourage self-reliance, self-esteem and self-confidence. Can you think of people you know who claim not to be able to look after themselves in basic tasks such as preparing a meal or washing clothes? Such people might have a reduced amount of work to do, but is this good for their self-esteem?

Feeding a child is much faster than encouraging self-feeding, but this tactic will not be appreciated when the child starts school and still needs help. Self-reliance is needed in a child when he or she starts school; a child has enough to deal with in adapting to all the new demands of school without the worry of not being able to use the toilet alone or not being able to cope with changing his or her clothes when it is time for PE.

Change and consistency

Have a look at the section in Unit 1, page 11, on bonding and socialisation. A child who has formed close bonds with several important people will be far more secure than a child who has not done so. Where there is a strong sense of security in a child, there is likely to be less emotional trauma caused by future changes in their situation.

A child may have to deal with a number of significant changes in their life at an early stage. These changes could include:

- a new brother or sister
- a new member of staff in placement
- the death of a pet or relative
- a change in placement
- a change in family circumstances, for example parental separation, new partner
- or moving home.

Think about it

How can you create opportunities for children to feel good? Think about games you plan for them. Do you make it possible for everyone to win sometimes? How does a child react if he or she does not win?

Think about it

Can you think of a time when a major change happened in your life? How did you feel and react? Perhaps you can remember the arrival of a new sibling or felt disturbed at the change from school to college. What helped you to adjust to the change?

If you are in a nursery placement, look at the procedure for moving a child on to school. Time should be taken to introduce the new place; a favourite toy might be taken and time spent with a familiar face in the new setting.

Look at some of the new children in a nursery or school. Why do you think some have settled in more easily than others?

Providing reassurance for change

It is very important to make sure that children know about changes that are going to happen. Their parents and carers in a setting should all make sure that the child is as well prepared as possible and time is allowed for discussion about worries the child may have.

Helping a child who has moved into a new child care setting provides a very good opportunity to observe the effects of self-esteem and self-confidence. A confident child with a high self-esteem is more likely to quickly settle into a new setting. Knowing that your main carer will be waiting at the end of the session to ask you all about your first day at school and will want to see your painting is a much better scenario than being made to feel a burden that you are bringing home yet another piece of rubbish.

Recognising insecurity and anxiety

Very often a child may seem to 'regress', for example starting to want a bottle again, or wet him or herself when highly distressed. Accept this as normal and recognise it as a call for help in making a transition or adapting to a new brother or sister. Sometimes a regression in behaviour may be the first sign you have at nursery about some disruption at home.

Sometimes the most well-adjusted child, who is outgoing and seems to be the obvious one to relish a positive change, can be the most upset by change. There are several possible reasons for this. There may be a number of minor changes happening in a short period of time, or a child may find it difficult to work out what the changes mean for them, no matter how well explained they are.

Being able to predict the effect of a change can be reassuring for some children, but not all. Some children (and adults) can become worried by the thoughts of what might happen and what might not.

Ways in which children display their anxieties:

- unusual sleep pattern
- unwillingness to eat or drink
- unwillingness to join in activities
- unusually subdued behaviour
- unusually upset when parent leaves
- unwillingness to leave one adult
- tearful.

Case study

Anxious behaviour

David, a six-year-old, is unusually quiet in the after-school club he attends. He does not want to join in any of his favourite board games and refuses a drink and biscuit at snack time. When his mother arrives to pick him up he is very tearful. Paul, the playworker, asks if there is a problem. His mother explains that their dog died the day before. Paul tells her he is glad to know as he can support David in the coming few days.

1 Is David displaying any anxieties typical of a child of his age?
2 Do you think his anxiety might have been understood earlier by Paul?
3 How do you think Paul will support David?

When you are reassuring and comforting distressed children the key factors to remember are:

- remain calm
- provide comfort
- be sensitive
- show respect
- provide reassurance
- be honest
- keep to normal routine where possible.

Socialising

Socialisation is all about learning to cope in the family and society we live in. The socialisation process will vary from family to family and in different societies. Primary socialisation takes place within the family in the first years of a child's life. Secondary socialisation starts when children come into regular contact with people and settings outside their home. This includes playgroup, nursery and school, and continues throughout life.

Socialisation teaches children about:

- society's views of gender roles
- how to interact with other adults
- how to interact with peers
- the views of peers
- the 'rules' of society, what is acceptable and what is not.

Children learn the skills to get on with each other through watching and experiencing the results of interactions.

Social skills

There are all manner of ways to help children to gain confidence and skills in socialising. They can do this through sharing and turn-taking in games, role playing in the home corner and by mixing with other

Think about it

How does your placement promote socialisation in the children who attend?

children and adults within the setting or in other settings. Respect for other cultures is an important point of socialising and joint activities with other settings is an ideal way to promote this.

Backgrounds

In your child care career you will encounter children, carers and parents from many different backgrounds. You will discover different ideas and preferences about food, leisure activities or religion, as well as expectations about children's behaviour and development.

Differences in cultural backgrounds can be due to any or all of the following:

- religion
- race
- gender
- education
- age
- social class.

A good rule of practice is to celebrate the diversity of experience among the children you meet in placement. Good child care and development workers use diversity to support children's understanding of the community they live in and welcome the differences they see. It is important not to judge parents' culture and values in your dealings with the children, even though they may be totally different to your culture and values.

Child care settings should be full of different experiences for children. The home corner in nursery, for example, should have provision for children to role play meals sitting at the table using knives and forks as well as sitting at a low table using chopsticks or using their hands.

Think about it

In a small group, discuss how you feel about the two different expectations of young children described below.

Child A, aged four, appears to be a 'model' child. At home he is expected to play in his own room. At mealtimes he eats everything that is put in front of him, and is allowed a dessert only if he has eaten all his main course. Bedtime is 7 pm sharp, after a bath and a story read by his father. He already understands that he has to fit in with the routine of his parents.

Child B is also four, and would be regarded as a very unruly child by A's parents. Her play takes place wherever she feels is best at the time. She is

always asked what she would like to eat and meals may be eaten while she is playing on the floor or occasionally at the table. There is no pressure to eat more than she wants to of any particular food. She usually goes to bed when her parents go to bed and often shares their bed.

- *Do you think one is preferable to the other?*
- *Which fits most closely with your own experiences?*
- *How do you think the cultural backgrounds of the children affect people's expectations of them?*

In the 1950s, child care experts would have been horrified by Child B, but very approving of A. Today's 'experts' tend to be more relaxed, and recognise that within certain boundaries it is more important that patterns of care and behaviour fit comfortably with the family. Those boundaries are matters that affect a child's health, safety and well-being. Within these limits, parents should feel free to develop a pattern of routines and behaviour that they are comfortable with. Children are not pre-programmed into acting in one particular way. A child whose parents work at night could easily develop a routine of sleeping all day and being awake at night. Problems might arise, however, when that child starts to go to nursery or school.

Expectations of intellectual development, too, can reflect wide cultural variations. In certain communities, four- and five-year-olds are expected to be making rapid progress towards fluent literacy. In other communities, they would be expected to be developing skills through free expression. Different theories of nursery and primary education, such as the Steiner or Montessori system, reflect different cultural expectations.

Child care workers should recognise and respect cultural differences in expectations and should ensure that these differences are reflected in activities in the care setting.

Assessment activities

Assessment Activity 10

The environment is not just physical. It is also about the atmosphere created by the spirit and views of the early years workers.

When Rona first comes into the Nursery she has little self-esteem and lacks confidence. She has spent a lot of time in hospital and her family have done a lot for her and not given her opportunities for any independence. Describe how you can help Rona by taking into account the following aspects:

- encouraging her to take part in activities
- acknowledging and praising her achievements
- helping her to recognise her own achievements
- giving her confidence in her achievements and abilities
- helping her to make progress and achieve in a way that is appropriate to her age, needs and abilities
- helping her to be more independent
- helping her to feel good about herself
- helping her to be more self-confident.

continued ▶

Assessment Activity 11

Consistency is something that is needed by children. Describe why it is important. You should include the following:

- ability to predict
- effects on confidence
- effects on security
- importance of reassurance.

However, it is inevitable that children will have to cope with change.

All new children to your child care setting will be experiencing change and there may be changes in the child care setting itself such as a new member of staff or a move to another room in the setting.

Describe the ways you can help a child cope with these changes. You should include:

- explanations
- being clear and honest
- providing reassurance
- giving comfort.

Assessment Activity 12

Describe the ways in which you can encourage children to socialise with each other and with adults, for example turn-taking in a game, mealtimes, play.

Assessment Activity 13

Describe how you can help children to be positive about their own cultural backgrounds. This should include positive images and celebration of all cultural backgrounds in all aspects of the child care setting.

When you have completed Activities 10, 11, 12 and 13 you will be ready to meet Pass criterion 4 (P4), which requires you to describe how to maintain an environment that builds children's confidence and resilience.

Assessment Activity 14

You can now explain (describe in detail what, how and why) the important elements of maintaining an environment that builds children's confidence and resilience. This enables you to meet Merit criterion 3 (M3).

4.4 Know how to support routines for children and integrate play

This section covers:

■ provision of food and drinks

■ consistency

■ balance

■ children's personal care.

Provision of food and drinks

Why do we need to eat? For many people eating is an enjoyable experience but everyone needs food and water for a number of reasons. We need food for:

■ energy and growth

■ all bodily functions

■ development of healthy bones, teeth, skin, muscles, nervous system

■ establishment of good eating habits and prevention of digestive problems

■ helping general behaviour patterns, for example sleeping, concentration and alertness

■ sensory experiences

■ fighting infection and healing the body.

Different food groups

When they are small, children need help to ensure they have the right amount and balance of food. They are incapable of providing food for themselves and to begin with they are unable to eat without help. Everyone needs to eat a **balanced** diet to help to maintain health. The important parts of a healthy diet are shown in the following table.

Nutrient	Function	Sources
Carbohydrates	Energy for growth and activity. Aid digestion of other food	Potatoes, pasta, rice, pulses, sugar, fruit
Fats: Saturated from animal sources Unsaturated from vegetable sources	Energy, body heat Contains vitamins (A, D, E and K)	Butter, cheese, meat, olives, vegetable and fish oils, nuts
Proteins	Growth and repair of the body	Meat, fish, soya, pulses, cheese, eggs, nuts, cereals
Vitamins: Fat soluble (A, D, E and K)	A – promotes good vision and healthy skin	Fat soluble – oily fish, cheese, tomatoes, carrots, milk, liver, egg yolk, green vegetables
Water soluble (C and all Bs)	B – aids blood formation, nerve and muscle function C – promotes healing D – encourages growth of bones and teeth E – protects cells from damage K – allows blood to clot	Water soluble – fruits, juices, meat, leafy vegetables, beans, eggs
Minerals: Calcium, sodium, potassium, magnesium, sulphur, fluoride, trace elements	For healthy bones and teeth, balance of fluids, energy production, control of nerves and muscles	In nearly all foods in differing amounts Sodium in salt, meat, fish and bread Fluoride in water supply
Fibre	Adds bulk to food to keep bowels functioning Thought to help in protection against heart disease and cancer	Oats, wholewheat bread, beans, leafy vegetables, prunes, apples
Water	Maintains fluid balance Helps in waste elimination	All foods and drinks in varying amounts

■ *The features of a healthy, balanced diet*

It is important that food is eaten in well balanced proportions with variable portions from each of the following groups of foods:

■ oils and fats

■ high protein foods

■ milk and dairy products

■ fruit and vegetables

■ potatoes and cereals.

Oils and fats (group 1)

- A concentrated source of energy, but too many saturated fats (animal fats) may cause heart disease in later life.

- Use unsaturated fats where possible.

- Found in sausages, cheese, chips, crisps, pies and biscuits.

High protein foods (group 2)

- Essential for body growth and repair.

- Foods include meat, fish, poultry, eggs, tofu, quorn and pulses.

- Meat, eggs and pulses contain iron for healthy blood formation.

- Oily fish and liver contain vitamin A.

- Children need two portions per day.

Milk and dairy products (group 3)

- Contain protein and vitamins A and B (for the healthy working of the nervous system).

- A rich source of calcium for the formation of healthy bones and teeth.

- Foods include milk, yoghurt, hard and soft cheeses.

- Children need three portions per day.

Fruit and vegetables (group 4)

- Provide rich sources of vitamins and minerals as well as fibre.

- Fibre helps digestion and prevents bowel problems such as constipation.

- Citrus fruits and potatoes have a high vitamin C content for healing and healthy skin and blood formation.

- Green vegetables contain iron.

- Children need five portions per day.

Potatoes and cereals (group 5)

- Provide energy as well as some protein, vitamins, minerals and fibre.

- Foods include bread, pasta, rice, breakfast cereals, and potatoes.

- Children need five portions per day.

Sugary foods

Sugary foods, including sweets, chocolate, snack bars etc. are not essential for a balanced diet and so are not included in any of the food groups. They are a source of rapid, short-lived energy and have little or no other nutritional value. Too many sugary foods may cause a child to become overweight or suffer tooth decay. If they are offered to a child they should not replace foods from the other groups. Naturally occurring sugars, such as those found in fruit and fruit juices, are the only ones necessary for health.

Salt

Salt occurs naturally in many foods, so a well-balanced diet should contain all that is necessary. Too much salt, such as adding salt when cooking or at the table, can cause ill health in later life and should be avoided with children. For babies and young children it can cause kidney problems.

Liquids

Liquids are just as important as foods in a healthy diet. Many squashes and fizzy drinks have a very high sugar content and no other value. Water is a far better alternative or natural fruit juices. However, a mixture of different drinks may be more realistic, including milk. Sugar should not be added to drinks as this will encourage a 'sweet tooth'.

Additives

Additives are substances added to food to preserve it or to improve its look or taste. All manufactured foods are required by law to list any additives in the food. These are all coded with E numbers so that they are recognisable.

Eating a healthy balanced diet

'Junk' food is often dismissed as not providing a healthy diet, yet a home-made burger or pizza or fish and chips can be an acceptable part of a child's diet. The secret is variety. Just as a constant diet of shepherd's pie or curry and rice would not meet all dietary needs, eating nothing but burgers is unlikely to give you a balanced diet.

However, many children do not eat a healthy balanced diet. There is growing concern that too many children are eating a diet that is high in fat and processed foods and are becoming overweight and unhealthy.

Poor diets in children can be part of the cause of a number of development and behaviour problems and research has shown that improving a child's diet can result in improvements at school. Even something as simple as drinking more water improves concentration levels significantly which is why most schools now have access to drinking water around the building.

Appetites

People have a range of appetites and food requirements from very small to large and remain healthy and active. This pattern starts in childhood and can also be affected by illness, stress or excitement. Changes in appetites can be due to many things:

- it could be the first sign a child is ill

- a toddler starts to walk and is too busy to eat

- an exciting event looming, such as an outing from school or a party.

For many children there is much more excitement in playing than eating. A good rule to follow is that if a child is hungry and the food on offer is palatable, he or she will eat. If the child is not hungry, he or she will not eat and no amount of persuading will change that.

Did you know?

Jamie Oliver, a well-known chef, investigated school meals in England and found that many of them were of very poor quality often using products that provided poor nutritional value and contained too much salt, sugar and additives. As a result of his campaigning the government increased the amount spent on the average school meal.

Think about it

Keep a record of your diet for two or three days, writing down everything you eat. How does your pattern of eating meet the suggested requirements shown above? Should you be making some changes?

You could also have a look at the menus in your placement. How much do they contribute to a healthy diet for the children?

THE HENLEY COLLEGE LIBRARY

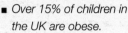

Did you know?

- *Over 15% of children in the UK are obese.*
- *Many children consume 50% more than the recommended adult levels of salt.*
- *83% of children consume more than the recommended adult levels of sugar.*
- *92% of children consume more than the recommended adult levels of saturated fat.*

Source: Feed me Better, 2005

Best practice in your work placement

Child care workers have a big part to play in encouraging positive eating habits. It is also important to follow the policies of your placement about food. Meal times are a potentially dangerous time, with the risk of choking, allergies and hot food and drink. Make sure you think about these points.

- Do any of the children you are working with have any food preferences or allergies?
- Supervise young children closely when eating raw foods such as carrots, apples, etc. in case they choke.
- Check that all stones and pips are removed from food for young children to avoid choking.
- Encourage children to eat a healthy diet as this will help to ensure that they grow into healthy adults.
- Do not make a fuss if a child is not hungry and does not want to eat.
- Keep sweets and snacks for after meals.
- Never use food as a bribe.
- Recognise how children can be tempted to try different eating experiences, for example with friends, in a café or picnics.
- Set an example by eating healthy foods.
- Children should be involved in choosing, cooking and serving their own food as much as possible.

Dietary needs

As with any other aspect of a child or young person's needs there are many different dietary needs. Some of these are culturally based, for example vegetarian or specific diets related to religious background, or they may be medically based. Children also simply have different tastes in food.

You must work closely with parents when a young child has specific dietary needs and respect their wishes and views. However, as children get older they will often know their own needs, especially if they have a medical condition and will be able to make suggestions about their diet.

Medical conditions

Diabetes
Diabetes means that the pancreas cannot regulate the body's sugar levels. Children need to avoid sugar but should have regular meals and snacks. Each child's needs are different and it is important to work closely with parents to support a diabetic child.

Coeliac disease
Coeliac disease is another medical condition which means that children cannot absorb their food normally and do not develop as expected. By avoiding **gluten**, which is found in cereals such as wheat,

flour, etc. most children subsequently develop very well. Coeliac disease is usually detected after a child has been weaned from breast milk.

Food allergies
Some children have food allergies. This means they cannot tolerate certain foods and may become very ill if they eat them. Common food intolerances are:

- lactose – found in milk and dairy products

- histamine – found in strawberries and ripe tomatoes

- tartrazine – found in yellow food colouring and some drinks and sweets

- nuts and nut products which can be hidden in many foods.

Religious or cultural variations
It is important to respect the diets of a variety of different religions. Look at the table below, but remember that only some members of that religion may eat those foods.

Did you know?

Some children can go into anaphylactic shock if they eat certain foods or even eat food that has been in contact with the substance they are allergic to. Look out for warnings on food labels and always follow instructions about foods that a child cannot eat. Anaphylactic shock can and often does result in the death of someone who has come into contact with something they are allergic to. Their face and throat may swell up and their heart and breathing stop.

Muslims	Eat **Halal** meat, fish and shellfish, which is slaughtered and prepared in a certain way. Do not eat pork or dairy products that contain rennet (used to set cheese for example). Fast during Ramadan.
Jews	Eat Kosher lamb, beef and chicken which is slaughtered and prepared in a certain way. Do not eat pork. Dairy products are not eaten with meat. Eggs must not have blood spots. Fish should have fins, scales and backbones. Fast during Yom Kippur.
Sikhs	Rarely eat pork. Do not eat beef as the cow is a sacred animal. Some Sikhs eat chicken, cheese, fish and shellfish.
Hindus	Usually vegetarian. Do not eat beef as the cow is seen as a sacred animal. Do not eat dairy products that contain rennet. Some Hindus eat eggs and shellfish. Fish with fins and scales is eaten.
Rastafarians	Some Rastafarians do eat lamb, beef and chicken, but do not eat shellfish.

Personal preferences
Vegetarians do not eat meat or fish.

Vegans do not eat meat, fish or any other products that come from animals, such as milk.

Safe food handling

Food is an excellent breeding ground for bacteria! It is very easy to be responsible for an outbreak of vomiting and diarrhoea by not being careful about hygiene when handling food.

High standards of cleanliness and personal hygiene are very important when storing, preparing and handling food. It is a good idea to take a Certificate in Food Hygiene, not only for your personal development, but as a useful addition to your skills and knowledge for jobs. Anyone whose job involves the preparation or serving of food should have a Certificate and for many jobs it is compulsory.

Best practice in your work placement

Storing food

- 'Use by' and 'sell by' dates should be checked regularly and anything out of date thrown away.
- A fridge thermometer must be used to make sure that a fridge temperature is kept between 0°C and 5°C.
- Freezer temperatures should be below −18°C.
- Hot food should be quickly cooled before placing it in the fridge.
- Do not leave food out at room temperature. Store food as soon as you can.
- Raw meat and fish should be stored separately.
- Raw foods should be stored at the bottom of the fridge to avoid juices dropping onto other foods.
- Food that has begun to thaw must never be refrozen.
- All food in the fridge should be dated so that it can be discarded at the right time.

Preparing food

- Wash hands thoroughly before preparing food.
- Remove watches, bracelets, rings and other jewellery.
- Tie hair back and wear an apron.
- Cover cuts and wounds with a coloured waterproof dressing.
- Do not touch your nose or mouth, or cough and sneeze over food.
- Never smoke in a room where food is being prepared.
- The floor, work surfaces, sink, utensils, cloths and rubbish bins should be cleaned regularly.

- Waste bins must be kept covered.
- Disinfect work surfaces before preparing food.
- Wash tops of cans before opening.
- Wash equipment and utensils in hot soapy water before preparing raw food.
- Keep a separate cutting board and knife solely for poultry and wash them thoroughly after use.
- Use a separate cutting board for bread.
- Cook foods thoroughly according to instructions.
- Only reheat food once and ensure it is heated all the way through.
- Ensure that whites and yolks of eggs are cooked thoroughly and are firm.

Serving food

- Only use clean crockery and utensils that are not cracked or chipped.
- Children should be provided with their own cups and utensils.
- All children and adults should wash their hands before serving and eating.
- Ensure children sit down and are able to reach their food safely.
- Do not give younger children sharp knives for cutting their food.
- Children should be supervised when eating.
- Pets must not be allowed in the eating area.
- Meals and drinks should not be served too hot for young children.

Play activities

Play activities are an excellent way of using food in various ways. Whole themes can be built around food, such as shops and farms. Mealtimes should be fun and enjoyable. They can be started with a song, games can be made from pre-meal hand-washing and the topic is rich with language development opportunities.

■ *Most children enjoy cooking*

Most children enjoy cooking. Part of the enjoyment is creating something from a mix of items and learning about the changes that occur, and then there is the fun of eating the results. Some children may have experienced cooking with parents or carers at home, but many may not have done so. Adult supervision is essential, and because small groups are usual, there is an excellent opportunity to talk with the children about the task, where the food comes from or other issues. Children should be encouraged to do as much as possible themselves to encourage a sense of achievement.

Consistency

Consistency is something that everyone needs to have in their lives to some extent. Knowing that you will have enough to eat, that you will have clean clothes to wear and that when you arrive home from college, members of your family will be there, are all part of consistency and having a routine. When that changes, most people can feel uncertain and insecure until they are comfortable with the change or realise it is only temporary.

Did you know?

John Bowlby first researched the effect of different carers on children in orphanages after World War II. He found that children who had not had a consistent carer could not easily form bonds and relationships.

Most people have various fixed tasks and practices that are part of their daily routine and along with regular family and friends around, give a sense of consistency in their lives. These include washing, dressing, eating, travelling to work or school, relaxation time, watching TV, study, etc. Young children and babies also need a routine and consistent carers in their lives.

Best practice in your work placement

To provide consistency and help children to develop routines:
- keep children informed in a way that is appropriate to their age and stage of development to ensure that they are certain of what is happening
- always inform new children and parents of routines
- always inform children and parents of changes to routines
- ensure that children who have English as an additional language are supported
- ensure that children understand expected behaviour, for example during an emergency evacuation practice
- involve children in routine tasks, for example handing out drinks
- allow children to make mistakes
- help children to carry out routines, for example include footprints to the cloakroom
- turn routines into learning opportunities as they are part of the curriculum.

Think about it

What are the routines in your life? Think of a time when your routine has been changed unexpectedly. How did it feel?

List the children's routines in your placement. What would happen if some of the activities were neglected, for example washing hands before lunch? How would the children be affected?

Balance

Importance of physical play

Physical play encourages children to develop all their physical skills and to practise the skills that they already have. Your role in supporting a child's physical development will be to ensure that the child has a wide variety of experiences in a safe environment.

Any setting should offer a wide range of equipment that can be used both indoors and outdoors. It is important that children are given opportunities to develop their gross motor skills indoors as well as outdoors. Such opportunities may be provided by designated areas such as a soft play area or by activities such as drama.

Some settings may be lucky enough to have designated areas for physical play or have the opportunity to use other facilities. These could include:

- a soft play area
- a swimming pool
- a sensory room

- a games pitch, for example for football, netball or tennis

- a cycle path or course

- a climbing area

- an obstacle course or exploring area using things such as tractor tyres and concrete tubing.

Supporting physical play

Children with additional or special needs may have limited play opportunities. It is your role to ensure that they can do as many activities as possible. This support may be given by adapting equipment, for example:

- placing fluorescent strips on the steps of a slide for a child with a visual impairment

- ensuring that a child in a wheelchair has enough space to turn the chair in a game of catch

- providing large areas of soft landing cushions for a child who has a tendency to fall over.

Supporting children with special needs can be achieved by:

- discussing how they can be supported with their parents, professionals and the child

- encouraging children to support their peers with special needs

- having a positive attitude towards exercise for all

- referring to role models such as stars in the Paralympics.

Rest, sleep and quiet periods

Why is rest so important? We all need to have rest and sleep as part of our everyday routines, not only because we get very tired, but because sleep and rest have several functions, not least allowing the body to recuperate. If we are deprived of sleep, we soon start suffering from memory loss, irritability and even hallucinations. Parents will often say a child is very irritable when tired.

Children lead busy lives playing, learning, and eating. This is all hard work for the body so periods of rest are important.

By resting all children will:

- allow muscles and tissues to recover

- allow the heart to settle to a normal rate

- have a chance to reflect upon experiences.

There is no fixed answer to the question of how much sleep children need. Some babies sleep 18 out of every 24 hours, others only 12. Some toddlers can cope on 10 hours at night and a nap in the day, while others will sleep for 12 hours at night and then need two hours' sleep in

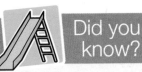

Did you know?

Some schools believe that games should be non-competitive and concentrate on the playing of the game rather than the result.

Think about it

How do you feel after a very late night if you have to be up early for college the next day?

Think about it

Talk to parents of several young children, all about the same age. How much sleep does each one need? How has this changed since they were babies?

the afternoon. Sleep patterns will change with changing routines and events in a child's life.

The body does not recuperate only by sleeping; rest is also needed during the day. Very few children will spend all day running around, actively playing, as they would rapidly become overtired and unable to concentrate. They will sit down sometimes and watch the world go by or ask to be read to or watch TV for a short time. These are all resting or quiet periods. The body regains strength as it rests. Many people can take a very short nap of 10–20 minutes and wake up feeling ready for action. Children are no exception to this.

Rest periods built into the day are very important for all children. Planning of activities is important to allow for short spells of quieter times during the day. Most nurseries and reception classes have a designated 'quiet' time in their daily routines to allow children to recoup their energy.

Most settings will have an area set aside for children to relax in. Some examples of quiet areas are given in the table below.

Setting	Quiet area
Baby room in a nursery	Carpeted area with subdued lighting, soft music and some gentle, tactile toys.
Foundation stage classroom	Book corner with cushions and screens that can be seen by adults, or a listening corner with story tapes and headphones.
Holiday club for children aged 11–16 years	Area in the shade with comfy chairs, snacks and magazines.

All children vary in the amount of rest they need and children tend to require less rest as they get older. The wishes of the child's parents must be taken into consideration, as must the routine of the setting.

Children's personal care

Supporting children and stressing the importance of health, safety and hygienic practices is all part of their personal care. From birth, a baby is totally reliant on carers until about three or four years old to help with their personal hygiene. This includes:

■ use of the toilet

■ hand-washing

■ care of the skin

■ care of the hair

■ care of teeth.

By the age of about eight or nine most children can fully care for themselves with the odd reminder about teeth cleaning or hair brushing. Part of any child care worker's role is to support children with their hygiene needs and to help them develop the skills to be independent in this.

Use of the toilet

Developing control of their bladder and bowel function is an important sign of growing up for a child. Most children are fairly reliably clean and dry by the time they are two and a half to three years old. This does vary from child to child and even then accidents easily happen if a child is tired, ill or just too busy to remember to go! Toilet training is covered in Unit 7 Care of Babies and Children Under 3. However, even if you only work with older children, at some time it is likely you will have to support them in their use of the toilet.

Many children have special names for their bodily functions, for example to describe the need to pass urine they may want a 'wee' or a 'pee' or they may just grasp at their genital area and wriggle! It is important to find out what each child will say or do if he or she wants to pass urine or empty his or her bowel.

Children often need reminders about appropriate times to use the toilet, for example before meals, at the end of playtime, before quiet or rest time.

Sensitive support is important, respecting a child's right to and wish for privacy. If appropriate, leave a child to deal with their clothing and cleansing alone. There are various steps, stools and seat adapters available to help children to use adult sized toilets. Use them to help with self-confidence.

If a child needs help, some points to remember are:

- protect yourself with apron and gloves
- make sure underwear is well pulled down before the child sits or stands at the toilet.
- pull the door to, to give some privacy until the child has finished
- if the child needs help wiping his or her bottom ALWAYS clean from the front to the back to avoid cross infection, especially for girls, and encourage that if the child is doing it by him or herself
- ensure the child is properly dressed and any wet or soiled pants are changed
- make sure the child washes his or her hands properly
- clean the toilet area according to your placement's rules
- wash your hands well.

Hand-washing

Thorough hand-washing is an essential part of good health routines. Our hands are full of bacteria that can be passed around our own bodies and very easily passed on to other people. Many bacteria and viruses cause serious illness and are transferred through the mouth, nose and eyes.

Did you know?

A survey found that almost a third of men and many women do not wash their hands after going to the toilet, vastly increasing the risk of food poisoning. Many of them are transferring germs straight from toilet to plate because they also do not wash their hands before preparing food. Estimates suggest as many as 4.5 million people suffered from food poisoning in the UK last year, although fewer than 100,000 cases were reported to the authorities.
Source: BBC website 2005

■ *Good hand-washing is essential*

Case study

Teaching children about hand-washing

Frank works in a pre-school group and wants the children to learn the importance of washing their hands as part of their toileting routine.

During a group time, Frank tells the children all about unfriendly bacteria. He then tells them about the importance of washing their hands using soap and water and how they must use paper towels to dry them.

He shows them some colourful notices he has made on the computer to remind them what to do. After the

group time he puts the notices up in the toilets at the children's height. Two children help him.

1 Do you think that Frank made the information fun? If so, why is this important?

2 How will the children understand the importance of hand-washing from this activity?

3 How will the children's confidence develop as a result of Frank's activity?

> Turn on the tap
>
> Put some soap on your hands
>
> Rub the soap all over your hands
>
> Put your hands under the tap and take all the soap off your hands
>
> Turn the tap off
>
> Dry your hands very well with the paper towels
>
> Put the paper towels in the bin

■ *The posters Frank used to encourage the children to wash their hands*

Caring for children's skin and hair

Carers need to make sure that children's skin and hair is appropriately cared for. Babies have different needs from older children. As children grow up they become more independent in their skin and hair care routines. In Unit 7 you will learn how to look after a baby's skin, including nappy changing. If a child has dirty skin, he or she will feel uncomfortable and may well develop a serious general infection if left unclean for too long.

It is important that parent's wishes are followed for a child's skin and hair care routine. Every family has different routines, needs and traditions and this may be influenced by a child's cultural background. The parents will also be able to advise on the best products to use on their child's skin if their child has an allergy or irritation.

Have look at the guidance for ensuring good skin care:

- show young children how to wash hands and praise them well
- when washing a child's face ensure flannels are only used by that child and are changed regularly
- encourage older children to wash themselves
- make sure all skin creases are carefully dried
- use soap carefully as it can dry skin
- use parentally preferred products if children have allergies or skin conditions such as eczema
- change nappies frequently and carefully to avoid soreness and infection
- encourage regular showers or baths to avoid sore areas and inflammation
- ensure water is not too hot; 63°C is a recommended temperature
- ensure feet are washed and dried properly and that footwear fits to avoid blisters and sores.

Haircare

Most people, including children, like their hair to look attractive and obviously younger children will need help in doing this. It is important, however, to check with parents about how a child's hair should be cared for if this is needed.

One of the commonest problems that children have with their hair is an infestation of head lice. Head lice like clean hair and can only crawl, not jump, from head to head by direct contact. The lice live on the scalp, suck blood from the scalp and lay eggs that they attach to the hairs with a very strong 'cement'. Treatment varies from combing with a fine tooth comb, to the use of lotions to kill the lice. Different lotions are needed from time to time to make sure the lice do not become resistant. The most effective form of prevention is twice daily brushing and combing of the hair to prevent the lice getting established in hair.

Did you know?

Around three million people catch head lice every year in the UK! Adults can catch them as well as children. Many grandparents catch lice from their grandchildren when they are sat on their knees!

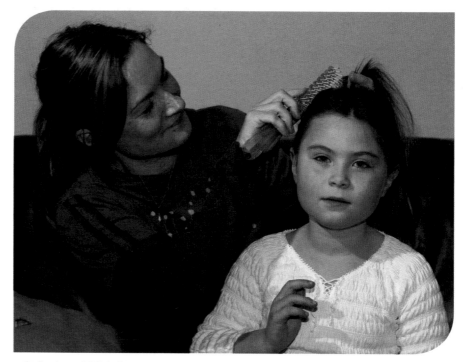

■ *Caring for a child's hair*

Case study

Head lice

One morning, 13-year-old Beth storms into the club and says she has caught head lice off Maria. Some of her friends tease Maria who asks to go home, although her hair has been treated. Two of the teenagers tell her she is dirty because she has lice.

In a group council session Graham, the manager of the scheme, informs the young people about head lice. He tells them that head lice are often attracted to clean hair and that anybody can catch them. He emphasises that it is important to treat people with sensitivity and not

name or blame them. He gives them informative leaflets about head lice. A discussion follows and the council agree on how they would support another outbreak. Beth apologises to Maria.

1 Why do you think Beth was angry?
2 Do you think Maria should have been upset?
3 Do you think that Graham ensured that the reaction to a future outbreak of head lice would be more appropriate?

Sun safety

Protection of the skin in the sun is essential as sunburn is not only sore and unsightly but it is also the basis for developing skin cancer later in life. Children's skin burns very quickly, even if they have sun cream on. While you will have to do more for young children, you will have to ensure that older children understand why they must protect their skin from harmful sun rays.

Best practice in your work placement

Children have delicate skin and you need to observe the following guidelines during summer. Even if it is cloudy, the sun can cause damage in the summer. How to protect children's skin against the sun:

- always keep babies under six months out of direct sunlight
- ensure children are kept out of the sun between 11 am and 3 pm
- cover children up using sun hats, T-shirts etc.
- children should use a high factor suncream with not less than 30SPF even when it is cloudy
- ensure faces are protected
- ensure older children understand the importance of protecting themselves against the sun.

Did you know?

Exposure to the sun can cause skin cancer (melanoma). There are over 7,000 cases of skin cancer in the UK every year.

In Australia the incidence of skin cancer has been high for some time now, but has reduced partly due to the 'Slip! Slop! Slap!' campaign. Slip on a long-sleeved T-shirt, slop on sun screen and slap on a hat. Sun hats are part of the uniform for all schools in Australia.

Caring for children's teeth

Teeth develop in a particular order and the way they are cared for is important to ensure healthy adult teeth. In Unit 7, you will find out more about how to help and comfort babies who are teething. Look at the diagram of the jaw to find out how teeth usually develop.

Think about it

Find out what the policies and procedures are in your placement for protecting children against the sun. Does your placement have any information for parents and children?

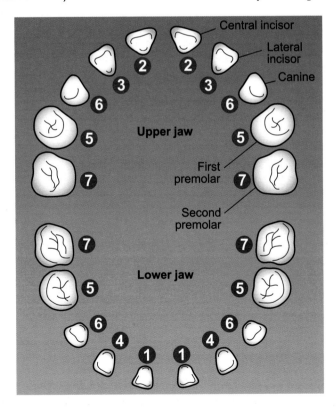

You should be aware of the following teeth facts:

- babies are born with teeth growing inside their gums
- the average age when teeth start to appear is six months

Did you know?

To build strong and healthy teeth, the children in your care will need a diet rich in:

- calcium
- fluoride
- vitamin A
- vitamin C
- vitamin D.

In areas where water supplies do not have enough fluoride, children should be given fluoride drops.

- there are 20 teeth in the first set of teeth which are called the milk teeth

- all milk teeth appear by the age of two to three years

- from the age of five onwards milk teeth begin to fall out

- permanent teeth start to come through when children are about six years old

- milk teeth are replaced by teeth that are larger

- the first permanent teeth to come through are molars and incisors

- the 12 extra molars make a set of 32 teeth

- sometimes permanent teeth are crooked and teenagers may need braces to correct this.

Chewing is good for the teeth but sweet and sticky foods can cause decay. Encouraging children to clean their teeth after every meal is important. You can make this fun. You could put a sequence of actions to music or make an attractive poster using pictures as well as words. By the time children are older, thorough teeth cleaning should be an accepted part of their routine. In the box below is an example of what you might put on a poster.

> Wash and dry your hands.
>
> Put water on your toothbrush.
>
> Place a little bit of toothpaste on your brush.
>
> Use a circular action to brush your teeth.
>
> Brush all teeth and inside edges.
>
> Rinse your mouth.
>
> Rinse your brush and place it in a clean place.
>
> Wipe your mouth.

Assessment activities

Assessment Activity 15

You need to describe the provision of food and drinks for children. The following need to be included:

- basic nutritional needs of children including water and food groups
- effects of poor diet
- cultural variations
- different types of food allergies
- importance of following the procedures of the setting to protect children

- importance of supporting children's food preferences
- basic information about safe food handling
- use of opportunities to support and encourage children's play.

You are now ready to meet Pass criterion 5 (P5), which requires you to describe the nutritional needs of children and the provision of food and drink.

Assessment Activity 16

Describe the importance of consistency in children's routines such as personal care, rest times and meal times and how you can help to carry this out.

Assessment Activity 17

Describe the need for balance in children's activities including the need for physical play with particular reference to children who have limited opportunities for physical play through disability or home environment, the provision of quiet times or rest periods and both support and encouragement for children to play.

Assessment Activity 18

Describe the ways you can support children in the use of the toilet, hand-washing, care of skin and hair, the use of toiletries, the need for sun safety and the development and care of teeth. Also describe how opportunities for play can be used.

After completing Assessment Activities 15, 16, 17 and 18 you are ready to complete Pass criterion 6 (P6), which requires you to outline (briefly describe) how to support care routines and integrate play into routines.

Assessment Activity 19

You should now explain (describe in detail) how play can be integrated into all care routines. This will enable you to meet Merit criterion 4 (M4).

continued ▶

Assessment Activity 20

Now you are ready to consider Distinction criterion 2 (D2).

In order to meet this criterion, you will need to look back at your notes for P4 and M3 as you are required to analyse (pick out the important aspects of) the role of the environment and care routines in building children's confidence and resilience.

5 Professional development, roles and responsibilities in child care

Introduction

Work placement is an essential part of any child care and development course. The theory you have been learning is directly related to the NVQ qualification at Level 2 in Children's Care, Learning and Development which is based on showing that you have the skills to work as an assistant with children from birth to 16 years.

Think back to the first occasion you spent time with a group of children for a few hours. Was it as you expected or did you end the session totally exhausted and shocked at just what is involved in supporting a lively, intelligent and challenging group of young people?

There is a world of difference between baby sitting for a child for a few hours in their home environment and working in a group setting on a continual basis. Throughout your work experience you will be constantly observing and learning how to work with children. You will be learning:

- from watching other staff
- from talking to other staff about their work and the children

- through experience of trying to put the theory you have learned into practice
- by going away from placement and finding out about something new that you have observed or heard about
- from discussions with your placement supervisor and tutors about your experiences.

This unit helps to consolidate all this knowledge and skill development, to help you reflect on your progress and to demonstrate that you are developing the essential skills to work in the field of children's care and learning.

If you complete the full First Diploma you will have experienced a total of 300 hours in placements with children and young people and recorded your increasing knowledge and skills in the 'Work Experience Journal'.

- 240 hours are directly related to this unit on Professional Development.
- 30 hours are linked to Unit 1 Children's Development.
- 30 hours are linked to Unit 3 Communication with Children and Adults.

The BTEC First Certificate requires you to experience 60 hours in placements:

- 30 hours are linked to Unit 1 Children's Development
- 30 hours are linked to Unit 3 Communication with Children and Adults.

However, you will also be using the opportunity to apply the knowledge from other units to your placement. Every single unit in this qualification is far better understood if you have experienced children in real life! The Work Experience Journal has specific pages for Units 1, 3 and 5 and blank pages for you to use for any other units that you wish to record your practical evidence against.

This unit:

- talks about how to effectively use your work placement
- explores a range of roles and responsibilities (safe and ethical practice, learner, assessor, care setting manager responsibilities, communication with parents/carers)
- identifies opportunities for you to collect evidence
- provides you with the space to gather your evidence
- helps you to present the evidence for assessment.

There are also useful pages in the Journal to help you to gather:

- a weekly workplace attendance record including participation in tasks, hours attended, supervisor's signature
- verification of workplace assessment tasks you have carried out.

This unit covers the following areas:

1 Understand support systems to develop own practice
2 Understand new knowledge and skills relevant to own practice
3 Understand own roles and responsibilities within the team
4 Understand values and ethics in child care working practice.

Each section will summarise the detail of the outcome and give some direct information and some links to other sources of material. This unit is very

5.1 Understand support systems to develop own practice

This section covers:

■ support systems

■ use of feedback

■ professional development

■ use of reflection.

Support systems

Use of feedback: clarification of own role in the team

No one will expect you to be confident in your first days in placement. In fact being over-confident is not a good idea! Can you think why?

Always remember that you are a student. You do not know everything about working with children, which is why you are on the course. You may not like every day in placement. In fact, you may find that some placements are a better experience than others. If you are feeling like this, then ask to discuss the situation with your tutor or co-ordinator. Ask for feedback from your placement supervisor and other colleagues about your performance. Ask what else you can do if you feel that you are not being sufficiently involved. There should be a clear understanding between you, your tutor or work experience co-ordinator and supervisor about your role. Placements are all different and the exact role of students in different placements varies. If you are unsure about exactly what you can or cannot do – ask.

Think about it

How do you think you will feel when you first make contact with your new placement or how did you feel if you have already made contact?

Your feelings may well be like those when you first started college or a new school or even this course!

will I like it?

frightened

nervous

looking forwards

excited

will they like me?

worried

Support in the work setting

There a number of people who are there to help you to settle in and gain the best possible experience from your placement.

- Your tutor from college can help you with issues about course work, how well you are doing, suitability of the course for you, helping with extra support for literacy or numeracy skills, where to find information.

- Your work experience co-ordinator (this may also be your tutor) can help you by visiting you regularly (find out how often he or she will visit) with issues in your placement, talking about examples of practice, observations, planning of activities.

- Your placement supervisor can help you with information about the placement, about the children, by giving verbal and written feedback on your work in placement, information on in-house training you can take part in.

- Other students (in college and in placement) can help you by being there just to talk to, exchanging experiences in placement, supporting each other with work, supporting each other in difficulties.

- Other staff in placement can support you by demonstrating good practice in early years work, encouraging you to shadow them, encouraging you to share ideas with them and ask for guidance.

The first part of your Work Experience Journal asks you to find out who your work experience co-ordinator and placement supervisors are and what the system is to support you. The table below shows the type of information you should include in your Journal.

Skills (what I can do)	Knowledge (what I have learned)
Use support systems Systems for supervision, for example tutorials, tutor placements visits, placement supervisor or mentor. Support in the work setting and at school or college. Use support systems to ask for constructive feedback on peformance; how to use new knowledge and skills in the work setting.	My work placement supervisor at the Laurels is Julia Howitt. I meet with her every week on my placement day to talk about what I am doing and again at the end of the day to review the day and think about next week. Robert Potts is the co-ordinator from college who went with me to arrange my placement and comes to see me in college and placement to talk about how things are going. He was very good at the beginning when I was unsure if I really did want to work with children.
Evidence (How I can show this)	**Follow up (what I need to do next)**
Tutorial records from Robert's visits. Reflective notes in my work diary. Evidence of work plans following discussion with Julia. Notes on my performance from end of day review.	Think about how I have developed as a result of using support systems. Reflect on my plans for working with children.

■ *Recording information in your Work Experience Journal*

It is important that you have someone in your support group with whom you can talk about how placement is going and express your feelings and concerns. Some things must be immediately reported to your supervisor, for example a problem with a child. However, for other things, for example, feeling impatient with a child or someone being sharp with you, it may be better to discuss it with your tutor or in some cases with a friend or family member.

Constructive feedback

An important role of your supervisor is to provide you with good feedback. Feedback should always be constructive which means that you are told what is positive about your performance as well as what can be improved. Use your supervisor to ask **how** you can improve and also for chances to try out some of the ideas you have been learning about in college.

Use of feedback

Everybody can improve their performance at work, whether they are just starting their careers as you are or are very experienced. Starting off being prepared to learn and improve is a very positive way of working. As a student you have a lot of different people observing your practice and being able to offer the benefit of their experience to help you to improve and develop your skills.

It is important to be realistic about the progress you should expect to make. Remember you are on a Level 2 course which is training you to work as an assistant in a setting not to be in charge of an area. So, you should be aware of what this means in relation to the level of skills you can hope to develop.

Knowing exactly what you can do in each of your placements is a good starting point for identifying what you can expect to gain experience in. You should make sure that this is made clear before you start in placement. Some placements may have a list of your role and responsibilities while in placement.

All of the support and supervision networks are there to offer suggestions for improvement. Feedback should always be constructive, pointing out your strengths and suggesting areas for development.

It is a good idea to always think about how well an activity has gone and what could have been done differently to make you more effective. In identifying improvements you may well identify a need for improved skills or knowledge.

Your supervisors and tutors should point you in the direction of information and guidance from other sources if needed but it is your responsibility to ask if you are unsure about how to get extra help or information.

This should develop into a routine of continuous self-development as shown in the following diagram. Reviewing your work in this way helps you to become more self-aware and know your areas of strength and weakness.

Think about it

Do you know exactly what you can do in your placement? Make sure that you read the Student responsibilities sheet in the Work Experience Journal and complete the checklist for each placement you attend.

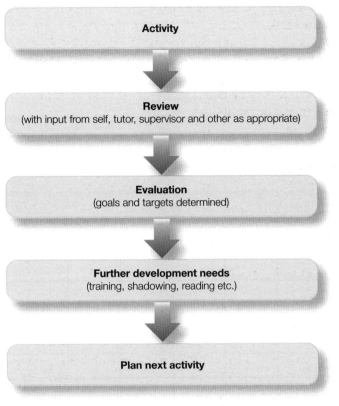

■ *Reviewing your work helps you to develop self-awareness*

Case study

Using a wheelchair

Jed is interested in how the school he is working in will be able to support the needs of a new child who has been for a visit with his parents. Joel, aged five years, uses a wheelchair to move around in and the school is quite an old building with steps between rooms and no other child using a wheelchair. His supervisor is very helpful in discussing the challenges the school faces in making it a welcoming and useful environment for Joel

and points out that there are many sources of information about disability on the internet such as the Disability section of the Direct Gov website (www.direct. gov.uk/DisabledPeople/ts/en).

As a result, Jed found out a lot of information about disability that he had never thought about before and it helped him to understand how to support Joel when he started.

Think about it

Use the following charts to self-assess against some of the skills needed to be an effective child care worker. Ask other people for their views as well and add other skills that are relevant at this time to you.

When you have identified where your skills fit on the 1–10 scale, think which are the two or three that are most in need of development. How are you going to improve them? Who can help you and when should your target date be for improvement? Use the second chart, which is the action plan, to help with this. Two examples have been completed for you. You will also find copies of these forms in the Work Experience Journal.

	Strength			Weakness	
Skill	**10**	**5**		**1**	**Improve by?**
Organisation					
Time keeping				3	Immediately
Listening skills					
Planning activities					
Taking feedback					
Observation skills		2			End of term

■ Self-assessment plan

Action planning is very easy to do. However, you must make sure you carry out what is needed. It is very easy for good intentions to fall to one side, especially if your actions do not go to plan. The Work Experience Journal has a further section on carrying out your action plan.

Skill	**Action needed**	**How/with whom?**	**By when?**
Time keeping	Catch earlier bus	Set alarm 15 mins earlier	Tomorrow
Observation skills	Improve detail noticed when doing observations	Do joint observation with supervisor and compare findings	Next placement day

■ Action plan

Skill	**Action**	**Contact/ arrangements made (date)**	**Comments**
Time keeping	Set alarm 15 mins earlier/catch earlier bus	January 25th batteries ran out in alarm	Buy new batteries today
Observation skills	Do joint observation with supervisor and compare findings next placement day	Very short staffed in placement so not able to do joint observation	Planned for following week

■ Action taken

Professional development

Your course is all about your professional development both at college and in your work placement. During your course, you will learn the background theory and practical skills at Level 2. However, the setting you have your placement in will be very different to that of your friends even if you are working in the same age group. Many settings have a constant programme of staff development for their own staff, information about other short courses or reading that can be done. You should try to take advantage of suitable development material and training opportunities that may be available in placement as these will help your progress and make your training even more enjoyable. For example, if you are working with under-threes your placement may have a training day on the government's initiative 'Birth to Three Matters'. Taking advantage of this type of training can help you to further develop your knowledge and skills. You can use this in your assignments and in your Work Experience Journal.

Case study

Skills development

Lou spent part of her placement in an after school club. Two of the children who attended had communication difficulties and used Makaton, which is a form of sign language using symbols. Lou was fascinated by the way the two boys communicated and was pleased when her supervisor pointed out that she could go on a course being run for workers at the school and club. Although it was hard work fitting in the course with college and placement, Lou really enjoyed it and hopes to be able to continue developing her Makaton skills.

Use of reflection

You should have spent time reflecting on your strengths and weaknesses in relation to working with children in the previous section. It is also useful to be aware of the way in which you learn.

Identify own learning style

There are many different styles of gaining and absorbing information, such as reading about it, listening or experiencing something. It is important to know how you learn best and adjust your study skills to this. Think about if you learn best by:

- listening
- reading
- working practically
- experiences.

Think about it

When thinking about your learning style, there is an obvious link to your work with children. If adults have different learning styles, then so must children! When you are in placement, see if you can work out how some of the children learn best. Given a range of options a child will naturally pick the type that suits him or her best.

There are a number of tools to check learning styles such as that developed by Honey and Mumford. They divided learners into reflectors, theorists, activists and pragmatists. You should have had an assessment of your learning styles when you started your course. Look again at your results – were you surprised? Have you changed anything about the way you learn as a result?

It is also important to be aware of how you work best:

- in short stretches
- longer chunks of time
- on your own
- with friends
- can you take notes easily?
- do you need support with literacy or numeracy?
- do you plan your work well ahead or under pressure of time?

Once you have identified how you learn and work best, it should be easier to plan your studies. No doubt, through your school years teachers have been saying you must plan revision and assignments. As an older student, hopefully you can now see the benefits of doing this. Take time to organise your study and work time to fit the way you work best.

If you know that you need support from staff at school or college, you must ask for it and make the best use of it. Think about the barriers to development that can affect children. If you have a barrier to progress this is an ideal time to make good use of the help that is available.

Case study

Time management

Janine is keen to do well on her new course at college. She works part time in a supermarket near home and knows it is going to be hard work to fit all her college work in. Janine spent some time thinking about how she enjoyed learning and working and realised she worked best on her own in fairly long stretches of time. She planned a timetable that enabled her to study three evenings a week and all Sunday morning plus two hours to organise notes and plan for placements.

Jess works in the same place as Janine and is also keen to do well on her new course at college. Jess does not like working on her own in silence and when she has tried it in the past she has just ended up reading magazines or ringing her friends. Jess arranges to stay at college on three days for one hour to work with Louisa, another friend on the course, before going to work. After work, she then works for another half an hour at home on her own and meets up with Louisa at the weekends to spend another two hours at her house working together.

Both Janine and Jess found learning styles that helped them to study to their best ability. Both examples work well and show that everyone needs to work in the way that best suits them.

Background and experience

We are all made up in part of our past experience. Unit 1 looked at what can affect a child's development and you will probably be able to think of experiences that have affected you. As development throughout life continues (particularly emotional and intellectual), experiences continue to influence that development. It is also important to realise that your own experiences of being cared for, relationships with siblings etc. will affect how you relate to children you care for. Your experiences of play are important – you need to have experienced good play if you are to support children in playing!

It is important that you start to be aware of how your background and experiences might influence the way you work in the field of child care and education.

Think about it

What are your experiences in these areas of day-to-day life:

- *play*
- *reading books for pleasure*
- *birthday celebrations*
- *celebrations such as Christmas, Eid, Diwali, Hannukah etc.*
- *the response you have from close family to your achievements*
- *being cared for as a child?*

How are your experiences different from those of your friends?

Assessment activities

Assessment Activity 1

You need to find out about and record the support systems for supervision to help you develop your own practice in a child care setting. You should record these in your Work Experience Journal on an ongoing basis and then use this as evidence for meeting the requirements of this unit.

You need to record and describe the following:

- tutorials
- tutor placement visits
- placement supervisor or mentor.

You must also find out about and describe:

- how you are supported in the workplace
- how you are supported at school/college
- the use of support systems to ask for constructive feedback on your performance

- the use of support systems to help identify areas of practice that need development
- goals, targets and development opportunities, such as other ways of undertaking professional development and development needs in relation to the team
- your own role in the team (see page 2 in the Work Experience Journal and page 4 for work placement expectations of your role in the team)
- the use of new knowledge and skills in the work setting.

When you have completed Activity 1 you will be ready to achieve Pass criterion 1 (P1), for which you are required to describe the use of support systems to develop your own practice in a child care work setting.

continued ▶

Assessment Activity 2

You need to reflect upon your practice in the child care work place.

■ What are your strengths and weaknesses?
■ What is your own learning style?
■ What is the effect of your own background and experiences on your practice?

You are now able to meet Pass criterion 2 (P2), for which you must identify the strengths and weaknesses in your own practice. You may wish to do this on an ongoing basis throughout your course.

Assessment Activity 3

Towards the end of your course and after you have completed Assessment Activities 1 and 2, you should be able to meet Merit criterion 1 (M1) for which you are required to explain (describe in detail) how support systems have helped you to develop your own practice in child care work.

5.2 Understand new knowledge and skills relevant to own practice

This section covers:

- new knowledge and skills
- feedback.

New knowledge and skills

The previous section should have started you thinking about developing new knowledge and skills and using feedback constructively.

As a student you will be faced with many different ways of developing new knowledge and skills. Information from your college tutor and from this book is only the starting point for you to apply knowledge to practice. You should be constantly feeling that there is so much more to learn and find out about!

Think about a child of three or four years old; they are constantly asking 'why', 'what' and 'how' questions about the world around them. You should be developing the same questions in relation to your time in working with children.

Think about it

How many ways of finding out information can you think of? List them and compare your list with the rest of your group. Do you know how to access all the different types of information?

Case study

Mel's puzzle

Mel had been on her course for four weeks when she had her first week in placement. Her tutor had spent a lot of time with them on development and supporting play and learning. After her first two days Mel was puzzled about the differences in the development of two of the children who were aged two years. Her supervisor explained that Joe, who was not walking confidently, had been born very early at 26 weeks.

Mel planned some time for herself to research prematurity. She looked in a number of early years text books in the college library and used a search engine on the internet to do this. As a result, Mel realised the effect that being born prematurely can have on development in the early years.

Think of an example of a new skill you have learned. How did you learn this skill?

Skill development is gained in a number of ways. Think about:

- observing a number of more experienced staff
- reading about the skills involved
- planning to work alongside an experienced colleague to practise a new skill
- trying a new skill out for the first time
- asking for feedback on your performance.

Feedback

Think of an example of someone who has given you feedback. What happened? Was the feedback helpful? How did you change your practice as a result?
If the feedback was not helpful why was this the case?

Feedback is important for everyone: without it how can anyone know if they are effective? It is important as an early years practitioner to constantly be looking for ways to improve your knowledge and skills. Feedback can be gained from a number of sources:

- other staff and students
- supervisor
- college tutor
- placement visitor
- children.

To be effective feedback has to be:

- constructive – gives positive points as well as areas to improve
- not destructive
- given in an appropriate setting not in front of others.

Assessment activities

Assessment Activity 4

Throughout your work placement and your course you should be taking the opportunity to gain new knowledge and skills relevant to your work in an early years setting.

Identify and make a list of these new skills and knowledge. Record your use of these new skills and knowledge and the use of support systems to ask for feedback on improvements

in practice. You should also be recording this on pages 12 and 13 of your Work Experience Journal.

You are now able to meet Pass criterion 3 (P3), for which you are required to outline (briefly describe) new knowledge and skills relevant to your own practice in child care work.

continued ▶

Assessment Activity 5

Towards the end of your course you will then be able to meet Merit criterion 2 (M2), for which you must explain (describe in detail) how new knowledge and skills have affected your own practice.

Assessment Activity 6

At the end of your course and when you have completed P1, P2, P3, M1 and M2 you will be able to meet Distinction criterion 1 (D1). To meet this criterion you must evaluate (describe and give reasons) the development of your own practice in the child care work setting.

5.3 Understand own roles and responsibilities within the team

This section covers:

- teams
- roles and responsibilities
- interactions with the team
- commitments
- dealing with conflict.

Teams

One of the first things you must do in each placement you spend time in, is to find out what the placement does. There are many different types of settings that work with children and young people aged 0 to 16. Each type has a different aim and purpose and may be funded from a number of different sources. Some are single purpose, for example day nurseries, and others are multi-purpose, for example Sure Start centres, and are staffed by one organisation or several. Have a look at the following summary list of some of the settings you may encounter and the way they may be funded and staffed.

Setting or purpose	Funding	Staff
Playgroup (early play or socialisation)	Voluntary (paid by parents) or charitable	Volunteers Paid manager
Day nursery (full care and some education)	Private or local authority	Nursery nurses Apprentices Employed by owner or local authority
Nursery class or school (pre-school education)	Private or local education authority	Nursery teacher Nursery nurses Apprentices Employed by owner or local authority
Sure Start Centre (support development of child and sometimes family, education, health etc.)	Several streams	Include education, health and social services staff Support staff

continued ▶

Setting or purpose	Funding	Staff
School (compulsory education)	Local education authority or private	Teachers, classroom assistants etc. employed by local authority or owner Support staff
Extended school with after school and community activities	Several funding streams	Range of staff according to provision
After school or holiday club (care/ activity after school/during holidays)	Various – private, charitable, local authority	Play workers

■ *Staffing and funding of different types of setting*

This list is not complete and you may find variations in different areas and settings.

Objectives and purpose of the team

As local authorities develop their 'Children and Young People's Plans', as a result of 'Every Child Matters: Change for Children', you will start to see exciting ways for organisations and settings to work together to improve the chances of children and young people. As a result of this, there will be changes in the objectives and purposes of settings and in the roles and responsibilities of staff.

This means that the organisations involved with providing services to children, from hospitals and schools to police and voluntary groups, will be teaming up in new ways, sharing information and working together to protect children and young people from harm and help them achieve what they want in life. Children and young people will have far more say about issues that affect them as individuals and collectively.

Over the next few years, every local authority will be working with its partners and through children's trusts, to find out what works best for children and young people in its area and act on it.

(Source: Every Child Matters website)

Own roles and responsibilities in the team

As well as knowing about the setting you are spending time in, it is equally important that you know about your roles and responsibilities in your placement.

The following list covers general points that apply to any setting. The Work Experience Journal has some questions for each responsibility. Make sure you complete one for each placement.

Think about it

Within the first few days in placement you should complete the Roles and responsibilities sheet in your Journal. Make sure you know what the setting is there for, who is who and what they do.

Did you know?

Every Child Matters: Change for Children is a new approach to the well-being of children and young people from birth to age 19. The government's aim is for every child, whatever their background or their circumstances, to have the support they need to:

■ *be healthy*
■ *stay safe*
■ *enjoy and achieve*
■ *make a positive contribution*
■ *achieve economic well-being.*

- Go to the right placement, on the right day and ask for the right person.

- Arrive punctually at placement.

- Wear appropriate clothing.

- Be open, friendly and approachable to staff, children and parents.

- Learn the names of the children and staff.

- Use good communication skills with children.

- Use good communication skills with adults.

- Complete any forms or documents that are needed.

- Turn up for all shifts and complete each one.

- Use time in placement to best effect to gain skills and experience.

- Always follow the values and ethics of working with children.

- Follow rules on confidentiality.

- Understand the placement's polices and procedures on relevant issues for example health and safety, illness, missing children.

- Work within the routines and expectations of the setting.

- Ask for advice and support when it is needed.

- Abide by placement rules relating to smoking and use of mobile phones.

- Keep up to date with all college and placement work.

- Finish the placement with a completed placement work book.

Depending on the situation there may be specific points for a setting that need adding. It is important that you know about any of these in your placement.

You should spend some time with your supervisor at the start of your placement agreeing what type of activities you will be expected to help with. Use your Placement expectations sheet to record these. This will help you to be clear about what is expected of you and the level of involvement in activities with the children. Your supervisor can then share this with staff you will be working with to avoid confusion or you being asked to do unsuitable activities.

Learning and performance

Knowing what you will be allowed and expected to do will help you to plan what you hope to learn from this placement. Use your Skill development sheets along with the Expectations sheet to plan your time. Be realistic, however, and be prepared that some opportunities may not happens, but equally unexpected events may happen from which you learn new skills. It is important to be flexible within your plan for developing skills and knowledge.

Remember you are a student on placement and you will be working with a number of different staff and also quite likely with other students or trainees. If you are working with people working towards an NVQ as part of an apprenticeship for example, they may have more involvement in planning and carrying out activities. This is important for their qualification as they have to practically demonstrate all aspects of the NVQ standards.

Interactions with the team

Although you are an extra person in the team at your setting, you are an important extra. You will make a difference while you are there and make an impact on the children you work with.

Working with children is not just about close one to one interactions with them; it is also about team work. You should be closely observing how the team work together in your time in placement and making notes for your Journal.

Teams are important in early years work because it is hard to provide good-quality care on your own. Support and help from others is needed to provide constant, effective care. Good teams share values and understandings about the purpose of care.

Look at the following examples of two placements.

Did you know?

As a student, you must never be left alone with children in your placement. You also should not be counted as part of the staffing cover in a placement. These are legal requirements to protect children and you.

Example 1

You arrive for your first day in a day care centre and are greeted by your supervisor. She is very friendly and has time to spare. She starts by getting you a drink and sits down with you. She tells you about the centre and explains who the children are and how the centre tries to provide good-quality care. She talks about the importance of understanding the underlying principles such as celebrating diversity and working in partnership with parents.

You are invited to sit in on a team discussion. The meeting includes some administrative issues but also a discussion of some of the children's developmental needs. Each member of staff looks interested. All the staff do not necessarily agree, but they all listen to each other. You can tell from the smiles and eye contact that the staff care about each other's feelings. They also care about how you feel and are very concerned that you should feel included in their group even though you do not know much about the centre. The manager seems to get on well with the staff and there is some humour in the group. At the end of the meeting you feel welcome and you feel good about working with the managers and staff.

In the first example, the staff work as a team. The team:

- show respect for individuals
- value equality
- respect the self-esteem needs of people
- have good communication skills
- believe that to give good-quality care you have to receive a caring approach from others
- believe that children, staff and managers have rights.

In the first example, the staff share professional values about caring and early learning which means they also work effectively with children.

Example 2

When you arrive for your first day in a day centre, no one knows who you are or why you are supposed to be there. One staff member says: 'You want to work in early years care, you must be mad. Anyway you can come with me and I'll show you what to do – I could do with some help. We just haven't got enough staff you know. There are far too many kids for us to handle. It's all paperwork nowadays; the senior staff spend all their time in the office. They haven't got time for the children as they have to get their reports done. If you are on a college course, then I suppose you will end up with a sort of job. After a while it gets to you – all the paperwork and all the screaming kids. I do not know how I ever had kids – it's enough to put you off having them you know. We do not have time for talking to each other usually here; we pretend that we have meetings and go on courses and all that but we do not really have time for all that stuff.'

In the second example, the worker outlined no longer seems to enjoy working with children and there is no team work.

As a result the staff:

- do not spend time talking to each other
- might not really be concerned about the principles of good practice
- might not feel that they are doing a worthwhile job
- do not get a sense of self-esteem out of their work
- might not care about the self-esteem of a person doing a placement.

Team values and expectations

Teams in early years settings should value:

- the diversity and equality of people

- anti-discriminatory practice (being prepared to challenge discrimination)

- the rights of children, especially self-esteem and independence

- confidentiality.

Together with these values, most teams will expect members to:

- present themselves in a way that shows respect for children, parents and other staff

- present themselves in a way that shows an understanding of safety issues

- maintain health and safety for all

- be reliable, punctual and show commitment to the team, including attending meetings

- maintain the security of children

- join in both the practical work and the administrative work that the team has to do

- understand their own role and be able to prioritise what is important in the job (time management) and show flexibility where necessary

- be able to review their own skills, recognise limitations and ask for help from others when necessary

- be willing to listen and communicate effectively with others, including being able to report and record events.

Good team practice

Most teams of staff have a heavy workload so if you turn up late or not at all, or if you do not let people know where you are, this leaves other people to do work that they were expecting you to do. Even if other people can cover for you, it sends a message: 'I do not care about the team – I do not want to be with you anyway.'

It is not always possible to be punctual, and sometimes transport problems prevent people from getting to work or meetings on time. However, it is always important to apologise and offer a brief explanation for lateness. This sends the message 'I do care about colleagues'. If you are ill, you should always telephone to explain and let people know the situation, so that they can plan ahead. This also lets people know that you care about belonging with them. It is unprofessional if colleagues are expecting you and you do not let them know when you cannot keep an appointment.

It is very easy to disrupt a team working by failing to fit in. Try to avoid this in your placements by observing and asking if you are unsure about what you should be doing.

Good practice working in a team involves:

- observation

- communication – especially asking if your plans are appropriate and listening to feedback and responses

- knowledge of roles and responsibilities of other team members

- being pleasant and helpful

- leaving personal problems outside placement

- being willing to help whenever possible

- carrying out instructions correctly

- informing other staff about your activities

- contributing to ideas when appropriate

- respecting other staff

- sticking to your responsibilities

- avoiding getting involved in gossip about other staff

- remembering that you are there to learn.

Very occasionally you may find that you are not very well supported in your placement and that you are not enjoying or learning from it. Although this is rare, if you are unhappy with the way you are being supported you should speak to your tutor or work placement co-ordinator about it. Sometimes it can be that there has been a change of staff or your supervisor is unsure of his or her role and the issue can be readily dealt with. Do not keep quiet about this situation. Always ask for help if things are not getting better.

Most students gain lots of skills and knowledge from placement. Working with experienced professionals, seeing different ways of working and trying out your developing skills is one of the best ways of applying the theory from college into practice. Use the experience of others by:

- asking for advice and using it

- asking for explanations of activities

- asking 'what if. . .' questions

- offering your ideas where appropriate.

Commitments

Most settings have a smooth timetable for the different attendance patterns of each of the children. It is important that children have all their needs met and that promises of plans are kept to. With good preparation and discussion, you should know how you fit into this timetable and what your role within it is.

One of the skills of being a good team member is only agreeing to the amount of work that you can complete. As a keen student it can be too easy to agree to take on too many tasks and then find you cannot do them all. If you do find that this is happening, you need to discuss it with your supervisor and learn to say 'no'. However, it is important that if you recognise you will not be able to do something that you tell the person concerned as soon as possible so the work can then be reallocated.

Dealing with conflict

Differences of opinion are healthy. If a group of intelligent people from different backgrounds and experiences are working together it would be very odd if there were never differences of opinion. In fact, learning can take place from other people's opinions and views but sometimes it can be difficult to avoid conflict over differences. Differences of opinion can be dealt with by:

- showing respect for the other person's point of view

- listening to their point of view

- being prepared to change your opinion

- being ready to agree to disagree politely

- accepting that your opinion may be wrong

- referring to a senior person if the differences may affect the children

- remembering never to get into an argument in front of the children or other staff.

Remember that as a student you are in placement to learn. By asking questions about things you are unsure of in an appropriate way and discussing issues with your supervisor, you should avoid situations of conflict.

■ *Ask other staff in your placement for guidance when you need it*

Sometimes it can be useful for staff to sit down and work through the difference of opinion in a team meeting in a constructive way, especially if it is about something serious that could impact on the children. Sharing views and exploring further can help to clarify situations and help everyone to reflect and learn.

There are some situations however where a difference in opinion may be about practice that is either illegal or dubious. Everyone working with children has an obligation to report such behaviour even though this may be difficult, especially when you have to carry on working with that person. However, it is essential that you discuss anything that worries you about the practice of others. You are not 'telling tales' but protecting vulnerable children and young people.

Case study

Reporting improper behaviour

Adam was very upset when he saw one of the staff in the nursery he was on placement in slap a child on her legs because she would not put her coat on. It was even worse because the member of staff was the owner's daughter. After thinking about it, he told his college tutor about the incident. His tutor followed this up immediately with the nursery owner without identifying who had told her and action was taken.

Assessment activities

Assessment Activity 7

You need to find out about the team you are working with and record its objectives and purpose, and the roles and responsibilities of the members of the team. You can record this in your Work Experience Journal on page 12.

Assessment Activity 8

Continuing this examination of team working you need to be clear about and record the following:

■ your own roles and responsibilities in the team
■ your own contribution to the overall activities
■ realistic responsibility for your own development, learning and performance.

You will be able to record this on page 13 of your Work Experience Journal.

Having completed Activities 7 and 8 you are now ready to meet Pass criterion 4 (P4), for which you have to outline (briefly describe) your own roles and responsibilities as a member of the team in a child care work placement.

continued ▶

Assessment Activity 9

From considering roles and responsibilities in the team you need to consider your interactions with the team. You will need to describe how you undertake the following:

■ support the effective functioning of the team
■ inform other team members of your own activities

■ accept and use suggestions and information constructively to improve your own practice
■ support and offer constructive assistance to other members of the team including suggestions, relevant ideas and information.

You should record this on page 14 of your Work Experience Journal.

Assessment Activity 10

As part of your interactions with members of the team you should be able to show commitment by:

■ completing commitments to other team members according to work priorities
■ informing appropriate members of the team if any commitments cannot be completed.

You also need to show that you can deal with conflict by:

■ showing respect for the views of others

■ having a constructive approach to differences of opinion and conflicts.

You should record commitments and dealing with conflict on pages 15 and 16 of your Work Experience Journal.

You are now able to meet Pass criterion 5 (P5) for which you must describe your own interaction with the team in your child care work placement.

Assessment Activity 11

Having completed Assessment Activity 10, towards the end of your course you will also be able to meet Merit criterion 3 (M3), for which you must explain (describe in detail) how you have supported the functioning of the team in your own work setting.

Assessment Activity 12

When you get to the end of the course and having completed Assessment Activities 10 and 11 you will be able to meet Distinction criterion 2 (D2). For this you must evaluate (describe how well, giving reasons and examples) your own contribution to the functioning of the team in the child care work setting.

5.4 Understand values and ethics in child care working practice

This section covers:

■ communication

■ being trustworthy

■ anti-discriminatory practice.

Communication

The key points to remember about successful communication in placement are about treating all team members:

■ equally and inclusively

■ as individuals

■ with respect for their dignity, culture, backgrounds and values

■ respecting confidentiality and the sharing of information according to the policy of the setting.

Unit 3 Communication with Children and Adults covers the important issues about these aspects of successful communication in placement. As part of this qualification you have to show that you can communicate effectively with adults in children's settings. Your Work Experience Journal gives you the opportunity to record and reflect on your evidence for this.

There is an old American Indian saying about understanding others by walking in their shoes, which is a good basis for your dealings with anyone in any situation. Always consider how you might feel if you were on the receiving end of an interaction, and think about what you can learn from others.

Being trustworthy

Children depend on adults to be there for them and to provide them with the support and guidance they need when they need it. To do this children need adults to be:

■ reliable

■ trustworthy

■ honest

■ straightforward.

It is likely that your tutor asked for references from people who know you before you started the course to check that these words could be used to describe you.

At some stage in your career, and certainly when you get your first job in a children's setting, you will be asked to complete an enhanced disclosure Criminal Records Bureau (CRB) form. This form is checked by the police and social services to ensure that you do not have any convictions or issues that mean you are not suitable to work with children. It is a legal check on your trustworthiness and honesty and will be regularly checked throughout your career.

Anti-discriminatory practice

One of the key skills that any person working with other people needs to have is a good working knowledge and understanding of the importance of diversity.

Diversity is about:

- difference, variety and individuality
- appreciating that we are all unique
- treating people as individuals.

Examples of these differences are:

- gender
- race
- ethnic origin
- physical and sensory ability
- sexual orientation
- age
- religion
- family or marital status.

Being aware of and understanding diversity helps to reduce **prejudice** and discrimination against personal differences.

■ *Every person is an individual*

Did you know?

From September 2005 disabled children and students have the same rights to education in the same settings as other children and in the same way access to any other services in Britain. Where possible reasonable adjustments have to be made to allow access to a mainstream school for a child who is disabled.

It was not until an Act of Parliament in 1981 that many disabled children received an education at all. They were often seen as not being capable of being educated, just because they had a disability.

It is very important to recognise how discrimination can happen and to make sure that we do not discriminate in our own professional practice. Professional early years workers also have a duty to challenge any discriminatory behaviour that they see. Anti-discrimination means taking action to stop other people being harmed or having their rights ignored.

Discrimination means telling things apart – knowing the difference between similar things. You can discriminate between, say, a pair of shoes that you do not like and a pair that you do. Telling things apart is a vital part of life – if we did not do this we would not be able to live independently.

Discriminating against people has a different meaning; it is important to realise that people are all different – with different life experiences. Discriminating against people means giving people unequal service or treatment because of their differences. There are a number of laws that protect people against the effects of discrimination including:

- The Sex Discrimination Act 1975 (amended 1986)
- The Race Relations (Amendment) Act 2000
- Disability Discrimination Act 1995 (DDA)
- Special Educational Needs and Disability Act 2001 (SENDA)
- Employment Equality (Religion or beliefs) Regulations 2003
- Employment Equality (Sexual Orientation) Regulations 2003
- The Human Rights Act 1998.

People who work in care have to be interested in learning about other people; interested in diversity and difference. Early years workers cannot divide people into 'types that I like' and 'types that I do not like'. Seeing the world in terms of 'us and them' leads to certain kinds of thinking. Discrimination sometimes comes about because of assumptions that people make in their thinking. People will sometimes stereotype or label others.

People may make assumptions based on stereotyped thinking. For example, an adult might say: 'I do not know how you do your job – working with noisy children all day – they would drive me nuts!' This person might be making assumptions based on the stereotype that young children are all 'difficult, naughty and noisy'.

When people say 'all women are ...' or 'all black people are ...' or 'all gay people are ...' they will probably go on to describe a stereotype of these groups.

Another way in which discrimination can be shown is labelling. Labelling is similar to stereotyping, but labels are brief and simple. Instead of having a set of fixed opinions about a group to which a person may belong, the person is summed up in just one word or term.

Sometimes people communicate in a way that does not show equal respect and value for others. A member of staff may not want to sit next to someone he or she has a prejudice about. People may use different body language when they have a prejudice towards someone.

Discrimination is not always obvious – very often carers simply make assumptions that everyone does or should think like they do, and this can come out in conversation.

Think about it

Imagine you go to a nursery school in December. The walls are full of artwork about Christmas. There are pictures of Jesus being worshipped by shepherds and artwork representing presents, Father Christmas, reindeer and the North Pole. All the people in the artwork have white faces. The children are learning to sing Christmas carols. There is no evidence of any other religion other than Christianity, and no evidence of any other ethnic group other than white people.

What would children learn from such an experience? Why does it matter that there is representation of diversity if all the children are Christian and white? How might a young child who belongs to a different ethnic group or religion be likely to be affected if he or she experienced such a day centre?

It is unlikely that you will ever find a centre like this nowadays, although older people may remember such things from many years ago.

Best practice in your work placement

Equal opportunities

■ Always be a good role model; mix girls and boys evenly in a group; ask a child who may be slow in moving to help you set out an activity.
■ Always challenge discriminatory behaviour, especially from other children. You can do this by making it clear there are words and actions that will not be tolerated.
■ Put yourself in the shoes of someone who has been the subject of offensive remarks.
■ Be ready to question your own attitudes and beliefs, challenging them if necessary.
■ Use any opportunity to extend your own knowledge about cultures and groups other than your own.
■ Be clear and consistent about what is acceptable and unacceptable behaviour.
■ Double-check plans to ensure you are not inadvertently excluding or offending anyone.
■ Be prepared to report incidents to your supervisor.
■ Celebrate the diversity of the children you work with.
■ Always consider every child as an individual with his or her own needs.

Think about it

Some years ago there was a school for children with learning difficulties. When it came to meal times, the children had to sit down for their meal. The 'slow' children were allowed to start first because they took longer. Staff would label children 'slows'. The 'slows' knew who they were, and sat down when 'slows' were called for. Some children were not very skilled with holding plates, etc., and these were labelled 'clumsies'. Children would describe themselves as 'slows' or 'clumsies'.

What effect do you think describing him or herself as a 'slow' or a 'clumsy' would have on a child's development of self-esteem?

Think about it

Imagine you are watching children playing. Some of the children are calling others 'names'. One child looks different from most of the other children and he seems to be 'picked on' most of all.

If this boy feels unwelcome and 'picked on' what effects could this discrimination have on him?

Assessment activities

Assessment Activity 13

Here you need to show that you understand, by describing and then explaining, the values and ethics in child care working practice.

You need to describe the values and ethics involved in communication. This should include the following:

- treating all team members equally and inclusively as individuals

- respecting the dignity, culture, backgrounds and values of all members of the team
- respecting confidentiality
- sharing information according to the policy of the child care setting.

You can record this on page 17 of your Work Experience Journal.

Assessment Activity 14

You also need to show that you are trustworthy. You should describe how the values and ethics of child care working practice include being:

- reliable

- trustworthy
- honest
- straightforward.

You can record when you do this on page 18 of your Work Experience Journal.

Assessment Activity 15

Finally you need to describe anti-discriminatory practice, including being able to challenge:

- discriminatory actions
- discriminatory comments
- discriminatory practice.

- You should record this on page 19 of your Work Experience Journal.

Having completed Assessment Activities 13, 14 and 15 you are now able to meet Pass criterion 6 (P6), which requires you to describe the values and ethics of child care working practice.

Assessment Activity 16

Having completed Activities 13, 14 and 15 and recorded your own practice in your Work Experience Journal you are now able to meet Merit criterion 4 (M4), for which you are

required to explain (describe in detail) how values and ethics are put into practice in child care work.

6 Supporting children's play and learning

Introduction

Play is essential for the development of all children. It is so important it is recognised in the United Nation's Convention on the Rights of the Child. Children develop and learn through their play. It is important for adults to know the importance and value of all types of play, to be as effective as possible in making provision for play, encouraging children in their play and knowing when to be involved and to intervene in children's play in order to ensure that children gain as much benefit as possible.

Children play throughout their development and this unit covers play for children from birth to 16 years of age.

In this unit you will learn:

1 how to support children's play

2 how to help to provide opportunities for children's imaginative and creative play

3 how to help to support physical play

4 how to encourage children to explore and investigate.

6.1 Understanding how to support children's play

This section covers:

■ understanding play
■ resources
■ encouragement
■ supervision
■ involvement
■ curriculum.

Did you know?

As early as the 1800s a famous writer named George Bernard Shaw recognised the importance of play for everyone, even adults when he said: 'We do not stop playing because we grow old; we grow old because we stop playing.'

Think about it

Think about a baby of about three or four months old playing with a rattle. The sound of the rattle helps the baby to learn about sounds and because it is interesting it also makes the baby want to reach out and touch it. Every time the baby grasps and shakes the rattle, the baby is learning control of the hands.

Understanding play

Play is a key way in which children learn about themselves and others. It is also an important way in which children learn many skills that will help their development.

The United Nations Convention on the Rights of the Child recognises the importance of play for children around the world in Article 31 of the Convention.

Children have the right to rest and leisure, to engage in play and recreational activities appropriate to their age, and to participate fully in cultural life and the arts. Appropriate and equal opportunities shall be encouraged in the provision of cultural, artistic, recreational and leisure activity.

As play is crucial to development and is something that nearly all children appear to do instinctively, it is an important skill to develop to work with children. Children use play to make sense of their lives, especially through role play. Through play children can:

■ copy adults
■ improve their skills and abilities
■ work through emotional upsets
■ express their feelings
■ make friends
■ practise relationships
■ learn about rules and taking turns
■ learn about how things work
■ enjoy themselves.

Play helps older children to develop different skills. It helps children feel in control and learn how to problem solve and to be with others. These are important skills as they help children in later life learn how to be independent, to negotiate and to socialise.

Playwork

One type of work with children and young people is playwork. You may work with playworkers if you have a placement in an after school club or holiday play scheme. The National Occupational Standards for Playwork are based on two important assumptions.

> *Children's play is freely chosen, personally directed behaviour that is motivated from within; through play the child explores the world and their relationship with it, elaborating all the while a flexible range of responses to the challenges they encounter; by playing, the child learns and develops as an individual.*

> *Whereas children may play without encouragement or help, adults can, through the provision of an appropriate human and physical environment, significantly enhance opportunities for the child to play creatively and thus develop through play. In this way the competent Playworker always aims to provide opportunities for the individual child to achieve their full potential whist being careful not to control the child's direction or choice.*

Different types of play

Play can take many forms, but a play activity will often fall into several categories as shown below:

Type of play	Examples	Benefits
Physical play	Running, skipping, cycling, rough and tumble, football, climbing frames and all other physical games using large equipment	Encourages and promotes physical and social development Understanding of concepts such as area, energy, space
Creative play	Painting, modelling, cooking, puzzles, junk modelling, dancing, music making	Hand–eye co-ordination, creativity, self-expression, emotional release, learning about colour, shapes, mathematical concepts such as size and volume
Imaginative or pretend play	Role play, domestic play, dressing up, puppets	Coming to terms with their world, learning their own and others' role in the world, release of stress, communication, countering gender-role stereotyping
Exploratory play	Exploring new ideas and objects, for example magnets, old telephones Water play Cooking Gardening	Intellectual development and creativity, learning about colour, shapes, mathematical concepts (for example size and volume)
Constructive play	Using Lego bricks, Meccano, K'nex, old materials	Fine motor skills, imagination, sense of achievement, numeracy and science skills
Messy play	Cornflour and water, sand, water, mud, play dough	Exploring textures, colours, understanding properties of materials. Release of stress and inhibitions

■ *Categories of play*

Children of all ages and stages of development can enjoy play of all types, appropriate to their level of skills. Skills, knowledge and understanding are not limited to one type of play. Children learn mathematical skills from physical play (size, relationships of objects) exploratory play (volume, size) and constructive play.

Interpersonal skills are developed in most play with others. Social and emotional development is probably best seen in development in role play which is a good example of imaginative, pretend play.

Stages of play development

Learning to play with other children happens gradually. Until the age of two, children usually prefer to play alone but with the support and reassurance of adults nearby. Eventually, by the age of seven, most children can play well with others and follow complex rules of games. To reach this sophisticated stage of social interaction children's play goes through several stages:

■ **Exploratory play**, which is the play of young babies observing their surroundings and making movement to reach out and grasp and play.

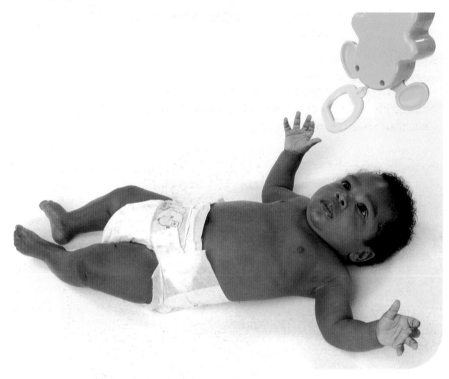

■ *Exploratory play*

■ **Solitary play**, which is the first type of play seen in a child and is predominant until approximately 15–18 months.

■ *Solitary play*

■ **Parallel play**, which occurs when a toddler will often play alongside another child, showing some awareness of them but without sharing the activity.

■ *Parallel play*

■ **Associative play**, which develops from about the age of two and a half years and is characterised by watching others and copying, for instance younger children may observe older children playing.

■ *Associative play*

■ **Turn-taking/sharing**, which occurs from about three years of age when play becomes more complex as simple rules start to be used.

■ *Turn-taking play*

■ **Co-operative play**, which is the final stage when children actively play together; they talk about their play and make decisions together, for instance 'Let's play dressing up!' or 'Shall we make a tower?'

■ *Co-operative play*

From the age of about two years, play can be a group activity, often called social or group play, or children can play by themselves.

Older children's play develops in complexity and becomes more involved with the adult world around them as they grow through their teens. Young people between 13 and 16 may often play using technology, for example computer games and play stations, but many are equally passionate about football or tennis, with single user sports like golf gaining popularity.

Resources

Supporting play involves providing resources, materials and equipment. It is important to involve the children in deciding what resources they want to have, especially older children. Resources can be limited by the amount of money available and a sum may need to be in reserve for replacing materials.

Toys do not have to be expensive, complex items with only a short lifespan in terms of interest and durability. Media advertising bombards children with images of the latest inventions of toy manufacturers, many centred on the latest craze or pop group.

Think about it

When did you last enjoy playing? Can you remember what you used to enjoy playing at different times in your childhood? What do you enjoy playing now?

Many seemingly ordinary items, such as empty cardboard boxes, provide potential play opportunities for children. A look around your home will reveal many resources for a child to play with: kitchen pots and pans, packets of food for playing shops, furniture for making dens, dressing up clothes, water in sinks with plastic utensils, the list is endless. Many of these items can be used in the nursery or classroom. The outdoors is an unlimited play area, although it may require additional supervision, especially for younger children.

Most children will effectively use a selection of toys available for play, ranging from the most simple to highly technical, for example paper and crayons, dolls, bicycles, construction toys and technical computer equipment and games. There are a few basic rules for choosing a successful play resource or toy. It should be:

- right for the stage of the child
- strong enough to be used
- safe to play with
- suitable for a range of play.

Children should be encouraged to try all sorts of toys without gender or culture bias. Boys can enjoy the home corner, cooking or doll play, and girls can enjoy construction, climbing or car play. Child care workers have an essential role in encouraging equal opportunities in all areas including play. Many useful books have been written about play and some toy manufacturers produce catalogues that are worth studying.

Did you know?

In order to help children play effectively, you need to have experienced using the materials yourself and know how to play. Ask your tutor if you could have a practice play area or ask in placement if you can try dough, plasticine, painting, Lego or anything you have not used before.

Play environment	Suggested resources
Craft area	Paint, malleable materials such as clay and dough, crayons, boxes, fabrics, shells, pebbles
Role play area	Simple dressing up clothes including hats and scarves, cooking utensils, pretend food
Quiet area	Books, CDs, soft cushions
Soft play area	Large soft foam shapes, bean bags, balls
Computer corner	Computer with appropriate software, games plus printer and possibly scanner Content control on computer
Construction area	Small and large scale construction materials such as boxes, cardboard tubes, glues, tape Commercial equipment such as Lego, Duplo
Music area	Instruments, radio, CDs, dance mats, karaoke machine
Physical areas (indoors/outdoors)	Large and small equipment such as climbing frames, swings, wheeled toys, bicycles, bats, balls, skipping ropes, football nets, basketball rings
Games	Board games, quiz games
Food area	Cooking equipment, utensils, chairs, tables, snacks and drinks

■ Resources for play

Encouraging play

Adults have an important role in encouraging play. They should facilitate play, not organise it. This means that the adult provides resources if necessary, ensures a safe environment, allows time for play and does not interfere with or direct the play.

The children and young people you work with in placement may all have different interests and needs. The play setting should reflect this by providing a variety of environments and resources that will encourage children to choose play opportunities themselves. An effective child centred setting, where children and young people feel they have some control and input to the opportunities, has a number of common features as shown below.

Attractive

An attractive environment will:

- show good wall displays of work done by children

- involve the children in the decoration and displays

- use materials and displays that reflect a relevant range of interests and ages.

Stimulating and challenging

The setting should:

- have activities children can succeed at but be challenged by

- recognise effort and achievement

- use praise and encouragement

- review and develop the layout and décor

- change opportunities and provision frequently to maintain interest.

Friendly and open

A friendly and open setting can be achieved by:

- workers being enthusiastic

- showing an interest in all the children

- seeking to meet each child's needs

- using a range of techniques to welcome children and to create a welcoming atmosphere

- inviting to children to join in.

By encouraging children to explore and choose play activities and adapt ideas to their needs, a good play environment can effectively support children in many different ways.

Did you know?

John Locke writing about child care and planning for children's play in 1693 stated that children should have lots of different 'playthings' but that they should only be allowed to use one toy at a time so they learn to look after them. He also felt that rather than buying toys, children should be encouraged to invent their own 'playthings'. For example, if they were given a top, children should be encouraged to make the stick and leather strap with which to spin the top.

■ *How involving children in choosing play helps them to develop*

Supervision

Child care workers are facilitators of play for children. To facilitate means to make easy or more easily achieved. Just think about what this means for supporting and supervising play.

Case study

Using your initiative

A group of ten eight-year-old children were very frustrated that they could not go out to play football in a holiday club as it was raining hard and the ground was very muddy. As a result, they were starting to interfere with some of the other children's play. Yasmin had a word with her supervisor and took the group of children into the empty school hall. Luckily there were some small football nets, which were usually used outside, stored at the back of the hall. With the children's help

she put these up in the hall and got some bean bags out of the equipment store. After a discussion with the children about basic ground rules for safety, the group had soon devised their own version of a relay football crossed with a rugby game using four of the bean bags. At their request, Yasmin was the referee.

1 Why was this a good experience for the group?
2 How did Yasmin act as the facilitator?

Values of playwork

The underlying values of playwork apply to all levels of facilitating play with children. Read through them and think how they can be applied to the children you have experience of.

Child at the centre of the process
The child must be at the centre of the process; the opportunities provided and the organisation which supports, co-ordinates and manages these should always start with the child's needs and offer sufficient flexibility to meet these.

Empowering children
Play should empower children, affirm and support their right to make choices, discover their own solutions, to play and develop at their own pace and in their own way.

Self-directed play
Whereas play may sometimes be enriched by the playworker's participation, adults should always be sensitive to children's needs and never try to control a child's play so long as it remains within safe and acceptable boundaries.

Opportunities for risk, challenge, growth of confidence and self-esteem
Every child has a right to a play environment which stimulates and provides opportunities for risk, challenge and the growth of confidence and self-esteem.

Health and safety
The contemporary environment in which many children grow up does not lend itself to safe and creative play; all children have the right to a play environment which is free from hazard, one which ensures physical and personal safety and a setting within which the child ultimately feels physically and personally safe.

Individuality
Every child is an individual and has the right to be respected as such; each child should feel confident that individuality and diversity are valued by the adults who work and play with them.

Consideration and care
A considerate and caring attitude to individual children and their families is essential to competent playwork and should be displayed at all times. Play should offer the child opportunities to extend her or his exploration and understanding of the wider world and therefore physical, social and cultural settings beyond their immediate experience.

Co-operation
Play is essentially a co-operative activity for children both individually and in groups. Playworkers should always encourage children to be sensitive to the needs of others; in providing play opportunities, they should always seek to work together with children, their parents, colleagues and other professionals and, where possible, make their own expertise available to the wider community.

Legislative framework
Play opportunities should always be provided within the current legislative framework relevant to children's rights, health, safety and well-being.

Access
Every child has a right to an environment for play and such environments must be made accessible to children.

Think about it

Which of the values of playwork listed would help you to stimulate play effectively?

It is important that supervision should support the values of playwork for a number of reasons:

■ to make sure that children are in a safe environment

■ to support play where necessary

■ to intervene when needed

■ to meet legal requirements.

Setting ground rules for play

Children should be aware of basic rules about their play. Ideally children should be involved in deciding what the rules are as they are far more likely to understand them. Rules should be as simple as possible and there should not be too many of them. They should cover:

■ turn-taking

■ safety aspects, for example pushing or running

■ ending play and clearing away.

Think about it

Has your placement got a set of rules for play? If not ask your supervisor if you could work with the children to devise some.

Our Outdoor Play Agreement

Let everyone take turns with the football

Only go down the slide one at a time

Only go down the slide sitting up facing forwards

Make sure there are no people too near you when skipping

Only ride the bikes and scooters on the special path

Always wear a helmet when riding a bike or scooter

Wear shoes with rubber grip soles on the climbing frame

Encouraging and stimulating play

Supporting play involves providing resources, materials and equipment. The greater the involvement by the children themselves, the more child centred the play is likely to be.

Children need support and help to encourage their development in all the areas we have been looking at. The role of an adult is to support the children without interfering in their play. To do this the carer needs to:

- allow plenty of time for play
- avoid over-organising and allow children to lead their own play
- provide a wide range of materials and show ideas for how to use them
- test out new ideas first before introducing them to children
- make sure that activities and equipment are safe to use
- be ready to help to adapt activities for different ages and abilities
- check there is enough space for the activities and the number of children
- help with rotas where needed so that all children can safely take part
- ensure that all equipment is in working order and suitable for the activity
- make sure there is enough of all materials for all the children involved
- use as many opportunities as possible for children to meet people and see examples of creativity
- avoid the use of templates, pre-drawn outlines, colouring books and tracing
- be a helper in play or activity, not a leader.

Intervention may be needed to move play on and to offer new ideas or alternatives. Children may have started to play a game and then become 'stuck' in the progress of it, some children may not be taking part and may need support to move into another form of play.

Intervention may also be needed if the play is not suitable for the majority of the children, for example if an older child has taken over and is excluding younger children.

Sometimes intervention can help to move play on and extend play according to their interests. An autumn outing in the local woods could stimulate a child's interest in the outdoors. A suggestion from you to collect some of the seeds and leaves to try to identify the trees would be an intervention.

Enabling accessibility for play

Some children may need adaptations to help them to take part in an activity. When you are planning an activity of any sort, you should always consider all the children who may be joining in. To a child who is timid about large groups, a boisterous game of chase or playing on the climbing frame may be very daunting and you should think of ways of helping the child to join in. You may need to think about providing two parallel activities, if staffing and numbers allow, in order to meet all the children's needs.

The climbing frame will not be suitable for a child who is a wheelchair user, without having a helper with the child at all times. Padded matting

Think about it

You are in charge of a group of eight energetic five year olds, five girls and three boys. Samir is slower than the others in walking, due to a condition affecting his muscles. Joseph does not like rough games and is reluctant to join in groups. Lucy likes any game that is noisy and rough but she broke her arm last week and has it in plaster. The weather has been wet and windy all morning and now the sun is starting to shine. The class teacher asks you to take this group outside and organise some play for them in the grounds of the school for half an hour.

How would you plan your half an hour to include all of the children? What play and exercise would you provide, and what would the benefits be for the children?

may be needed underneath the frame in case of falls. A child with reduced vision could enjoy using the frame if paired with another suitable child or assisted by you.

By using your imagination and thinking about the safety issues, you can help most children to enjoy most activities and equipment. They can usually be adapted to suit all children without losing the aim of the exercise. Careful thought must be given to making sure that no one is discriminated against in play and exercise.

There are many ways to include a child who is disabled. Many manufacturers make suitably adapted play equipment, for example tricycles with bucket seats. Equipment specifically designed for children with disabilities can usually be used by all children. The manufacturers of 'ball pools' and huge foam wedges in different shapes originally designed them for children with disabilities but they now feature in most adventure playgrounds for younger children. Careful use of foam mats can take much of the risk out of physical exercise for all children, so that falls do not have hard landings.

It goes without saying that, at all times when you are caring for children, you have the responsibility for their safety. This applies especially when children are playing with or on equipment. Think about a child's stage of development and ability. Is the activity suitable for the child, without being too protective? Good play opportunities stretch a child's ability and help in his or her development.

Involvement

There are times when you need or are invited to take part in play with children. It may be to join in or to support the children. You should only become involved in the following circumstances:

- if invited to do so by the children, which is a real compliment, but do not try to take over

- if help is needed such as physical help or to collect materials or equipment or to support a child with a particular need

- to reduce potential hazards and assess risks

- if conflict starts that the children cannot resolve (try to support the resolving of the conflict through negotiation and compromise and then withdraw if possible)

- if children are looking bored and uninterested

- during a team game if a member has to leave but do not be determined to win.

Think about it

Have you been invited to join in children's play? Can you remember an adult trying to join in uninvited when you were younger? What did it feel like?

Best practice in your work placement

How to join in play

- Wait to be invited to join in.
- Do not use equipment that is only designed for children.
- Do not take over the game or activity.
- Do not be too competitive.
- Be aware of health and safety issues.
- Try to encourage the children to be in control.
- Check that you are not inhibiting the play and withdraw if you are.
- Encourage and enthuse the children.
- Be a good role model.

Curriculum

When play is being planned for a child of any age it is important that the demands of the relevant curriculum should be considered. Play is an important aspect of all the different levels.

Curriculum	Key development features	Role of different types of play
Birth to three matters 0–3 years	Strong child Skilful communicator Competent learner Healthy child	Play is the main method of developing all aspects in this age group Physical and manipulative Imaginative and creative play are important
Foundation stage 3–5 years	Personal, social and emotional Mathematical Knowledge and understanding of the world Communication, language and literacy Physical development Creative development	Children still doing most of their learning through play to gain skills for the next stage All types of play important – increased value of exploratory and role play
National curriculum Key stage 1 (5–7 years) Key stage 2 (7–11 years) Key stage 3 (11–14 years) Key stage 4 (14–16 years) Key stage 5 (16 years)	Core subjects of English, mathematics and science, with a range of other subjects including physical education, art and design and music	Play becoming less of a feature in the curriculum though still strong in some areas, for example physical education All types of play important in informal settings

■ How play relates to the curriculum framework

Think about it

If you are in a Foundation stage setting, how is social and emotional development encouraged through play in your placement?

How important do you think play is in supporting social and emotional development in Key stages 1 to 4?

Assessment activities

Assessment Activity 1

Describe the following different types of play:

- physical
- manipulative
- imaginative
- use of basic materials, for example sand
- exploratory, for example objects, materials or equipment of interest
- creative
- therapeutic.

You have now met Pass criterion 1 (P1) for which you must describe the different types of play.

Assessment Activity 2

Describe the role of the adult in providing resources or the provision of materials and equipment for play. Examples of resources provided by an adult are dressing up clothes, natural materials and constructional apparatus. You should be able to add a number of other resources to this list.

Assessment Activity 3

A more thought-demanding aspect of the adult's role is to encourage play. Describe how play can be encouraged by enabling children to explore and choose play opportunities for themselves and to adapt ideas and resources for themselves without interference or direction by the adult.

Assessment Activity 4

Describe an adult's role in the supervision of play which should include how an adult:

- should be available but without intruding on children's play
- should offer new ideas, resources or alternatives to encourage, stimulate and help develop play
- should enable accessibility
- should set ground rules, for example not throwing sand
- should ensure that all play is suitable for children's ages, needs and abilities.

When you have completed Assessment Activities 2, 3 and 4 you will have met Pass criterion 2 (P2) for which you are required to describe the role of the adult in the provision, encouragement and supervision of children's play.

Assessment Activity 5

You can go on to consider Merit criterion 1 (M1), for which you must explain (describe in detail and why) how children should be encouraged and supervised in their play.

continued ▶

Assessment Activity 6

Briefly describe how adults should be involved and intervene in children's play.

This should include the following but you may want to include other ways of doing this:

- taking part in play with children if this is what they want (try and think of an example of this happening to you or one of the early years workers in your work placement)
- allowing children to develop their own play ideas without over or under protection
- ensuring access for all children
- ensuring there is enough time and adequate resources to enable to develop and deepen play according to their interests
- being aware of the relation of different aspects of play to relevant curriculum frameworks, for example one-to-one correspondence in role play.

Assessment Activity 7

At this stage, using the notes you have made for Activities 2, 3, 4, 5 and 6 you can start to consider Distinction criterion 1 (D1) for which you are required to evaluate the role of the adult in all aspects of children's play.

6.2 Know how to help to provide opportunities for children's imaginative and creative play

This section covers:

- resources
- intervention
- encouragement.

Resources

Creative play encourages children to create and explore. Creative play supports children's development through them:

- exploring the properties of different materials through their senses
- developing physical, social, emotional and intellectual skills
- gaining satisfaction and developing confidence and self-esteem.

Provision and selection of materials

There is a wide range of materials and equipment available for creative activities, many of which are available in most settings. A lot of creative materials can be 'salvaged' from home, such as clothes, hats, empty kitchen roll tubes, boxes and other people's work-packaging materials. Child care workers can be very good at retrieving materials other people see as rubbish to use with the children they work with! Have you started yet?

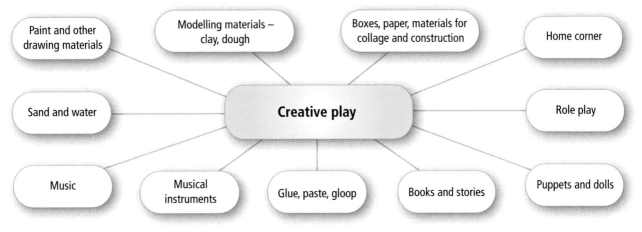

■ *There is a wide range of materials for use in creative play*

The range of creative materials is common to all age ranges, but can be focused into the different curriculum stages up to the age of eight years to meet the developmental stage of the children.

Curriculum stage	Features	Creative materials
Birth to three matters 0–3 years	Learning through senses and movement	Finger paint Crayons Playdough Water play Sand
Foundation stage 3–5 years	**Early learning goals**	Wet and dry sand Water Construction materials Clay and dough Paints, crayons, pens Cutting and sticking activities
Key stage 1 5–7 years	**National Curriculum requirements**	Materials used to develop specific skills including following instructions for example model making Creativity to learn about other topics

■ *Creative materials by curriculum stage*

Think about it

Have a look in your placement. What sorts of materials are provided for creative play? Are they all commercially bought ones or have staff brought in materials from home? Have a look in equipment catalogues at the range of materials available.

Did you know?

When Maria Edgeworth was writing in 1789 she thought that a nursery should be filled with toys that led to experimenting. These included sturdy carts, gardening tools, printing presses, looms and furniture that can be taken to pieces and put together again, pencils, scissors, tools and workbenches. How does this compare with the toys and equipment at your placement?

Equipment and props

All resources for play for children should be in good repair, clean and safe to use. Children should never be presented with toys or games that are broken, dirty or have parts missing. They will not enjoy playing with them, they could be dangerous and a child will be frustrated with a jigsaw that has a piece missing. Washing paint and glue pots and brushes is an important part of early years work.

Toys and equipment must be checked before the children have access to them. This should be done as they are put away and again as they are put out for use. Equipment that is broken should be attended to straight away and broken toys should be thrown away. You should also ensure that everything that will be needed for a particular activity is available and ready for use.

Health and safety issues have been covered in Unit 2. It is essential that you keep the principles of health and safety in mind when you are providing resources for activities. Being constantly on the alert for possible dangers will help to prevent accidents and illnesses in children. As soon as you spot a potential hazard, do something about it. Remove a broken toy, mop up a spillage and report anything that you cannot deal with to your supervisor. If you do not do so and a child is injured, you could be held responsible under the Health and Safety at Work legislation.

Paints and other drawing materials

Paint can be bought in a number of different types and forms, from powder paint to ready mixed acrylics in a plastic bottle. Always make sure tops are on properly and powder paint is kept dry. Paints can be mixed with all sorts of materials, such as glue, glitter or sand to provide different textures.

Different sized and textured applicators are available. Think about using paint:

■ with brushes (size appropriate to the child)

■ with sponges

■ with potatoes

■ with rags or newspaper scrunched

■ with rollers (bought and old bottles)

■ with straws to blow it

■ over shiny surfaces, for example wax crayon.

The surface that the paint is applied to matters. This can be anything from a plain sheet of paper to plastic, wood and different thickness and types of paper. Try some of the different materials and techniques out so you can help children to use them effectively.

Water

Children start to play with water as soon as they enjoy having a bath as a baby. Plain water in a paddling pool, bowl or water tray will engage children. Add in bubbles, coloured water, containers and other equipment and it may be difficult to encourage them into another phase of activity! Washing up painting equipment can be fun for children to do. They won't see it as a chore.

Safety considerations are important with water play. Make sure that children are never left unsupervised as a young child can drown in a few centimetres of water.

Sand

Most early years settings have a sand tray. It can be used wet or dry and played in with a range of containers, diggers, rakes, scoops and other equipment. As with water, children can share their imaginative play in a sand area which can be inside or outside. Special sand that is safe for children and does not stain should be used. Outdoor sand areas need careful protection to stop animals getting into them.

The home corner

Most early years settings, including the Foundation Years, have a home corner. The ideal home corner changes its features on a regular basis to provide a range of materials and stimuli to encourage children to explore their environment. The home corner is where you are likely to observe children engaging in 'symbolic play' and role play.

Think about it

Have a look at the range of drawing materials:
- *paint*
- *pencils*
- *charcoal*
- *wax crayons*
- *felt tips*
- *chalks*
- *coloured crayons.*

Can you think of any more?

Did you know?

Frederich Froebel lived from 1782 to 1852 and founded the first kindergartens. He was a strong believer in symbolic play, for example by using a stick as a gun or an empty pot as a cup.

Did you know?

Many suppliers of equipment have a range of specialised dressing up clothes, for example nurse or fireman. Although useful they can limit a child's imagination and it can be far better just using a hat or a length of material to symbolise the role. Hats are one of the most important imaginative play resources for children of all ages.

A well-equipped home corner is likely to have the following features:

- accessible to all children including any wheelchair users
- use multicultural resources, for example cooking utensils
- areas for sleeping and eating
- washing up facilities
- cooking facilities
- eating equipment
- telephone
- cleaning materials, such as brush, vacuum cleaner, dusters
- clothes washing equipment
- range of multicultural and gender dolls
- clothes, hats, scarves, shoes and bags.

The home corner should move into different areas of the setting including outdoors in good weather, if possible. Supervision is important in the home corner to limit the number of children if necessary and observe the usual safety precautions. Equipment and resources need regular checking to make sure that they are clean and in good repair.

Songs, music, rhymes and stories

From birth, many children hear a carer singing lullabies and rocking songs. As children grow they delight in songs and rhymes; the constant repetition makes it possible for them to join in these familiar, sing-song types of communication. New songs and rhymes introduce new words and phrases which are quickly learned. Once a child is attending any sort of group, from toddlers to school, songs are an important activity. Used with actions or puppets, group songs allow a child to try joining in without being singled out. Songs and rhymes can fit very easily into themes and topics in the nursery or school.

Music is a medium to which most children respond. A piece of music can serve many functions including soothing children, allowing them to express themselves in movement, promoting dance and providing inspiration for a painting. All these are forms of communication and are especially important when a child has difficulties in verbal communication. Apart from listening to music, children love to make music, and again this can be used for communicating. Clapping hands is the simplest form of music making.

Think about it

Have a look at the range of musical instruments in your placement. Do they include any of those shown below? Try them out to see what type of noise they make.

You should develop your own library of songs, music, rhymes and stories that encourage communication and language development. Every time you hear or see a new example in a book, in your placement, etc. write down or copy the details. Create a resource file with various headings. Choose a theme, for example autumn or animals; an ideal theme would be one that is in current use at your placement. Collect as many relevant songs, rhymes and examples of music as possible and file them in your

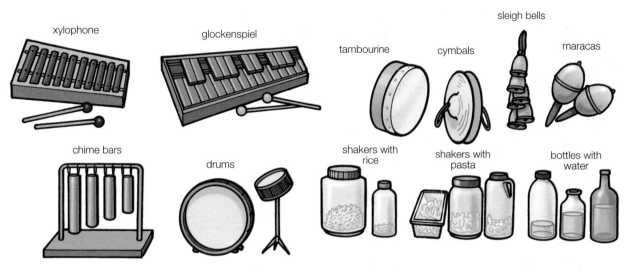

■ *Instruments suitable for working with children*

resource file. Choose one of each and try them out with a few children in your placement, making notes on the success of the activities.

Books

As with music, you should look at the range of books available to seek out ones suitable for helping language and development. Reading stories to children is an important part of communicating; very few children, if any, do not enjoy hearing a story, either as part of a group or on a one-to-one basis. Reading promotes all of the aspects of intellectual and language development.

Choosing the right book is important. The choice of book has to be related to the child's:

■ age

■ stage of development

■ ability to understand the story

■ interests and cultural background.

The same book can serve different age groups. A storybook with bright, attractive pictures will provide stimulation to a toddler who enjoys the pictures and an older child who enjoys the story. Books that open up discussion are an excellent medium for promoting language development. Examples include books that show familiar scenes, for example a shopping street. Such a book will help you encourage children to talk about their local shops and the goods inside or about lorries or vans.

Books can be central to developing a theme for further activities. *The Very Hungry Caterpillar* is an excellent example. This book describes the growth of a caterpillar into a butterfly, showing what the caterpillar ate on its way to forming a chrysalis. Work on food, growth, change, insects,

Did you know?

The government has supported a Bookstart scheme to encourage literacy from an early age. Every one- to two-year-old will receive a satchel containing books and every three- to four-year-old child will receive a treasure chest that includes books and crayons. Babies up to 12 months will continue to receive a free bag of baby books delivered through libraries and health visitors.

Think about it

Choose at least two different books and briefly describe them. Make a list of all the extra activities that can be linked to the books and how the book and the activities will help to promote language and intellectual development.

numbers and colours can all develop from reading this one book. It is a book with a story that is easy to remember, so it can help in memory development with children.

Having heard a story from a book, children can be stimulated to produce paintings, models and collages. Older children might develop their own related story. Children will enjoy verbally extending the story they have heard, or 'writing' their own story in pictures. These activities all help in the development of communication.

Best practice in your work placement

Supporting children's play

- Is there adequate adult supervision? Are more adults needed for certain activities?
- Are there any hidden dangers in the immediate area, for example tools, steep steps, poorly protected pools?
- If outside, are there any poisonous plants or berries within children's reach?
- Is the flooring safe? Are there any frayed carpet edges, loose rugs, splinters in wooden floors?
- Is all basic furniture and equipment in good condition and not liable to be pulled over?
- Are safety items in place, for example mats under climbing frames, safety gates and childproof locks?
- Are all toys and games safe to use and clean?
- Are spills cleaned up immediately?

Intervention

Remember what was discussed earlier – you are a facilitator of children's play. This particularly applies to imaginative play. A child's imagination will be stifled if he or she does not have the chance to let his or her imagination expand.

Imaginative and creative play can be helped by:

- providing the materials and setting for creativity
- encouraging children's imagination through stories, outings, activities
- valuing a child's results
- encouraging children to talk about their activity using open questions, for example 'Tell me about your painting' rather than 'Is that a painting of your dog?'
- praising a child for their efforts (never compare to another child)

- making sure there is no competition from other children (for young children)

- valuing the process of creation rather than the end product.

Allowing children to play freely helps children to explore their imagination and to build a basis for more structured learning. Free flow imaginative play is usually child led and is often unplanned. A chance remark or reference by a child or adult can lead into an imaginative game. A mention of a visit to the supermarket could result in the home corner being turned into the local branch or a child sharing details of his or her holiday during circle time could spark a free play activity on a journey.

Encouragement

Stereotyping

Stereotyping must be avoided in all aspects of play and activities including imaginative and creative play. Children should be encouraged to feel positive about themselves and their families. Displays and activities should be considered to make sure that maximum benefit is gained and that cultural diversity has been an important factor. All children should be growing up aware of the diversity of our country.

Think about these points:

- make sure projects and themes incorporate other cultures, such as food from around the world

- ensure various people are represented, for example an Asian female teacher, a Chinese doctor, a male nursery nurse

- include people with special needs in displays, posters

- use several languages in the messages on the display

- provide a variety of skin-toned dolls, paints etc

- involve parents from all cultures represented at the setting

- think how children growing up in a predominantly one-culture area can spend time with children from another culture.

Feelings and roles of other children

Role play gives children the chance to pretend to be other people. They act out situations, sometimes to make sense of their own world, sometimes for enjoyment. Children may need props to support their role play, for example dressing up clothes, hats, masks. At other times they will adapt what is around them.

Role play is excellent in encouraging language development. Children start to engage in role play from about two years old. Provision of areas such as a mock shop or café are good ways of encouraging role play. It can also be totally unplanned with a corner of a play area used.

Did you know?

Margaret McMillan (1860–1931) who was the founder of the first nursery schools believed in free play to encourage children's imagination and help their full development through active learning.

Free flow imaginative play is best encouraged by:

- allowing time
- allowing space
- ensuring other children are involved when appropriate
- making sure the play is fun
- supporting children to return to their play at another time
- intervening if the play becomes too rough
- providing ideas or equipment if requested by the children.

Think about it

Observe children in the home corner. Are they following stereotypes of behaviour, for example girls doing the cooking and cleaning? How could you intervene?

You may see children pretending to be their parents in role play or acting out their feelings about something that has happened to them. As a student you should be alert to passing on any worries you might have about role play you observe, such as excessive aggression or strange behaviour.

Role play is an excellent opportunity for children to develop other skills such as language development and numeracy skills. Pretending to go to a café supports numeracy skills when counting out cakes onto a plate, giving change or one cup of tea. Role play in cooking gives scope for size, changing properties, measuring weights, counting, etc.

Developing creative play

Children can be encouraged to develop their creative play through careful support. Introducing ideas to a child will usually result in them adapting the idea themselves.

Visits to art galleries and exhibitions or showing them pictures and displays can be an excellent trigger to a child. Older children are encouraged to experiment with different artists' methods in the National Curriculum key stages. Younger children's painting will show development after they have seen different styles and types of creativity.

Think about it

Write down the different skills children are practising the next time you see role play in action in your placement.

Case study

A visit to a gallery

A group of five-year-olds were taken to a local exhibition to see some bright and imaginative sculptures. They were given paper, pencils and crayons and encouraged to produce their version. Most of the children produced their version of the sculpture. Samir went off into a corner facing away from the exhibit. When his teacher had a look at his work it was a fabulous drawing, totally unlike the sculpture but using colour and shape in a similar way with a lot of Samir's own imagination.

1 Who do you think had benefited most from the visit?
2 How would you have arranged the time for the children to do their picture?

Painting, drawing and mark making are all precursors of a child eventually being able to write. There are many different ways of helping a child to become a writer. Encouraging them to tell you about their efforts and then you writing their response on a label attached to it is a good start. Many children will tell you they are writing by making marks and scribbles. Eventually this can develop in to recognisable words – probably not spelt as you would expect though! Giving children lots of opportunities to 'write' even at a young age can produce some amazing results and help in developing the skills they will need later. Of course, in order to write, children need to have seen lots of writing in books, on packets, adverts, bus destinations etc.

Assessment activities

Assessment Activity 8

Describe the range of resources, materials and equipment that need to be provided by an adult in helping to provide opportunities for children's imaginative and creative play.

There is a huge range that you can cover here but in this range you should include:

- home corner equipment and materials
- paint and paper
- glue and paste
- musical instruments.

Assessment Activity 9

You now need to build on previous assessment activities and describe the role of the adult in intervening in children's imaginative and creative play.

The role of the adult here should include:

- enabling children's imaginative play to flow freely

- enabling imaginative play to follow the children's interests
- ensuring the setting's requirements are being met
- not intervening unless requested by the children, when additional ideas or resources are required or when safety is a concern.

Assessment Activity 10

The role of the adult should also to be to give encouragement to children in their imaginative and creative play and avoid stereotyping.

Children can be encouraged to:
- make marks
- paint
- draw
- model

- print
- express their feelings in a safe manner
- explore materials
- explore the feelings and roles of others in imaginative role play.

You can now meet Pass criterion 4 (P4), which requires you to describe the role of the adult in providing for imaginative and creative play.

Assessment Activity 11

You can also go on to explain (describe why in detail) why it is sometimes important for adults to be involved and to intervene in

children's imaginative and creative play. This enables you to meet Merit criterion 2 (M2).

continued ▶

Assessment Activity 12

You can also add further notes, concerning adult involvement and intervention in children's imaginative and creative play, towards meeting D1.

6.3 Know how to support physical play

This section covers:

■ benefits of physical play

■ encouragement

■ supervision.

Benefits of physical play

Physical play does not only help physical development. There are many other benefits. Have a look at the diagram below.

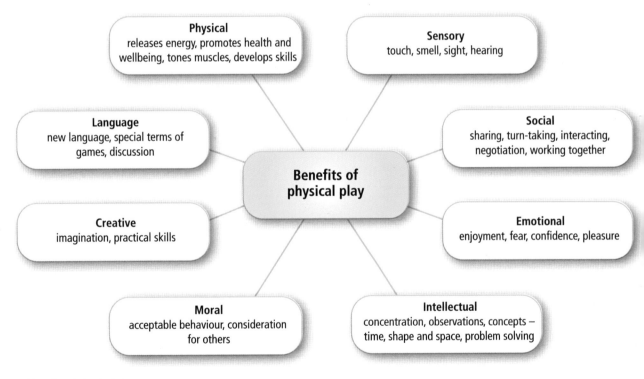

Physical
releases energy, promotes health and wellbeing, tones muscles, develops skills

Sensory
touch, smell, sight, hearing

Language
new language, special terms of games, discussion

Social
sharing, turn-taking, interacting, negotiation, working together

Benefits of physical play

Creative
imagination, practical skills

Emotional
enjoyment, fear, confidence, pleasure

Moral
acceptable behaviour, consideration for others

Intellectual
concentration, observations, concepts – time, shape and space, problem solving

■ Benefits of physical play

■ Exercise and play help to use the energy provided by the food a child eats. If exercise does not burn up enough energy, a child will gain excess weight.

■ Exercise helps to develop muscles. You can see how important this is if you examine an arm or leg that has been in a plaster cast after a fracture for six weeks; it will be very much thinner and weaker than the other limb as a result of not having had any exercise.

- The immune system is strengthened through exercise, so it can help a child to be less vulnerable to illness.

- Energetic play can be an ideal way for children who are angry or upset to work off their aggression. Ask any teacher about the effect of bad weather resulting in enforced indoor play. A group of young children may react badly to not having the chance to work off their energy in the playground.

Types of physical play

There are many types of physical play. Some can be solitary, for example construction, skipping and ball play, that you should be able to adapt to working with a child individually if needed. It is then easier to introduce them into playing with one or two other children and eventually larger groups.

Most types of physical play are excellent tools to encourage turn-taking and thinking about others, for example ball games, team games, or using equipment such as climbing frames or bicycles.

The table below shows some examples of physical play and how they can help children to develop.

Think about it

When you are in placement, observe children enjoying a physical activity. Which skills are they using or developing?

Type of play	Effect on health and development
Baby on changing mat without nappy kicking freely, rolling for toys	Nappy area exposed to fresh air aids healthy skin Physical stretching, building muscles in legs Development of mobility
Baby bouncing on knee of carer	Social interaction Developing strength in legs, practising standing
12–18-month-old child using push-and-ride toy	Practising walking with support Manoeuvring skills Independence Muscle movement
Rough and tumble play in a safe environment with foam mats, cushions, etc.	Developing gross motor control by physical activity
Five-year-old in the park running, playing on the swings and slide	Social interaction with other children Fresh air and sunshine builds up the immune system Developing gross motor control by physical activity
Swimming Gymnastics Dancing Football (any age)	Help to promote healthy development of bones, muscles and the immune system Develops social skills, team skills, self-esteem by achievement, co-ordination skills Learning about rules and turn-taking
Music and movement (any age)	Co-ordination of body to music. Creativity, imagination

■ *Development through physical play*

Encouragement

Most children need little encouragement to play and exercise. Play is a constant feature of a young child's life as children learn through play. However, recent studies have shown that many children do not get enough exercise, possibly as a result of parents transporting children everywhere by car, parents fearing to allow children to play far from their home and increasing use of TV and computer games. Some children may need encouragement to play by suggesting activities and facilitating games and other physical play.

A child may have barriers to spontaneous play, for example because of restrictions in physical movements or through shyness and reluctance to join in. Some children may need some direction to gain the opportunity to develop skills through play and exercise. Child care workers can help by suggesting and providing opportunities. Physical play is an excellent way to encourage the use of newly gained skills or to help further development of skills a child may be struggling with.

Equipment to support physical play

Large and small play equipment can be used to encourage children's physical development. Large-scale equipment will enhance gross motor development and co-ordination, while small play equipment encourages manipulative and fine motor skills.

The following types of physical play can enhance children's physical development:

- large equipment, such as bicycles, tricycles
- ball games, such as football, volleyball, catch, short and ordinary tennis
- team games including rounders, netball, basketball, football
- large-scale construction
- throwing and catching, skipping
- using space to run and dance.

All large equipment needs plenty of space if it is to be used safely. If equipment is overcrowded and unattractive looking children are less likely to want to use it. Encourage them by arranging different equipment into groups or themes.

Think about it

Which of the following equipment is in use in your placement?
Which play might be suitable for a child with difficulties moving?
Which play might be suitable for a withdrawn child who does not like noise and crowds?

- climbing frames
- play tunnels
- swings
- slides
- trampolines
- seesaws
- ropes and rope ladders
- sit-and-ride toys
- bicycles and tricycles
- large balls, hoops, beanbags.

How many times have you heard parents telling a child not to do something as they will hurt him or herself? How do you think that will affect a child's chance to explore his or her abilities?

Children will enjoy using it either indoors or outdoors, but wherever it is used you must think about:

- protective matting for the floor in case of falls and avoiding the risk of falls onto dangerous objects
- adequate adult supervision
- avoiding too many children trying to use the equipment at once
- adaptations and support for children with physical disabilities.

If your placement has a wide selection of equipment, try to find out how the adults decide which item is to be used and watch how they encourage children to join in. Children enjoy variety in activities and keeping a piece of equipment for occasional use will make it a treat. For example, a trampoline needs close supervision, so it can be used only at certain times. Large-scale equipment needs careful checking before use for loose parts, broken sections and cleanliness. If it is kept outside, covers should be put over it. If possible, equipment should be stored indoors to prevent spoilage.

Small equipment has fewer potential hazards and requires less space. It offers great potential for children to develop their self-esteem, as results are almost instantaneous. An important rule about selecting suitable small equipment is that smaller children need bigger pieces, while larger (older) children enjoy smaller pieces. The safety issue is obvious: small children can and will put small items in their mouths and may choke.

Smaller children should also be kept away from older children's construction and modelling work to avoid the accidental destruction of their efforts. Small play equipment includes:

- stacking beakers
- posting boxes
- Duplo, Lego
- jigsaws of many types
- interlocking train sets
- foam blocks
- wooden blocks
- construction straws, stickle bricks, Meccano.

For which age group might small equipment be suitable? Put an approximate age range against each type of equipment listed above.

As with large play equipment, you need to be selective in the amount of equipment you put out. Small play materials need to be carefully stored in boxes or trays, keeping different sized pieces separate. Tables should be arranged to confine each type to a separate area. In this way, toys will be kept in good condition and not get mixed up or lost.

Not all physical play involves the development and use of gross motor skills. It is useful to know how to provide activities using fine motor skills to encourage a child's manipulative skills including:

- small-scale construction blocks, Lego, Meccano
- puzzles

- threading cotton reels and beads
- manipulating the mouse on a computer.

Supervision

Physical play does need good supervision. It is important to balance the need to provide an acceptable level of challenge against the risks to children.

Children need to be encouraged to experiment and take risks to help them learn how to deal well with risks. It is the adult's responsibility to make sure those children are safe. Most children will not undertake something that they are not happy with. The danger lies in less confident children being encouraged by a bolder one to do something they are not comfortable with. For example, climbing to the top of the climbing frame. It is only when they are up there that the less confident child realises he or she cannot get down! Supportive encouragement by an adult to go a little further is a different matter and can help a timid child to surprise themselves.

It is very important that children are encouraged to challenge themselves. Many children are over protected and not allowed to test themselves. As we have already seen it is important to make sure that activities are suitable for all children in respect to their age, needs and abilities.

Did you know?

*A **risk** is a potential danger, for example a bicycle with poor brakes. By making sure the bicycle is in good working order the risk is reduced. A **hazard** is something that has the potential to cause harm, for example a patch of oily liquid on the ground where a child may ride the bike. Cleaning up the oil reduces the hazard and the likelihood of an accident.*

Case study

Climbing trees

Joel is aged nine and is very agile and enjoys climbing. He can climb trees and climbing frames with ease and more importantly get down safely! His friend Jem has never climbed a tree before, but does not want to appear 'soft' and so follows Joel up a tree that Joel has climbed many times before. Part way up, Jem looks down and becomes very frightened and cannot get down.

1 What do you think happens next?
2 If you had been there, what would you have done?
3 What, if anything, should be said to Joe and Jem later?

Think about it

Have a look at the available space in your placement. How useful is it for physical activity? Ask your supervisor how the need for physical play space has been dealt with.

Using space

Different settings will have very different amounts and types of space for physical play. Some may have good outdoor areas whereas other may have none. Careful consideration of the space available is important to make sure it is used well.

Sometimes settings have lots of space but it is not well used. School playgrounds can be a good example of this as they are often expanses of tarmac and/or muddy grass. There are some good ways in settings to help playground space to be used well. Have a look at these ideas that have been tried.

- Work with children to suggest games that can be formally organised in the playground. These are announced along with a brief explanation of how to play the games. Equipment and space is then provided in the playground.

- Playground buddies are children who are responsible for organising and supporting game playing in the playground.

- Different areas of the playground are marked out to help younger children to play organised games such as hopscotch.

- Limiting organised ball games (such as football) to certain days or times to allow all children to use the space. Girls are encouraged to join the ball games by practice work in physical education.

Think about it

How effective do you think the ideas listed above will be? Have any been tried in your placement?

Assessment activities

Assessment Activity 13

Maria has just started to attend your work placement. She had an accident to her leg about six months ago and although her leg is now better she is not confident in taking part in physical play.

What are the all-round benefits to Maria in taking part in physical play?

You should include not only physical benefits but also social, emotional, intellectual, moral, creative, communicative and sensory benefits.

Assessment Activity 14

Describe how encouragement from an adult will help Maria, for example in using her whole body.

Assessment Activity 15

How should Maria's physical play be supervised? You should include the following:

- without under- or overprotection
- ensuring the effective use of space
- ensuring that physical play is suitable for her age, needs and abilities.

continued ▶

Assessment Activity 16

You should now use your notes from Assessment Activities 13, 14 and 15 to meet Pass criterion 5 (P5) for which you must outline (briefly describe) the benefits of physical play for children and how this can be supported.

Assessment Activity 17

You should then go on to explain (describe in detail) how physical play can be encouraged for children's benefit. You will then have met Merit criterion 3 (M3).

Assessment Activity 18

You can also add to your notes towards meeting D1.

6.4 Understand how to encourage children to explore and investigate

This section covers:

■ resources

■ encouragement.

Did you know?

Maria Montessori founded a type of education named after her. She firmly believed that children learned best by exploring the world around them. She developed a range of equipment to help this exploration that is still in use in Montessori schools.

Resources

Children need to be encouraged to explore and investigate. It helps them to understand the world they live in and also helps them to get involved in their world. This is important for all ages but especially older children. Play has been limited for children over successive years. Adults who are over 40 remember playing out in their local area when they were younger. Now children are protected from perceived danger much more. Children played out in the street in urban areas and in fields and woods in the countryside. The street was not simply a physical space, it was a cultural space too that linked the street, the pavement, the gate, the front steps and the domestic door together. There were 'street games' and 'street rhymes', along with the 'freedom of the streets'.

Looking around the area near your placement may provide an interesting experience for children. In many early years settings, children are taken and collected by car and never see the surroundings.

Local communities usually have a variety of resources to encourage children to explore and investigate in a safe environment. Examples include:

■ urban parks

■ activity centres with facilities for investigating and playing

■ ecology parks with ponds and wildlife

■ areas of country parks

■ woodland

■ farms with open days for children

■ schemes to involve children in the design and development of provision.

Think about it

Have a look at your local environment:
■ Is there a local park or open area?
■ Are there interesting places to go on a bus ride or a walk?
■ Are there trees that you could safely use for bark rubbings?

Case study

The Groundwork Trust

One good example of an organisation that works closely with children and young people to provide a safe and enjoyable environment is the Groundwork Trust. They work in most areas of the country and actively involve children and young people.

Groundwork offers holiday play schemes to encourage young children to get out and about and explore the natural environment through joining in a series of fun-days. Activities range from bat walks to mini beast hunts, bird box building to pond dipping. The scheme aims to get children interested in nature from a young age as a way of educating them about their responsibilities towards the environment and creating active and dependable citizens of the future.

Groundwork has involved young people in improving a dilapidated and unsafe playground. The park now contains a redesigned children's playground, youth shelter, skate park and multi-games court. Young people continue to be involved in the park and have designed two ornamental gateways as entrances and are working with Groundwork on a series of art features.

Groundwork works with young people and children aged from 5 to 13 years old to encourage health and fitness. Groundwork provides a taster of different sports, such as basketball, to encourage participation in regular exercise while other activities like creating a healthy eating recipe calendar are designed to prompt the young people to think closely about the food that they eat and where it comes from. The scheme tackles childhood obesity by helping young people change their lifestyles in way that is fun and enjoyable in an informal learning environment.

Find out what sort of schemes like these there are in your area. What are they and who is supporting them?

Did you know?

The greatest single factor affecting children's play in the 20th century has been the loss of the street as a children's domain to the private motor car. There are now 32 million cars on the streets of Britain, compared with eight million children aged between five and 15.

Source: Tony Hawkead, Chief Executive of Groundwork

Think about it

Ask your parents or grandparents how they used to play outside. Do they remember the freedom of playing outside in the local woods or parks? Make a list of the sort of games they played.

Lots of other organisations and community groups are involved in similar schemes to those offered by Groundwork and many schools and groups get involved. Children learn about their environment through these activities and also develop personal skills and interests.

Short breaks to activity centres are a good experience for older children to experience challenge through activities such as climbing, water sports, caving. These are restricted by safety requirements and costs but if you are in a placement that has such an activity, try to find out what is planned.

It is very likely that your placement already has another excellent tool for children to explore the world by, which is the computer. Research on topics is possible in an instant by using the internet for children from quite a young age. Likewise, staff can also find out information and materials that they can use to explore with the children. There are many CD-Roms that are aimed at helping children to explore their world as well. See if your setting has any.

Children can explore their world within the setting by a number of ways including gardening. Gardening helps to develop children's knowledge and understanding of the world and does not need too much space as even a couple of tubs can be used to grow plants from seeds. Wildlife gardens can encourage birds and insects that can be watched and investigated by the children. Older children will enjoy preparing soil for planting, watering and weeding their area.

Gardening is a good reason to get children out of the setting to look at other gardens for ideas and also to involve family members in helping out in a larger venture.

Safety issues are important with gardens:

- tools must be safe and the appropriate size for the children
- check that the soil is free of chemicals
- be aware of plants that are poisonous if eaten
- ensure hands are carefully washed after gardening.

Encouragement

When children are being introduced to the world that exists outside their own experience the attitude of the adults doing this is very important.

Children will easily pick up on the enthusiasm of an adult and want to find out more. Sharing information on holidays is a good activity. A postcard from somewhere is a good reason to gather the children round the computer and look for some information on that place.

Stimulating interest in woodlands through a video or a story can be used very effectively to move on to planning an outing to a local wood.

Case study

Recording your day out

Neil planned a day for a group of seven- and eight-year-olds to a local beauty spot. It was part of a deep wooded valley and had a stream with stepping stones across it. As part of the outing he also planned to visit an outdoor sculpture exhibition using natural materials. The structure of the day was to include a walk through the wooded area exploring the trees and environment, time to play on the stepping stones and in the water and a chance to

look at the sculptures before finally encouraging the group to make their own art work out of materials around them. He captured all the events on camera and used the photos along with writing by the group and 'treasure' they brought back to mount a display of the day.

Make a list of all the skills the group will have used and developed.

Risk

Sometimes practitioners will not plan for outdoor activity with children because of the risk. As with any activity the risks need careful consideration and managing. All organised activities need staff that have been trained and checked to see if they are usually involved with children. A greater number of staff from the setting may be needed to ensure adequate supervision.

As with anything the risk has to be balanced against the benefits and if the risk is minimal, the benefits are well worth the extra effort and planning needed.

Remember the discussion on risk in the last section. Children need to be allowed to test themselves in a safe environment without over-protecting them. As with any other activity it is important to ensure that all children can participate and special measures taken to support those who need extra help. Children with disabilities may not have had the chance to explore the outdoors.

Assessment activities

Assessment Activity 19

Find out about resources to encourage children to explore and investigate.

Include:

- community resources
- ICT.

Assessment Activity 20

Describe how children can be encouraged to explore and investigate.

- Include information on engaging children's curiosity by providing interesting and stimulating activities and experiences. Give some examples from your own experience.

- Show an interest yourself in exploring and investigating. Again give some examples from your own work in a work placement.
- Provide opportunities for exploration and different experiences for older children. Give some examples here.
- Provide information on taking risks and under- and over-protection of children.

continued ▶

Assessment Activity 21

You can now meet Pass criterion 6 (P6), which requires you to describe how children can be encouraged to explore and investigate.

Assessment Activity 22

You should now be able to fully meet the Distinction criterion 1 (D1) which requires you to evaluate (that is to say how important and worthwhile) the role of the adult is in all aspects of children's play.

7 The development and care of babies and children under three years

Introduction

The rate of development in the first three years of life is very rapid. The influence of carers is important in this age group and can have lifelong consequences.

The care and development of babies demands particular knowledge, understanding and skills. This unit builds on the principles of supporting development in Unit 1, going into much more detail for the different stages from birth to three years.

In this unit you will learn:

1 the expected sequence and development of babies and children in the first three years of life

2 how to help provide physical care requirements for babies and children under three

3 how to provide play activities to encourage learning and development

4 how to communicate with babies and children under three, interpret their needs and respond to them.

7.1 Understand and observe the expected sequence and development of babies and children in the first three years of life

This section covers:

- development
- observations.

Development

Remember the basic principles of development from Unit 1 that apply to all children:

- development starts from the head and works down the body
- all development happens in the same order, but can occur at different rates
- all areas of development are linked together.

Although development happens at different rates, there are certain stages that most children will reach by a certain age. These are known as the 'milestones of development', for example, walking alone by 18 months, smiling at six weeks.

The four areas of development are:

- **Physical** development. This refers to the body increasing in skill and performance and includes:
  - gross motor development (using large muscles), for example legs and arms
  - fine motor development (precise use of muscles), for example hands and fingers.

- **Social and emotional** development. This is the development of a child's identity and self-image and the development of relationships and feelings about him or herself learning the skills to live in society with other people.

- **Intellectual** development. This is learning the skills of understanding, memory and concentration.

- **Communication and speech** development. This is learning to communicate with friends, family and all others.

'Birth to three matters'

Research has shown that even babies have highly developed learning skills and that the first three years are extremely critical in giving a child the best start in life. The importance of the first three years has been increasingly recognised in the changes to the expectations of child care provision. It is no longer enough to just provide care for babies and young children; the importance of supporting and enhancing a child's development and learning is firmly embedded now in all provisions from child minders to nurseries. In 2003, the UK government launched 'Birth to three matters' to provide a framework to most effectively support children from birth to three years. The framework looks at a child's learning, growth, development and environment in four areas:

- a strong child

- a skilful communicator

- a competent learner

- a healthy child.

Each area links in with four broad developmental age groupings:

- heads up, lookers and communicators (0–8 months)

- sitters, standers and explorers (8–18 months)

- movers, shakers and players (18–24 months)

- walkers, talkers and pretenders (24–36 months).

To work effectively with babies and young children you need to know the key developmental points of these age groups in detail.

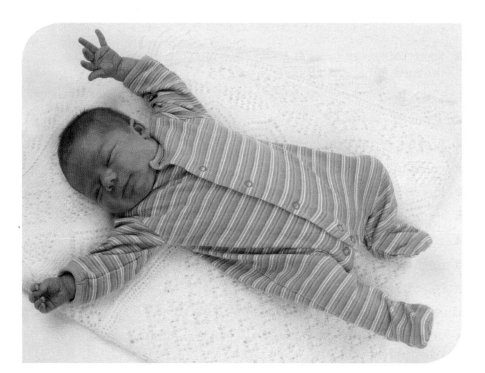

Heads up, lookers and communicators (Birth to eight months)

At birth

Movement

New-born babies have very little, if any, control over their bodies. They are scrunched up and will curl into the foetal position. Movements are reflex rather than deliberate.

Reflexes mean babies will:

- grasp an object that has touched the palm of their hand
- turn their head to look for a nipple or teat if their cheek is touched
- suck and swallow
- try to make stepping movements if they are held upright with their feet on a firm surface
- startle in response to a sudden sound or bright light
- stretch their arms suddenly and then bring them in if they feel they are falling
- recognise their mother's voice and smell
- cry when they are hungry, in pain, need feeding, changing or just cuddling.

Senses

Babies use their senses from birth.

- Smell and taste: babies respond to sour or sweet tastes.
- Hearing and communication: crying is a baby's only means of communication. Different cries for different meanings develop very quickly. Loud sounds make babies jump but they enjoy listening to voices.
- Sight: babies can focus at 20–25 cm which is close facial contact distance. Otherwise vision is fuzzy.

By one month

Babies of this age need:

- firm but gentle handling
- constant holding when awake
- lots of cuddles, touch, talking and singing
- feeding, bathing, changing
- music to listen to
- bright colours and mobiles within 20–25 cm of their faces.

Physical

The physical movements of a one-month-old baby are:

- lies on back with head to one side – arms and legs on face side outstretched

- head lags when pulled up to sitting position
- when held sitting, back is a full curve
- primitive reflexes, such as rooting, sucking, stepping, grasping are still present.

Social and emotional

The responses of a one-month-old baby are:

- responds positively to main carer.
- imitates facial expressions.
- stares at bright shiny objects.
- gazes intently at carers.
- social smile at carers (by six weeks).

Intellectual

A baby:

- blinks in reaction to bright light
- turns to soft light
- stares at carer
- cries when basic needs require attention.

Communication

A baby:

- cries when basic needs require attention such as hunger, tiredness and distress
- 'freezes' when a bell is rung gently close to the ear and moves head towards the sound
- stops crying at sound of human voice (unless very upset)
- coos in response to carer's talk.

Three months

Physical

- kicks legs and waves arms
- brings hands together over chest or chin
- watches movements of own hands, plays with own hands
- holds rattle for a few seconds if placed in hand
- can lift head and upper chest and turn when on front.

Social and emotional

- fixes gaze on carer's face when feeding
- smiles, starting to engage and vocalise with carers
- recognises preparation for routine, for example bath, feeding.

Intellectual

- follows movements of large and smaller objects.

Communication

- becomes quiet and turns head towards sound of rattle near head
- sudden loud noises can still be upsetting
- cries when uncomfortable or annoyed
- vocalises when spoken to and when alone
- sucks lips in response to food preparation
- shows excitement at sound of voices, footsteps.

Six months

Physical

- sits with support
- rolls over
- pushes head, neck and chest off floor with arms when on front
- holds arms out to be lifted up
- held standing, bears weight on feet and bounces
- uses whole hand in palmar grasp, passes toy from one hand to another.

Social and emotional

- starts to show interest in other babies, smiling
- becomes more interested in social interaction, depending on amount of time spent with other children and his or her personality
- fear of strangers and distress at separation from carer
- interacts differently with various family members
- uses comfort object, such as a blanket
- puts hand to bottle or cup and pats it when feeding
- seeks attention.

Intellectual

- is very curious, easily distracted by movements
- immediately fixes sight on small objects close by and reaches out to grasp them
- puts everything in mouth
- finds feet interesting objects
- watches toys fall from hand within range of vision
- immediately reaches for rattle when offered and shakes it to make sound.

Communication

- makes singsong vowel sounds
- laughs and chuckles and squeals aloud in play
- screams with annoyance
- responds differently to different tones of voice
- turns immediately to main carer's voice
- starting to respond to noises out of sight with correct visual response.

Eight months

Physical

- sits alone for 10–15 minutes without support
- reaches out for toys when sitting
- may crawl or shuffle
- pulls body to stand but cannot lower body so falls backwards
- pokes at small items with index finger
- uses index and middle fingers with thumb in pincer grip to pick up small items
- will take and hold a small brick in each hand
- lifts block but can only release by dropping.

Social and emotional

- very interested in all around
- recognises familiar and unfamiliar faces
- shows stranger anxiety
- takes everything to mouth (mouthing, from six months)
- holds, bites and chews a firm object, for example a biscuit.

Intellectual

- looks in correct direction for falling toys
- might find toy hidden under a cushion or cup if he or she watches it being hidden
- holds toy out but cannot release.

Communication

- vocalises for communication, shouts for attention
- babbles loudly and tunefully using dual syllables in long strings, for example dad-dad, baba, mam-mam
- imitates adult vocal sounds, for example coughs, smacking lips
- understands 'no' and 'bye-bye'
- instant response to hearing test conducted 1 metre behind child, out of sight.

Sitters, standers and explorers (8–18 months)

Twelve months

Physical

- pulls to stand then can stand alone and starts to walk holding on (cruising)
- mobile through crawling or shuffling
- enjoys self-feeding and holds cup with help
- neat pincer grip – picks up anything tiny from the floor
- starting to show hand preference
- clicks two cubes together
- puts cubes in box when shown.

Social and emotional

- strong attachments to carers
- shows definite emotions and is aware of emotions of others
- will play alone
- starting to develop object permanence.

Intellectual

- will hold two cubes, one in each hand, and click together in imitation
- drops toys deliberately and watches them fall **(casting)**
- looks in correct place for toys that have rolled out of sight

- will crawl to retrieve rolling ball
- recognises familiar people at 6 metres
- watches movements of people, animals, cars etc. with great interest.

Communication
- knows and turns to own name
- jargons loudly in 'conversations', includes most vowel sounds
- understands about 20 words in context, for example cup, dog, dinner, and understands simple messages, for example 'Clap hands', 'Where are your shoes?'
- may hand adult common objects on request.

Eighteen months
Physical
- can walk alone with legs far apart
- drops from standing to sitting
- pushes and pulls toys when walking
- can walk downstairs with hand held
- tries to kick a ball, rolls and throws ball
- squats to pick objects from floor
- assists with dressing and undressing
- can use spoon with increasing skill
- uses delicate pincer grasp for tiny objects
- can build tower of two cubes
- holds crayon in primitive tripod grasp and scribbles
- turns handles
- pulls off shoes.

Social and emotional
- becoming more independent
- joyful and full of fun
- starts toilet training
- start of tantrums when upset
- has separate sense of self (egocentric – only concerned with his or her own view of the world)
- little idea of sharing and strong sense of 'mine'
- more demanding and assertive, emotionally volatile
- expresses rage at being told 'no'
- may have a comforter, such as soft doll or teddy.

Intellectual

- turns pages of books, several at a time, enjoys picture books and can point to a named object

- points to interesting objects outside

- points to parts of the body

- understands use of everyday objects, for example vacuum cleaner.

- helps to undress

- enjoys pretend play, for example talking on the phone.

Communication

- first words appear – uses six or more recognisable words, understands many more

- echoes prominent or last word in sentences

- tries to join in with nursery rhymes

- responds to simple instructions: 'Fetch your shoes,' 'Shut the door.'

Movers, shakers and players (18–24 months)

Two years old

Physical

- walks up and down stairs with both feet on one step

- climbs on furniture

- runs and changes direction

- opens, shuts doors and turns handles

- kicks ball without falling
- builds tower of six bricks
- uses spoon for self-feeding
- puts shoes on
- draws circles and dots
- starts to use preferred hand.

Social and emotional
- enjoys other children's company but reluctant to share toys
- needs clear boundaries and routines
- able to choose from limited range of options
- may show concern when another child is upset
- engages in parallel play (alongside others)
- remains egocentric
- becoming emotionally stable, but still prone to mood swings
- learning to separate from carer for short periods, for example while at nursery
- knows own identity.

Intellectual
- names and points to parts of the body
- recognises self in mirror
- draws and makes marks
- imitates household tasks
- is extremely curious
- enjoys simple puzzles and building towers.

Communication
- two words linked together
- uses more than 200 words by two years
- makes simple two-word sentences
- refers to own name, talks to self during play
- telegraphic speech – using key essential words and missing out connecting words
- rapidly expanding vocabulary, including plurals
- holds simple conversations
- enjoys repetition of favourite stories
- counts to ten.

Walkers, talkers and pretenders (24–36 months)

Three years old

Physical

- stands and walks on tiptoe
- can kick a ball confidently and throw overhead and catch with arms out
- jumps from low steps
- pedals tricycle
- turns single pages in book
- can copy a circle
- builds bridges with blocks when shown and tall towers
- undoes buttons
- threads large beads.

Social and emotional

- greater social awareness
- will play in twos or threes, sharing ideas
- may have close friends

- a lot of mixed play of the sexes
- stable and emotionally secure
- friendly to other children, increasing independence, but still needs support from adults
- fears loss of carers
- sense of gender, ethnic and cultural identity
- less anxious about separation but easily upset.

Intellectual
- copies circle and cross, draws man with head
- matches two or three primary colours
- can sort into simple categories
- paints with large brush, cuts with scissors
- will talk about paintings
- constantly asks 'why'
- confuses fact and fiction
- development of role and fantasy play
- remembers songs, rhymes and stories.

Communication
- imitates adult speech
- increasing vocabulary
- can listen well if interested
- grammar developing
- can describe feelings at simple level, for example happy, sad
- talks to self in play
- can be understood by strangers
- short, grammatically correct sentences
- knows parts of body, animals
- still making errors of tenses.

Theories of development

Over the years there have been several different theories about how and why babies and children develop. Some of these theories have influenced advice and guidance given to parents and carers. It is interesting to look at old child care books and see the differences in advice on leaving babies to cry, how often they should be played with and whether mothers should go back to work. All these points have been hotly debated in the past.

The general themes of developmental theory that you explored in Unit 1 obviously apply to babies and the under threes. However, some of them are especially relevant.

Bonding, attachment and communication

All babies need to develop close links with at least one important adult within the first year of their life. This is the start of a person's emotional security. John Bowlby (1907–90) was made famous by his research finding that if a baby has long separations from the main carer, or does not form an attachment to a main carer, there would be serious problems for the child in later life. It is unusual for this to happen, as all child care professionals are aware of the need to encourage the development of close bonds with consistent carers. It is usual for most babies to have close emotional links with several people.

The first close emotional bond is usually with the baby's mother. Before birth, the baby has been listening to the mother's voice, hearing her heart beat, and generally becoming familiar with the rhythms of the mother. In a normal delivery, the mother often holds the baby while the placenta is being delivered and a breast-feeding mother may start to feed at this point. If there are complications in the birth, every effort is made to ensure that the mother can hold or touch the baby as much as possible, even if the baby has to be in an **incubator**.

All this helps with the process of 'bonding', which is strengthened by:

- skin-to-skin contact
- eye-to-eye contact
- familiar sounds of voices
- familiar smells.

It is important for a baby to develop relationships with significant others. This not only allows more flexible caring, but is part of the process of primary socialisation. We cannot learn to develop relationships and mix with people in society generally until we have developed a range of relationships in our early months with different family members and other close carers. Ideally, a baby needs one or more constant caring figures, usually mother and father or grandparents. A good bonding relationship can and does develop with non-family members; you will see this yourself as you progress in your work with babies. If a baby is cared for outside the home, then the carer should not be constantly changing. Many settings now use a key worker system, where one person has the prime responsibility for a child.

Case study

Louie and Leila

Louie, aged nine months, attends a day nursery every day from 8 am to 6 pm. The baby room is staffed by whoever is available from the main nursery. Louie's mother is concerned because she never seems to see the same person when she drops Louie off or picks him up. Louie seems to be losing interest in nursery and cries or is miserable most of the time.

Leila is also aged nine months and attends a different nursery from 8 am to 6 pm. The baby room has its own team of staff, with two key workers responsible for each

baby. They are never on duty together, but have a good communication system to inform each other of how the babies are progressing. There is also a meeting once a week for the key workers to discuss 'their' babies. Leila's mother feels confident that she is leaving Leila with the same people all the time and Leila greets her carers with a big smile every morning.

Why do you think Leila and Louie react so differently to their day care?

Nature/nurture debate

One of the key debates about the potential for development is whether it is already predetermined by our **genetic** inheritance (nature) or influenced by our experiences and environment (nurture).

Many experiments and studies have been carried out, including studies on identical twins who have been separate since birth. After many years of debate a fairly balanced view is that we do inherit some aspects of development, while others are more influenced by our upbringing and environment.

Even our height can be influenced by the quality of our diet and may be affected by illness. Parental involvement and access to learning materials will influence the intellectual achievement of a child.

Have look back at Unit 1 where we explored the different influences on development.

What do you think has influenced aspects of your development?

Policies and procedures

Working with babies exposes you to humans during their most rapid period of development. Remember that all babies and children develop at very different rates. It is important, as a student, that you do not voice concerns about a baby's stage of development to parents or carers. It is very easy to upset parents unnecessarily by a casual remark, for example that Jane seems late in sitting up without help and that Ellie who is a month younger is already doing so. Any concern about any child you work with should be passed to your supervisor. Your concern may be about development or other issues, for example feeding or state of clothing but they should all be passed up the line. Some information may need recording in the child's day book, for example 'refused feed', but again always pass that information on. Information on babies is subject to the Data Protection Act. Parents can and do ask to see what is written about their child – be sure it is accurate and factual information.

Check out the policy and procedures in your setting.

Observations

Observing the progress in the development of a baby or young child is a fascinating activity and an excellent way to learn about the development of children and their needs.

Observations are also a requirement of the Foundation stage guidance for children aged three to school age and are included in the 'Birth to three matters' framework. However, there are a few ground rules that are vitally important to follow to protect the child and yourself:

- make sure you have a clear understanding of the normal range of development for the child you are observing

- remember the wide normal variations that can occur in any child's development

- always report any concerns you may think there are about any child's development to your supervisor, never directly to the child's parents

- never pass information about a child's development to anyone who does not need it, always go through your supervisor

- be sure to keep to the policies and procedures of your placement relating to observations

- remember that personal information on children and their parents is subject to the Data Protection Act and so is restricted in its distribution.

The term 'observation' can be used in a number of ways. An effective, skilled child care worker is constantly observing the children he or she works with. In being observant you can often identify things that need further investigation or simply note points of development. Observations can be:

- formal or

- informal.

Think about it

Find out what the Data Protection Act means to your placement. Look it up on the internet and ask your supervisor about the settings policy.

Informal observation

Case study

Informal observation

Jake was supervising a small group of toddlers. He noticed that Ruby, who was one and a half and usually very happy when playing, was very unsettled and kept crying. He then paid particular notice and noted that she seemed very flushed. When the session was over, Jake discussed Ruby with his supervisor. She had noticed that Ruby was not as settled as usual and ate very little lunch. That evening the supervisor had a word with Ruby's dad when he picked her up. He thanked the supervisor for noticing and said they would keep an eye on her at home. The next morning Ruby's parents rang the nursery to say that she was not well and they were taking her to the doctor.

This is an example of Jake and the supervisor making good use of informal observation. Can you identify the number of points they both noticed through informal observation?

Formal observation

Go back to Unit 1, pages 30 to 38. This section covers the important features and types of observation that apply to all observation activity. Can you remember these key points?

- observing is spending time to watch and record certain things about a child and then drawing conclusions from that record

- observations should be objective

- observations should be confidential.

Best practice in your work placement

How to carry out observations
- Always ask your supervisor before carrying out any observation on a child.
- Make sure that parents have consented to observations being carried out on their child.
- Carry out observations and assessments in line with your placement's policy.
- Make sure that you have everything you need to hand.
- Observe children sensitively and without them noticing.
- Write up your observations in a sensitive and non-judgemental way.
- Avoid making any negative judgements about children.
- Make sure that any conclusions are based directly on the observations.
- Share your findings with your supervisor so that they can be passed on to parents.

Think about it

There are a number of different observation techniques. Can you explain what these are?
- *checklists, tick charts*
- *written records/ snapshot observations*
- *time samples*
- *event samples.*

Assessment activities

Assessment Activity 1

You need to describe the development, including communication, of babies and young children in the first three years of life. You will need to build on what you already know from Unit 1.

You need to include the following:

- different aspects of development
- sequence and expected pattern of development
- acceptable range

- current theories, for example the nature/nurture debate
- current frameworks of effective practice, for example 'Birth to three matters'.

When you have completed this activity you will have met Pass criterion 1(P1), which requires you to describe the development, including communication, of babies and young children in the first three years of life.

Assessment Activity 2

You now need to know how to observe babies in the first three years of life.

In the first place you need to briefly describe the differences between formal and informal observation, explaining the need for formal observations.

Secondly, it is vital that you obtain permission from your supervisor and from the parents of the child you wish to observe.

You now need to carry out a few observations of babies and children, ensuring that you record your observations clearly and accurately using the format required by the setting.

Assessment Activity 3

Having observed and recorded your observations, you should share the information you have about the developmental progress of the babies and young children you have observed with your supervisor.

You should also report any concerns according to the procedures of your child care setting and identify areas of development that would benefit from more support.

Assessment Activity 4

Briefly describe the legislation relating to the use of personal information, for example the Data Protection Act.

When you have completed Activities 2, 3 and 4 you will have met the evidence required for

Pass criterion 2 (P2), for which you need to outline (briefly describe) what needs to be considered when observing babies and young children in the first three years of life.

continued ▶

Assessment Activity 5

You should now go on to explain (describe in detail what, how and why) how to undertake observations of babies and young children under three years. This enables you to meet Merit criterion 1 (M1).

Assessment Activity 6

You need to identify what can be learned about babies and young children in the first three years of life through observing them. When you have done this, you will have met Pass criterion 3 (P3).

Assessment Activity 7

You may now go on to justify (give the reasons for) the use of observation of babies and young children in the first three years of life. This will enable you to meet Distinction criterion 1 (D1).

7.2 Know how to help provide physical care requirements for babies and children under three

This section covers:

■ feeding

■ routine care

■ physical signs of illness.

Did you know?

As cows' milk was often contaminated before the mid twentieth century, many babies died if they were not breast fed. Wealthy families used 'wet nurses', working class women who were prepared to feed someone else's baby as well as, or instead of, their own baby. It was not until the early 1900s that milk started to be treated to make it free of bacteria and viruses.

Feeding

Infant feeding

National guidelines relating to the feeding of babies clearly state that breast feeding is best for babies until they are six months old. From three to four months, solids may be gradually introduced, avoiding cows' milk, wheat, nuts, eggs, salt and sugar. Weaning is dealt with in greater detail later in this section. The debate between breast and bottle feeding has raged on for many years. Until modern baby milks were produced, babies who could not be breast fed had to be fed on cows' milk which is totally unsuitable for babies under one year. Modern infant formula milks are scientifically modified to make them as near to human milk as possible.

Advantages of breast feeding

The main advantages of breast feeding are the following:

■ breast milk contains the right amounts of **nutrients**, at the right temperature, and is always available without risk of contamination

■ breast milk contains **antibodies** to boost the immunity gained in the uterus

■ it is less likely to result in an overweight baby

■ it helps delay or prevents eczema

■ it has little additional cost

■ it helps in the bonding process

■ it helps the uterus shrink more quickly

■ it delays the return of the mother's periods.

Advantages of bottle feeding

Although breast feeding is the ideal way of infant feeding, not all mothers wish to use this method, or they may not be able to breast feed, for example if they are taking certain prescription medication. There are claims that bottle feeding has some advantages in comparison to breast feeding:

- it is obvious how much milk the baby is taking

- there is no risk of embarrassment with public feeding

- other people can feed the baby, such as the father

- it helps a mother who is returning to work.

Parental choice

A child care professional's role in the choice between breast and bottle feeding is only to give impartial information if asked, and then support the parents in their choice. The choice about feeding is a personal one for the parents of the baby, with support from midwives, health visitors and doctors.

Breast feeding is one of the most natural functions of motherhood and when established is an immensely satisfying experience. It can take some time to establish a good feeding pattern and milk supply. Mothers who are breast feeding need support to ensure they have enough rest and a good diet to promote good milk production.

Mothers who are breast feeding may need help to find some privacy when feeding their baby. Discreet public feeding is possible, as mothers can usually find a quiet corner away from the public gaze and if some thought is given to clothing it is quite possible to feed a baby without anyone really being aware.

Never suggest or support a suggestion that a mother could use a public toilet to feed; would you like to have your lunch in such a place? Being informed about breast feeding and offering support is a role of child care workers.

Returning to work may need some thought if a baby is being breast fed. Some enlightened employers are supportive of mothers taking feeding breaks if the baby is near to mum's place of work. Working mothers can express milk and may use a breast pump. The milk should be kept in a sterilised bottle in the fridge until needed and then warmed and bottle fed to the baby. Some babies find it very difficult to adapt to taking milk from a rubber teat as it is a very different prospect to a human nipple. You also need to make sure that all the usual hygiene rules related to bottle feeding are followed to avoid the risk of contamination and infection.

Formula feeds

Current formula infant feeds are almost a replica of breast milk as they are manufactured to match the protein and salts in breast milk. In one important respect, however, formula feeds cannot match breast milk: the antibodies that are passed on from mother to baby in breast milk cannot be replaced in formula milk. However, a well-prepared formula bottle given in a caring environment with close interaction between baby and feeder can be a satisfying experience for both parties.

Poor practice in bottle feeding can, however, be dangerous and unsatisfying for a baby. Poor hygiene and preparation of bottle feeds can lead to potentially fatal gastro-enteritis. 'Prop' feeding can result in choking, and not stimulating the bond between carer and baby can lead to emotional problems.

Equipment for feeding

Large chemists and baby shops have a wide range of bottles, sterilisers and associated equipment that, if added together, would be very expensive. There are some essentials for formula feeding:

- feeding bottles: up to 12 to allow rotation and advance preparation

- teats with holes of a suitable size to allow milk to flow without choking the baby

- covers for the teats, usually a top for the bottle that allows the teat to be put upside down in the bottle during storage in the fridge

- bottle brush and teat cleaner

- sterilising equipment

- clean surface to prepare feeds

- a clean and safe water supply (especially important in developing countries).

Sterilising the bottles and equipment used in bottle feeding is essential to kill the bacteria that thrive in warm milk. There is no substitute for sterilising and it must be done after each use of a bottle and teat. The first stage in sterilising is a thorough wash in hot soapy water, paying particular attention to the inside of the teat and the curves and edges of the bottle using a bottle brush. After rinsing, the equipment then needs sterilising.

There are several methods of sterilising:

- steaming, using a special device, takes about ten minutes and equipment is then sterile for up to three hours

- cold water sterilising uses a solution made from tablets or concentrated solution; the bottles should be soaked for a minimum time, usually 30 minutes, and they remain sterile for up to 24 hours

- boiling for at least five minutes; this tends to damage plastic bottles if used regularly and equipment will need re-sterilising if not used within three hours

- microwaving, using a special unit that fits in the microwave, takes about ten minutes and the effect lasts for two to three hours.

Following the common sense rules of hygiene is the first step on the road to safe feeding. The table below examines the principles of good practice.

	Action needed	Comments
Environment (kitchen)	Clean, dry worktops No other foodstuffs around Keep pets, etc. from surfaces	Contamination can easily occur due to carelessness
Operator (person preparing feed)	Always wash hands before starting work Do not touch any surface or equipment that will come into contact with milk Avoid touching the head, face, etc. during preparation Carefully read and follow the exact instructions on formula and sterilising solution packets Exact quantities of milk powder and water should be used	Risk of contamination and bacteria Very easy to make a feed that is too strong or too weak as proportions are carefully calculated by the manufacturer
Equipment (bottles, teats, etc.)	All should be assembled before the start of preparation All bottles, teats, jugs, spoons must be thoroughly cleaned in hot soapy water, rinsed and left fully immersed in sterilising solution for minimum recommended time Formula should be checked as fresh and within date of use on packet Check that the water supply is a safe supply and water is boiled before use	Milk and milk residue is an ideal medium for bacteria to breed Even a tiny amount of residue under a bottle rim can be enough to cause illness in a baby if bacteria multiply Any food stuff deteriorates with age and may cause harm if not within the use-by date Water supplies can carry bacteria that can cause gastro-enteritis. This can kill small babies due to the dehydration caused by vomiting and diarrhoea
Storage	Packets of formula should be kept in a dry cupboard, tops safely and securely closed Bottles should be kept in refrigerator when made, teats covered Bottles should never be left out at room temperature Contents of part-used bottles should be disposed of	All important to prevent contamination and potential gastro-enteritis

- *Rules of good hygiene*

Giving a baby a stronger feed is dangerous because the feed will contain too much protein and too many salts; a baby's body cannot cope with this and convulsions and brain damage could occur as the body dehydrates. Too high a concentration of salts can lead to kidney damage. To avoid accidentally making the feed too strong:

- always check the number of scoops of powder that are needed

- only use the scoop provided in the packet

- do not be tempted to use heaped scoops; level off the powder with a plastic knife

- always read and follow the directions on the packet.

Giving the feed

There is no nutritional benefit in warming a bottle feed, but if it is heated to a suitable temperature it will be more enjoyable for the baby.

- Heat the bottle in a commercial bottle warmer or in a jug of water. Never use a microwave oven as there is a serious risk of hot spots in the milk in the bottle that will scald the baby's mouth and digestive tract.

- Check the temperature is correct and not too hot. A test of the temperature should always be carried out (not by having a sample yourself). Your inner wrist is a sensitive area of skin and this should be used for testing purposes. The feed is at the correct temperature if a few drops sprinkled on the inside of your wrist feel comfortable.

- Sit in a comfortable position with the baby. Be sure he or she can see your face and is in close contact. Talk to the baby while you are feeding.

- Make sure the bottle is tilted to ensure the teat is filled with milk – this will prevent air being swallowed with the milk. If the baby swallows a lot of air the resulting wind and pain will disrupt the feed. However, some air is needed in the bottle as the feed is taken because as the milk is taken in by the baby a vacuum (no air) results in the bottle and it can be very difficult for the baby to take the milk in.

- After a few minutes remove the teat from the baby's mouth and allow air into the bottle to prevent a vacuum forming.

- Whenever possible, the baby should be fed by the main carer, so that the same bonding will take place that breast feeding promotes. Whoever feeds the baby must ensure it is done in a comfortable position that allows for eye contact and close bodily contact. Talking and smiling to the baby is an important part of the feeding experience.

- Remember that a baby should never be left alone to feed from a bottle that has been propped up, because:
  - there is a high risk of choking
  - the baby is being deprived of important contact with the carer
  - too much air will be taken in.

Case study

Running late

Charlotte has slept in this morning. She is supposed to be meeting her friend in town for a day's shopping and is very late. Her baby is crying, so she rushes down to the kitchen and takes the last bottle of milk out of the fridge. She pops it in the microwave to heat and then props the bottle up with a pillow so that her baby can reach the teat and take her feed while Charlotte makes another bottle to take out with her. She puts the kettle on, grabs a bottle from the pile of dirty dishes beside the sink and gives it a quick rinse under the hot tap. She finds the formula but cannot find a measuring spoon so she scoops a few teaspoons of powder into the bottle before adding the boiling water. She quickly packs a couple of nappies and the newly made bottle into a bag before putting the baby into her pram and setting off to meet her friend and have a day out at the shops.

1 Make a list of all the mistakes that Charlotte has made.

2 What might happen as a result of these mistakes?

Weaning

Weaning is the term used to describe the process of changing a child's feeding from being dependent on milk to eating family foods. A new-born baby does not have the digestive system to cope with solid foods. A baby of one year has a more mature system able to cope with different foods. The process of learning to enjoy a wide range of foods can be an easy one or it can be difficult for carers and the baby alike.

The important thing to remember about weaning is the purpose of it, which is to safely introduce children into the normal eating patterns of their family by familiarising them with a wide range of new tastes. Trying to rush the process can at best overwhelm a child's taste buds and at worst cause health problems through the use of inappropriate foods.

Think about it

There are many fashions related to weaning. Ask your parents and grandparents when they weaned their children and what foods they used, and you will probably receive several different answers. Parents in the UK may say they started their child on baby rice, while parents in Israel may have used avocado pear as a first weaning food.

■ *Everyone has their own tastes!*

It is very easy for carers of children to transfer their own food dislikes to them. How difficult is it to feed a baby with something you dislike? Think about your body language and facial expressions if you are in that situation.

Starting the weaning process

There are national guidelines relating to the start of weaning and it is a good idea to try to collect some government leaflets from baby clinics to check on the latest guidelines. The UK and Irish Department of Health guidelines of August 2005 recommend that a baby should have nothing but infant milk for the first six months of life. The guidelines recognise that all babies develop at a different rate but advise that it is not a good idea to introduce solid food before they are twenty weeks old because the digestive system and kidneys are too immature to cope.

A baby could thrive very well on milk alone until the age of 12 months but at this age, the iron stores from birth will be diminishing and the baby will be at risk of becoming anaemic. Leaving the start as late as 12 months could make it difficult for a baby to make the change from a breast or bottle to eating from a spoon.

Within the guidelines, the best judge of when to wean a baby is the baby him or herself. Babies are ready to start weaning when they:

■ are still hungry after feeds

■ can sit up

■ show interest in solid food

■ pick up food and put it in their mouth

■ want to chew.

Sucking the fists is not a sign of being ready for weaning; this is a normal part of development as the baby has found how interesting his or her hands are.

There are several stages involved in weaning, as shown in the table below. Progress from each stage should be led by the baby. There is no clear age at which each stage should be reached but by their first birthday a child should be eating most family foods – even if some are cut up very small or mashed.

Weaning stage	Suggested foods
First stage (ideally from 6 months) Sloppy, slightly thicker than milk foods	Bland tastes Thickened milk – baby rice Pureed or stewed apple, banana, avocado
Second stage Thickness increasing, but no lumps	Increase variety and strength of taste First stage commercial foods Home-made pureed vegetables with gravy, for example carrots, yam, sweet potato Fruit and custard

continued ▶

Weaning stage	Suggested foods
Third stage Food less pureed – coping with thicker texture and some lumpiness Starting to finger feed	Introducing slightly lumpier texture
	Home-made food mashed with fork: potatoes, vegetables, fish, fruits
	Rusks, bread crusts, peeled pieces of apple, mango or banana, cubes of cheese
Fourth stage (by 12 months) Eating most family foods	Using family foods, avoiding tough or stringy textures
	Very little that cannot be offered

■*Stages of weaning*

Commercial and home produced weaning food

Nutritionally there is little difference between commercial baby food in jars or packets and home produced weaning food. Commercial food can be expensive and the consistency is often unlike ordinary food. As a result, some parents will only feed a baby home produced food, which is fine but can be difficult if the family is out for the day or the rest of the family are having a meal that is spicy or otherwise unsuitable. A sensible mix of commercial and home food is a good compromise. Home produced weaning food is nearer in texture and taste to the child's eventual diet, but can take time and effort to prepare.

Think about it

Investigate all the different commercial weaning food available in supermarkets, chemist's shops, etc. How easy do you think it would be to provide similar foods at home?

How to start weaning

1 Offer the first spoonfuls of a bland, very liquid mix, part way through a milk feed or near the end, when the first pangs of hunger have been satisfied.
2 Introduce new tastes gradually. Offer only one new taste a day in the first months of weaning and if a new food is rejected one day, try it again later; it may then be accepted with pleasure.
3 Gradually thicken food, eventually mashing it with a fork.
4 As the amount of solid food increases, the amount of milk feed offered should be reduced. By the time a baby is eating three substantial meals of solids a day, milk feeds should be reduced to night-time, with water or fresh juice between meals and at mealtimes.
5 As soon as the baby starts trying, let him or her join in feeding, even though everything will fall off the spoon and it will go anywhere but in the mouth.
6 Offer finger foods as much as possible, for example lumps of cheese, apple pieces, small sandwiches. (It is no coincidence that a baby is ready to start self-feeding when his or her gross and fine motor skills have reached the stage of sitting up and a pincer grip.)
7 A vital piece of equipment at this stage is a sheet of plastic to protect the floor if it is not washable.

A suggested day's menu as a baby progresses towards a normal family diet could be like the one shown below.

Time of day	Daily diet 6–9 months	Daily diet 9–12 months	Daily diet 12+ month
On waking	Breast or bottle feed	Breast or bottle feed	Drink of milk
Breakfast	Baby breakfast cereal with pureed fruit	Porridge made with 90 ml infant/follow-on milk	1 slice of toast, Weetabix with milk, well-diluted orange juice
Mid-morning	4 satsuma segments	2 breadsticks and cheese cubes	Carrot sticks and chickpea puree (hummus)
Lunch	3 tbs broccoli and potato with cheesy sauce, 90 ml infant/follow-on milk, chopped melon pieces	1 hard boiled egg with soldiers, 1 fromage frais, 90 ml water or well-diluted orange juice	Scrambled egg on toast, banana and custard, 90 ml water or well-diluted orange juice
Mid-afternoon	Half a small mashed banana or mango, water as a drink	Toast fingers, water as a drink	90 ml fruit smoothie, 1 pitta bread or bread with cheese or ham
Tea	Tomato sauce with mince and pasta shapes, 90 ml follow-on milk 1 small yogurt	Shepherd's pie with meat or lentils, broccoli, carrots 1 banana, water or juice	Fish pie and vegetables, seedless grapes or stewed fruit, water or juice
Evening	Breast or bottle feed	Breast or bottle feed	Breast feed or milk

■ *Suggested day's menu for 6–12 months plus*

Nutritional requirements

The general guidelines of a healthy diet that you looked at in Unit 4 apply to children and babies who are being weaned. However, there are one or two differences until their digestive system is fully mature.

- From nine months, each day a baby needs:
  - □ 3–4 servings of starchy food
  - □ 3–4 helpings of fruit and vegetables
  - □ 2 servings of protein
  - □ vitamin drops until they are five years old.

Babies have small tummies and need energy for growth.

- They should have full-fat dairy products but no cows' milk as a drink until one year old.

- Never give a child nuts until the age of five years as there is a strong risk of allergy and also of choking.

- Avoid products containing wheat until at least six months of age. Some babies are allergic to the gluten in wheat, resulting in coeliac disease.

- Eggs should be well cooked and only offered after six months.

- Citrus food and shellfish should not be given before six months.

- Never add extra salt at all and avoid salty products until 12 months.

- Avoid honey, soft and blue cheese until 12 months.

Feeding problems

It is rare for a child to make the transition to everyday family meals without a few tears and tantrums on the way. Many children are seen to have a food problem at some time. The approach that carers take is an important part of dealing with this.

Refusing food at a designated mealtime is not a problem. Any child who has food offered in a relaxed, thoughtful manner will eat as much as he or she needs if opportunities are provided. This continues throughout childhood; eating and not eating only become a problem if the child's carers see them as a problem. Babies have every right not to eat if they are not feeling hungry, in the same way as you have. Why would a toddler want to sit down and eat when he or she is in the middle of an exciting play activity or investigating what is in the cupboard in the hallway? Sometimes a child is simply too busy, too tired or still full from the last meal to want to eat. Simply removing the plate and letting the child go back to play is the best approach.

Supporting parents' wishes

Feeding a baby can be a difficult and emotional topic for parents. Many people see a thriving child as the sign of 'good' parenting. A child who does not eat well could be regarded as not being cared for properly.

We develop our attitudes to food from a very early age, from our parents and our own experiences. Parents can become upset about what their child is or is not eating and many parents come under pressure from grandparents. Despite being aware of the latest healthy diet issues, they may find it hard not to follow their own parents' suggestions. Child care workers may need to offer support to parents in encouraging healthy eating in their babies. However, it is important to remember that parents are responsible for their child's diet.

As far as possible child care settings should follow the wishes of parents in all aspects of care unless there are health and safety issues at stake. This applies particularly to food. Parents are the most informed about their children's needs and requesting they do not eat a certain food may be for a reason you are not aware of:

- Cultural variations should always be respected when you are designing menus for young children.

- Always avoid offering 'forbidden' foods, such as pork to Muslims or meat to vegetarians.

- Always follow instructions about children's allergies to certain foods as failing to do so could cause a child to die. Remember that the allergen could be hidden in a seemingly innocent food so you must always read food labels.

Did you know?

Many people who are overweight or suffer from eating problems, for example anorexia or bulimia, remember mealtimes as a battle zone in childhood.

Think about it

Survey the menus of all the babies at your placement. Do they all eat the standard menu of the nursery? If they do, find out what provision there is for following parents' wishes where they have different requirements for their child's diet. How would the nursery support those parents?

■ *Find out what children eat at home*

Routine care

Babies and children under three years need help with their personal hygiene including:

- washing and dressing
- care of the skin
- care of hair
- care of teeth
- changing nappies
- helping with toilet training.

At birth a baby may not like being disturbed and changed but by the age of three a young child will be doing much of the task involved for themselves with minimal support from adults. It is important to respond to the individual child in the way you handle them bearing in mind these important points:

- always be gentle when changing a baby, think about the way their limbs move and always lift them firmly under the arms using both hands
- always support the head according to the baby's stage of development
- keep undressing and handling for very young babies to a minimum
- encourage older babies to 'help' with dressing by pushing arms through sleeves

- remember that even young babies require attention to their dignity and privacy during changing

- make sure you are respecting parental wishes at all times with regard to lotions, clothes etc.

- always be sure you have everything you need before starting any task

- never leave a baby alone on a changing surface; ask someone else to fetch something you need.

Washing and care of skin

It is unlikely that you would be in a situation of bathing a baby in your placement as bathing is something that is part of parenting a baby and is usually done at home. However, babies and young children need frequent washing as it can be very dirty work being a baby!

A baby's skin can very easily become sore as they have very sensitive skin. Even with the highest standard of care, babies can get rashes or sore spots. The key principles for caring for baby's skin are:

- hands and faces must be cleaned after feeds

- never share cleaning cloths between children

- always carefully dry the skin

- nappy areas must be cleaned regularly especially when changing a dirty nappy

- skin creases, for example armpits, neck, groin need care to keep them dry

- avoid the use of perfumed products that can irritate sensitive skins

- use creams etc. as advised by parents

- never poke around in a child's ears with cotton buds; just clean around the outside with cotton wool if necessary

- baby boys' foreskins should be left alone and they should not be pulled back at this age.

Washing and changing a baby is a good opportunity to notice any skin problems. Some of the common ones are shown in the table following.

Dressing

Parents will have provided the clothes for babies in your care but there a few basic points about baby clothes that are important to remember:

- natural fibres are more comfortable to wear as they absorb perspiration

- two or three thin layers of clothing are better than one very thick layer; clothing can then be adjusted to suit the temperature

- overheating can be dangerous for a baby

- clothes that are machine washable are easier to care for

- clothes should be loose and easy to put on and take off

Problem	Description	Cause	Treatment
Sweat rash (milaria)	Rash of small red spots on face and chest	Overheating Immature sweat glands	Cool child down by removing clothes Use cotton next to skin and avoid synthetic fibres Avoid overheating with clothes and room heating
Cradle cap	Yellow/brown crusting on the scalp, particularly on anterior fontanelle (soft spot)	Build-up of sebum	Soften with olive oil or baby shampoo and rinse well – special shampoos are also available
Chafing	Soreness in body creases, for example neck, groin and armpits	Insufficient washing and drying of skin Excessive sweating	Prevent by good skin care, especially in the neck area due to baby dribbling. Apply mild cream, for example zinc and castor oil
Eczema	Sore red rash, may affect face or any part of the body, particularly skin folds – can be very severe, with bleeding and weeping due to scratching	Usually an allergic response, possibly to cows' milk or detergents	Requires medical treatment Avoid soap and using bio detergents for washing clothes. Keep nails short to stop scratching Use emulsifiers in the bath Breast feeding helps to lessen severity and delay onset

■ Common skin problems

■ avoid ribbons and cords that could easily cut off the circulation around a finger or neck

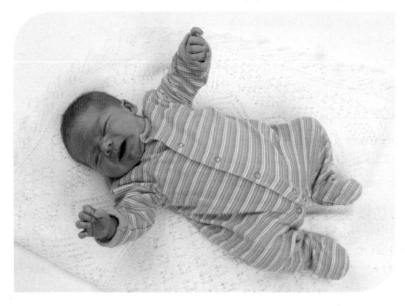

■ all materials should be flame resistant

■ care should be taken with clothes that have feet in them, for example stretch 'babygro' suits. It is important to check frequently that there is enough room for the baby's feet to move as wearing too tight a suit will damage the soft, growing bones of the feet.

Hair care

Babies have very fine hair and if it is fairly long it can tangle easily and need careful brushing. As they grow and start to eat solids, food can easily get mixed up in their hair in which case it needs careful sponging out.

If you need to brush a baby's hair ensure you use a soft brush which must be only used for that baby.

Some cultural groups have specific requirements for hair care. For example, many Afro-Caribbean babies have their hair braided into plaits that stay intact during washing.

Think about it

Find out about any particular hair styles and care that apply to children in your placement.

Care of teeth

Teething is a big event in the development of a baby. The arrival of a baby's first tooth is often a cause for celebration but also of discomfort for some babies.

The usual pattern of the arrival of teeth is:

- bottom front teeth at around four to seven months
- two middle top teeth
- teeth along the sides from front to back
- second molars at the back at around age 12 months.

By the age of three most children have a full set of 20 baby teeth which a child should keep until the second teeth start to appear around the age of six years.

Teeth need careful care even before they start to appear. Good care of the teeth includes:

- avoiding sweet drinks in bottles and soothers
- limiting the amount of fruit juice as it contains acid that can damage the teeth
- encouraging children to drink plain water
- avoiding foods with sugar
- wiping gums before teeth appear with a piece of gauze after feeding
- brushing teeth as soon as they appear with a soft brush twice a day
- only using a very small pea size amount of toothpaste under supervision to avoid swallowing.

Nappy changing

Disposable nappies have taken over in the past 20 years, with the result that millions of dirty paper and plastic nappies must be destroyed daily. Disposable nappies are convenient as they do not require washing or carrying around if you are out, but they are very expensive and present society with the big problem of disposal. A move back to using terry

Did you know?

When William Cadogen was writing about childcare in 1748 he suggested babies should be changed just once a day!

nappies is slowly gaining ground. You may find yourself caring for a baby who uses them, so being able to change one is a useful skill.

The best way to learn the mechanics of changing a nappy is to watch a competent person. The folding of terry nappies is almost an art form and there are many ways to do it depending on the size and sex of the baby. This is one of their advantages as the nappy can be folded to be thickest at the position of urination. The same sized terry serves a tiny 3 kg baby and a bouncing two-year-old. They need to be covered with some form of plastic outer to prevent wetness coming through and are often used with a thin paper lining to make the disposal of faeces easier. There are also tailored varieties of terry nappies available. Disposable nappies come in many different sizes and shapes with a range of special compounds to absorb wetness, built-in cream to prevent soreness, etc.

The following procedure for changing a nappy is recommended.

- Wash your hands.

- Collect all your equipment: nappy, water, soap, cotton wool or baby wipes, cream, changing mat, bucket or bag for the dirty nappy.

- Always wear gloves and follow the policy of the setting.

- After removing the nappy, clean the baby's bottom. If the nappy is a dirty one this will need greater care than if the nappy is wet. Using clean water is fine, but baby wipes contain a solution to neutralise ammonia and so help to prevent nappy rash.

- When cleaning female babies, always clean from front to back to avoid introducing infection into the vagina. With boys, try to avoid soiling the foreskin area.

- Apply a protective barrier cream if used. Be careful not to get cream on the adhesive fixings of a disposable nappy; if you do they will not stick.

- Put the nappy on, being very careful with nappy pins if used, and dress the baby.

- Dispose of the soiled nappy. Roll it up and put it into a nappy sack if disposable. If it is a terry nappy, dispose of the paper liner and put the nappy into a bucket of sterilising solution.

- Wash your hands.

Terry nappies should be washed after soaking in solution at a temperature of at least 60 degrees centigrade and in non-biological powder. They should be rinsed thoroughly.

Nappy rash

Nappy rash appears as a red, sore area over the buttocks. In severe cases it can look like chafing. Sometimes a baby can develop thrush on the buttocks; this can be seen as small outbreaks of spot-type lesions away from the main red area. Medical advice is needed to deal with a nappy rash caused by thrush.

Think about it

Have a look at the range of nappies used by babies in your placement. Are they all disposable or are some parents using terry nappies of some sort?

A barrier cream applied to the napkin area is useful to prevent nappy rash and petroleum jelly is a good standby. There are many different creams on the market, all claiming efficiency, but few babies will reach the age of two without ever having a nappy rash.

The first defence to prevent nappy rash is to ensure a baby does not spend too long in a wet nappy and certainly never leave a baby in a wet and dirty nappy. Applying a barrier cream is a second defence. All babies will benefit from spending some time each day without a nappy on. A warm room and a covered mat on the floor are a suitable place to let the child have time without a nappy.

Toilet training

Children are not in nappies for ever. As a child's body develops they start around 18–24 months to become aware when their bowels and bladder are full and need emptying. This is the ideal time to start toilet training.

There is often great pressure on parents to toilet train children as soon as possible, but trying to get a child to use the toilet too early can lead to many problems. Sometimes there almost seems to be a 'race' between parents to see whose child is 'dry' earliest! Early years settings too can often inadvertently put pressure on parents by admission policies, which only allow children over three who are toilet trained to come to the setting.

Remember these points when helping children with their toilet training:

- only start when the child is ready – this varies with every child

- toilet training takes time, for example it can take three months for the child to get the idea and then this will still only be daytime success

- girls appear to be easier to toilet train than boys, but no one really knows why.

A child is ready to start toilet training when the following signs appear.

- The child begins to have bowel movements more regularly and often at predictable times, for example in the morning after breakfast.

- The child can try to pull pants up and down and shows an interest in wearing pants rather than nappies.

- There are signs of awareness that a bowel movement is happening such as grunting, squatting, telling you, etc. The child has words for stool and urine such as 'poo' and 'wee' (it is helpful to find out what words the family uses for these bodily functions so that a child with minimal language can be readily understood).

- Toddlers begin to show that they understand the feelings they have in their bodies which mean they need to 'go'. Over time they will be able to signal or tell you that they need the potty or the toilet. In the early stages, signals such as the child holding him or herself in the groin area, wriggling, looking uncomfortable or pulling at clothing may all be letting you know that the child is aware of different sensations.

Think about it

Does your placement allow children over a certain age who are not toilet trained to attend? How do they support children and parents with toilet training?

- The child may dislike the feeling of being in a dirty nappy and nappies can be dry for a few hours at a time.

It is important that a child is starting to want to be independent and do things for him or herself. Being able to manage bodily functions is a huge step towards becoming independent.

The child must also be able to physically walk and sit down safely and comfortably. This may seem obvious but these are all skills that have to be learned.

There are some times in a toddler's life when it is not a good idea to try toilet training:

- if the family is moving house
- at the time of arrival of a new baby
- changes in parental relationships
- illness
- changes in care settings or even carers.

Toilet training requires a lot of learning and effort on the part of the child, so not asking them to cope with too many new things at once is helpful.

Did you know?

At one time parents were encouraged to put babies as young as two weeks old on a potty to try to turn the reflex post-feed bowel emptying into a habit!

Best practice in your work placement

Toilet training

- Parents' wishes should be followed to make sure there is consistency between home and setting.
- Take things slowly. Some children become dry during the day very quickly and others take much longer, so be patient.
- Do praise the child when successful but do not make such a fuss that the child begins to become anxious and fretful.
- Do not make a fuss if a child has an 'accident'. Toilet training like any other skill needs lots of practice so 'accidents' are bound to happen. **Never** make a child feel stupid or 'bad' if they wet or mess their pants.
- Do not put pressure on the child – slow and steady is the rule, and be guided by the child's pace. If the child starts to appear anxious or worried, do not persist.
- Gentle encouragement, stories, songs and fun potties or using the toilet with specially adapted seats and steps are all good ideas, so long as the child does not see going to the toilet as a 'performance' which must be achieved at all costs.

Hygiene, health and safety

Babies and young children are vulnerable and need protection. Have a look back at Unit 2 to remind yourself about how to keep all children safe.

There are some basic, essential rules which should always be followed when working with any child, but are particularly important with babies.

1   Always wash your hands:
   - before picking up a baby

   - before preparing or giving feeds

   - after changing a baby

   - after taking older children or yourself to the toilet

   - after playing with pets.

2   Poor attention to hygiene and safety can be serious:
   - never reuse a partly finished bottle of feed

   - never leave a bottle of feed out at room temperature

   - always keep bottle teats covered when not in use

   - always test the temperature of a bottle feed – check it on the back of your hand

   - do not allow other children or pets to touch spoons or dishes that are for a baby's food

   - never prop feed a baby, that is, leave a baby in a pram or seat with the bottle propped up on a pillow, etc.

   - never thicken a baby's bottle with rice or rusk otherwise babies may choke

   - always supervise an older baby when eating, particularly hard foods such as rusks or apple

   - never give a child anything containing a food product they are allergic to.

3   Always remember that young children and babies in particular, have no sense of danger. They need protecting from:
   - animals, even family pets

   - dangers from heat, household objects, etc.

   - falls as they become more mobile; a baby should never be left alone on a surface above ground level

   - other children who may injure them through exuberance or jealousy.

4   Avoid exposing babies to known infections, although this is not always easy, as many conditions are infectious before symptoms appear.

Think about it

What are the policies and procedures in your placement to protect babies and young children?

5   Always put a baby to sleep on his or her back, with the feet at the bottom of the cot, and use blankets that can be tucked in and will not billow over the face. This will help to prevent sudden infant death syndrome (cot death).

6   Never smoke in a room where a baby may be cared for or anywhere near to a baby or child. Apart from the risks associated with passive smoking, the effects of smoking by a baby's carers is a high risk factor involved in **sudden infant death syndrome**.

Physical signs of illness

Babies can become ill very quickly. Minor symptoms that an adult would not worry about can rapidly cause serious illness or death in a baby. If you are ever worried about a baby's health, speak to your supervisor as a matter of urgency.

Some conditions need urgent medical help by dialling 999 for an ambulance:

- stopping breathing or going blue
- not responding, floppy or glazed expression
- cannot be woken up
- having a fit or convulsion
- vomiting with a fever and/or diarrhoea
- any injury
- unusual or high pitched crying
- difficulty in breathing.

Babies are prone to many other types of health problems that can cause concern to parents and carers. If a carer is concerned, medical help or advice should be sought from the family doctor practice or through phoning NHS Direct or taking the child to an NHS Walk in Centre. This applies to the following conditions:

- fever with a headache or stiff neck
- fever that does not settle
- earache or discharge from ears
- pain in the head
- vomiting for more than 12 hours
- refusing several feeds
- any blood in the faeces
- painful urinating or blood
- any bad smelling discharge
- abdominal pain

- cuts or scrapes that ooze pus or are red and inflamed
- sudden rashes or large areas of blisters
- sore throat causing difficulty swallowing.

Always seek help if you are worried by letting your supervisor know in the first instance. Medical staff would far rather see a baby unnecessarily than risk a tragedy.

Assessment activities

Assessment Activity 8

You need to describe feeding for babies and children under three years. There is a lot to cover here and it must include the following:

- preparation of formula feeds according to the manufacturer's instructions
- correct sterilisation of equipment
- bottle feeding in line with current practice, parental wishes and the needs of the baby
- storage of expressed breast milk
- care of skin, teeth, hair
- help with toilet training.

Assessment Activity 9

Part of physical care is to know the signs of illness in babies and young children. Describe:

- the signs and symptoms of common illnesses
- how to recognise common illnesses
- the appropriate responses that should be taken.

You have now covered the evidence needed in order for you meet Pass criterion 4 (P4), which requires you to describe the feeding and routine care of babies and young children under three years.

Assessment Activity 10

You can now go on to explain (describe in detail) how babies and young children under three years should be fed and cared for safely. This enables you to meet Merit criterion 2 (M2).

7.3 Understand how to provide play activities to encourage learning and development

This section covers:

- play activities
- links with development
- procedures and practice.

Play activities

It is never too early to learn. Babies and young children benefit from new experiences and learn through a variety of activities, interaction with people and by exploring the world around them. If you think about the four features of the early years as defined by 'Birth to three matters' you have a good guide to the type of activities you can use to encourage learning and development in babies and young children.

A strong child

Between the ages of birth and three, a child finds out who they are, what they like and what they can do. They experiment with different ways of relating to those around them and need to be recognised and valued.

Play and practical activities include:

- providing a variety of mirrors in different places to help babies explore what they look like and who they are
- letting children make decisions about how and where to display their paintings or allow them to select which toys to play with
- using different voices to tell stories and getting children to join in wherever possible, using puppets or soft toys
- providing dressing up clothes and materials that help children find out what it feels like to be someone else
- providing experiences that involve using all the senses, such as relaxing music, soft lighting and pleasant smells.

Encouragement and support help children develop emotionally and respond to successes and challenges.

A skilful communicator

As a child grows, he or she becomes increasingly sociable, learns to communicate effectively, understand others and make choices.

Play and practical activities include:

- role playing and dressing up, visits to parks, shops, libraries, encouraging children to take on roles, meet others and express feelings and thoughts

- listening to tapes of rhymes and stories, spoken words; some that require children to respond, others that engage them to listen

- responding to what children show they are interested in and want to do by providing activities, stories and games

- providing opportunities for babies to make choices, for example which spoon to choose, which bib to wear, the size of paintbrush to use, whether to go outdoors or stay in.

A competent learner

Drawings, words and imaginative play encourage a child to explore and develop his or her creativity. Play and practical activities include:

- resources for babies to play with, for example pots and pans, wooden blocks, soft toys

- diaries or photographs where children record an important occasion such as visiting a special place

- opportunities to play with sand, water and play dough

- collections of everyday objects such as wooden pegs, spoons, pans, corks, cones and boxes that can be safely explored alone, shared with adults or other children.

A healthy child

As a child grows he or she learns to express feelings and cope with new situations. A child develops physical skills and learns about his or her body. They also learn about boundaries, rules and asking for help.

Play and practical activities include:

- stories, pictures and puppets which allow children to experience and talk about feelings

- a consistent approach when responding to challenging behaviour such as scratching and biting

- non-specific play materials such as boxes and blankets so that play can move in different directions.

Age groupings

The four age groupings are also useful to think about (see page 247). Some activities are difficult to classify as supporting only one aspect of development but many will have a key focus and it is worth trying to balance the activities throughout a period of time.

Heads up, lookers and communicators (0–8 months)

Aspect of development	Suggested activities
Motor development	Time to enjoy freedom of kicking in the bath or on a changing mat without a nappy
	Playing with hands and feet while changing or washing
	Noisy paper to kick against
	Finger games, for example 'This little piggy'
Hand-eye coordination	Mobiles hung over cot, chair, changing mat
	Objects to hold and look at with a range of textures
Social and emotional	Cuddles
Intellectual, including creative skills	Brightly coloured pictures and objects
	Watching trees in the wind
Language and communication	Singing and talking to baby
	Imitating a baby's noises and expressions
	Sound-making toys such as rattles
	Songs and movement

Sitters, standers and explorers (8–18 months)

Aspect of development	Suggested activities
Motor development	Stacking and nesting toys
	Playing ball
	New experiences using the body, for example swimming
	Encouraging mobility by putting toys slightly out of reach
	Push and pull toys, toys that make sounds or pop up when a button is pressed, etc.
Hand-eye coordination	Mirrors
	Building stacks and knocking them down using toy bricks, boxes
Social and emotional	Household opportunities, for example pots and pans, boxes, cans
	Games cleaning teeth, brushing hair
	Outdoor trips to the park, shops, to see the cows
Intellectual, including creative skills	Great enjoyment of water play, for example in the bath with toys, in small washing up bowl
	A treasure box made from a strong cardboard box with changing items aimed at different senses
	Large, easy-to-hold crayons with big sheets of card to scribble on
	Books with bright pictures to look at
	Simple hide and seek with increasing difficulty
Language and communication	Action songs, for example 'The wheels on the bus'
	Constant communication

Movers, shakers and players (18–24 months)

Aspect of development	Suggested activities
Motor development	Blowing bubbles and blowing out candles
	Riding toys
Hand-eye coordination	Music and rhythm toys, including 'home made' as well as bought instruments, music boxes and music tapes
	Peg boards and work benches
Social and emotional	'Grown-up' items such as keys, pens, bags and hats of all kinds
	Games that include getting, hiding and retrieving objects
	Make-believe games and resources to support fantasy play, such as materials from different cultures, dressing up clothes, props such as puppets, etc.
Intellectual, including creative skills	Show and label pictures – put the pictures in context
	Art supplies for mark making, painting, play dough or clay
Language and communication	Talking about what is happening now and what happened this morning, yesterday, what you might do together tomorrow
	Talking about the child's day-to-day experience such as 'What did you have for lunch today?'
	Reading and talking about books or picture books with repeated words, rhymes and phrases that a toddler can remember and will want time after time
	Pretend play such as having a conversation on a toy phone
	Talk to the child about the marks they make and the colours they may have used
	Point to familiar written words that occur naturally such as signs on doors, or when outside or on an outing
	Reading, singing, rhymes, clapping hands, etc.

Walkers, talkers and pretenders (24–36 months)
All as 18–24 months plus:

Aspect of development	Suggested activities
Social and emotional	Fantasy or imaginative play, for example pretending to be someone else either in the child's family or someone from a TV series or film
Intellectual, including creative skills	Dressing up with a supply of materials such as hats, pieces of material and bags

Even a young baby will have preferences for some activities rather than others. It is important to observe the response to an activity and adapt or change it if necessary.

The development of ideas and views is also rapidly happening at this age. Think carefully about avoiding stereotyping activities, even for young babies. Do not think in terms of boys' or girls' activities.

■ *Remember to give praise and encouragement*

Think about it

Listen to most adults with a baby or young child. When any degree of a new skill is shown, the adult will usually exclaim something on the lines of 'My word... aren't you a clever girl' to which the baby laughs and does it again. This is an excellent example of learning through reinforcement!

Did you know?

Observations of carers with young babies shows that boys are often handled much more firmly than girls and have the opportunity for more 'rough and tumble' play than their sisters.

All the basic principles of encouragement and supporting the building of self-esteem apply to young babies as well as older children. Always remember during play to:

■ praise

■ support

■ encourage.

Babies and young children, unless actively discouraged by adults or not given appropriate opportunities to explore their surroundings, are curious about everything. Motivation is not a problem! However, the role of adults is to provide safe opportunities for babies and young children and to give praise and encouragement so that their positive attitude remains. They will then continue to grow and develop in the best way they can.

During any developmental phase, you will want to encourage children while they are 'practising' a new skill and also help them to move on when they seem to have mastered the skill. For example, when they learn to walk they will have to practise a great deal before they can confidently walk away on their own. Children need practice and support in order to progress.

New and challenging activities

Everyone needs some challenge and babies and young children are no different. A challenging activity is one that is just a little bit more difficult than what the child is able to do at any one time. Activities that are challenging help to extend a child's knowledge or skills, in other words to fulfil more of the child's possible potential. The key factors that help babies and young children achieve more of their developmental potential are:

- to be given activities, which 'stretch' their current knowledge or skills a little further
- to be motivated to try something new
- to be encouraged by adults
- to receive praise and encouragement
- to be successful through their own efforts.

Placing an attractive toy just out of reach can encourage the newly crawling baby to make an extra effort, as can simply getting down to the child's 'floor level' and encouraging the child to come to you. The important thing is to observe, to find out what interests the child and to find out what development stage the child may be reaching so that you can support the child in the best way possible.

Procedures and practice

Babies and young children need to be kept safe while they are learning all their new skills of rolling, crawling, pulling to stand, etc. There will be a health and safety policy in your placement and you must be aware of this. You must also make sure that you understand the potential risks in your environment.

Special care is needed when babies start to crawl or shuffle. Just imagine, for around eight months or so they have been limited to looking at things in sight or reliant on others to bring things to them. All of a sudden they can move and reach all those interesting looking objects. A baby does not know that many of them may injure and hurt.

Think about it

Where is your setting's health and safety policy? Are there any special requirements for the care of young babies?

Check the rooms in your placement. Can you spot any potential danger areas or safety issues?

Make sure any activities you are involved with follow your placement's plans and check them with your supervisor.

Assessment activities

In this part of the unit you have to show that you understand how to provide play activities to encourage learning and development.

Assessment Activity 11

Identify and choose five play activities to support different aspects of learning and development. These areas of development and learning need to include the following:

- gross and fine motor development
- hand and eye co-ordination

- language development through listening and responding
- emotional expression and social competence
- intellectual skills and understanding
- imagination and creative skills.

continued ▶

Assessment Activity 12

Linking with the five activities identified and chosen for Assessment Activity 11, you now need to show how to provide these activities. You must include descriptions of the following:

- resources needed for the activities
- ensuring that activities are inclusive and value diversity
- meaning of challenge
- link between challenge and developmental progress
- ensuring that activities are challenging but achievable for the individual child
- helping babies and children to choose activities that meet their identified needs and interests

- importance of monitoring individual responses to different activities
- why it is important to give praise, support and encouragement
- importance of following procedures and practice regarding safety and risk assessment
- ensuring that activities are in line with the overall plans of the child care setting.

When you have completed Activities 11 and 12 you will have met the requirements for Pass criterion 5 (P5), for which you must identify five different play activities that help to support different aspects of learning and development.

Assessment Activity 13

You should explain (describe in detail) what is meant by challenge in play activities. This will enable you to meet Merit criterion 3 (M3).

7.4 Know how to communicate with babies and children under three, interpret their needs and respond to them

This section covers:

- development
- responding to children
- talking to parents.

Development

Babies need their carers to help them survive – without carers to feed them, change them, keep them warm and safe and provide them with bodily contact, babies would not survive very long. To make sure their carers know they need something babies need to communicate. Babies' first vocal communication is crying. The pitch seems to be particularly useful for attracting the attention of adults who (usually) quickly go to find out what is wrong, soothe and comfort. As a result of this, babies begin to make relationships with their carers. Babies learn about the world through what their carers do and the opportunities they give to babies to look at and feel objects.

Children all over the world develop the major features of communication skills by the time they are three or four years old. When they start school children can vary speech to suit the social occasion, know the meaning and pronunciation of thousands of words and use correct grammatical formats. So how does this amazing process take place?

At birth a baby's brain and senses are programmed for the task of acquiring language. Babies can hear before birth – they respond to noises while in the uterus.

Early language

A child's first words usually start around the time he or she takes his or her first steps. This is the same all over the world in all societies. The period before a baby starts to use words is called the pre-verbal stage – a baby is finding out how to communicate long before he or she says its first words.

This is through:

- gazing into the eyes of carers
- being sensitive to the emotional tones around them

Did you know?

Some researchers have shown that babies as young as 42 minutes can imitate someone sticking out their tongue. These babies watch and then, with a bit of effort, stick out their tongues too!

Think about it

Go back to Unit 1 page 17 and have another look at the chart outlining the sequence (order of) language development from birth. What do you think the most important thing is that you can do to support communication at each of the stages?

- 'turn-taking' in conversation by gurgles and other sounds
- making their needs known by crying, responding etc.
- babbling which later blends into early speech.

Talking and interacting with babies and young children helps them to socialise, to get to know other people and to learn about themselves. Babies learn from the way other people behave. It is very upsetting for babies if the adult they are with does not talk to them, turns away from them, pays attention to someone else and so on. They do not know the reasons and work very hard to try to get the adult's attention.

Age	Language and communication skills
Pre-linguistic or pre-verbal stage	**Birth to 12 months**
Birth to 4 weeks	Cries when basic needs require attention, for example hunger, tiredness, distress
1 month	'Freezes' when a bell is rung gently close to the ear, moves head towards the sound
	Stops crying at sound of human voice (unless very upset)
	Coos in response to carer's talk
3 months	Becomes quiet and turns head towards sound of rattle near head
	Vocalises when spoken to and when alone
6 months	Makes singsong vowel sounds, for example 'aah-aah', 'goo'
	Laughs and chuckles and squeals aloud in play
	Responds differently to different tones of voice
	Starts to respond to noises out of sight with correct visual response
9 months	Vocalises for communication, shouts for attention
	Babbles loudly and tunefully using dual syllables in long strings, for example 'dad-dad', 'baba', 'mam-mam'
	Imitates adult vocal sounds, for example coughs, smacking lips
	Understands 'no' and 'bye-bye'
	Has instant response to a hearing test conducted 1 metre behind child, out of sight
1 year	Knows own name
	Jargons loudly in 'conversations', includes most vowels sounds
	Understands about 20 words in context, for example cup, dog, dinner, and understands simple messages, for example 'clap hands', 'where are your shoes?'

continued ▶

Age	Language and communication skills
Linguistic stage	**12 months onwards**
12–18 months	First words appear – uses 6–20 recognisable words, understands many more
	Echoes prominent or last word in sentences
	Tries to join in with nursery rhymes
	Responds to simple instructions , for example 'fetch your shoes', 'shut the door'
18–24 months	Uses two words linked together
	Uses more than 200 words by two years
	Makes simple two-word sentences
	Refers to own name, talks to self during play
	Has telegraphic speech, that is, is using key essential words and missing out connecting words
2–3 years	Rapidly expanding vocabulary, including plurals
	Holds simple conversations
	Enjoys repetition of favourite stories
	Counts to ten

Think about it

Watch a parent or a colleague talking to a young baby. Notice how the adult gives the baby time to 'reply' and so keep up a conversation.

Best practice in your work placement

Supporting the development of communication

- Always give a baby your full attention or include them in conversations. Conversations with colleagues can wait until later.
- Watch, listen and respond to the baby.
- Talk aloud to the baby as you are doing something.
- Use simple gestures to support what you are saying.
- Make sure that the tone of your voice, the rhythm (how 'up and down' your voice goes), the pitch (how high or low) and the tempo (how quickly or slowly you speak) change as you speak to make you interesting and help the baby work out sounds.
- Talk and sing to and with the baby.
- Make sure that your facial expression matches your mood. Babies will look at your face and see a smile, a frown or a blank expression and they will sense your mood and respond to it. (Research has shown that babies show distress or worry when their normally responsive carer suddenly shows a very still or blank face.)
- Pay attention to what a baby is 'saying' to you by his or her responses.

- Take time to let the baby respond to you – they learn about turn-taking in the two way 'talking' and listening they do with a partner.
- Copying what a baby does helps to establish a 'dialogue' so that they can imitate and be imitated.
- Help an older baby or child to learn about the names of objects, colours etc. by naming them in a natural way, for example 'Oh look at the black dog/the red bus,' and so on.
- Repeat an older child's phrases without correcting to both check that you understand and to help the child hear the usual way of sentence construction, tenses.
- If English is not the first language, find out some phrases in the child's home language to encourage continuity between home and the setting. This will illustrate that the home language is valued and will support bilingual learning. Parents' views must also be taken into account.

Other methods of communication

Some children may be visually or hearing impaired. They require special attention to ensure they do not miss out on communication and learning. It is vital that all staff respond to the child's cues which signal a need for interaction or to explore. Think about:

- opportunities to involve touch in communication for blind children

- visual cues for deaf children, careful positioning of the head and body so that the baby or child can clearly see mouth movements and eye direction, will be very important

- making sure that lighting is good to maximise the child's vision

- using exaggerated facial expressions to support meaning

- making sure noise levels in the room are not disruptive

- using games, such as peek-a-boo, or 'round and round the garden' where the same actions are repeated which is suitable for all children but especially for a deaf child.

Sign language

Young children who are deaf may well be learning an alternative form of communication. The earlier sign language is taught, the more 'natural' and fluent the signing.

There are different sign languages such as:

- BSL – British Sign Language

- ASL – American Sign Language

Different countries have their own sign language but some movements are common to many, such as a headshake meaning no. Men and women may use different signs and there are regional variations in signing for the same objects.

A signing method known as Makaton is often used instead of BSL with people with learning difficulties. Makaton also uses speech alongside signing. This method helps children to link a word to an action or object and is an aid to communication.

BSL is a language with its own grammar and is used fluently by deaf people. In the UK, Makaton signing is based on BSL; it takes the signs from BSL. As with spoken languages, where there are regional variations of dialect and accent, there are also variations in the signs that are used throughout the UK. The signs from BSL matched to Makaton have been standardised to those used in the South East/London region. This standardisation is to avoid confusion for Makaton users if they move around the UK.

Source: Makaton website

Have a look back at Unit 3 Communication. Do you remember the section on non-verbal communication? Babies and young children are very good at picking up non-verbal communication. You do not have to say anything for a baby or young child to recognise that you are feeling sad, angry or happy.

Learning how to respond to children's communication is important for any child but for babies it is even more important. Most parents quickly learn what the different cries of their baby mean:

- hungry
- tired
- in pain
- nappy needs changing
- bored
- in need of a cuddle.

Test yourself with a baby you are caring for: what are they telling you? What happens if you do not respond correctly?

With toddlers it can be very difficult to interpret their speech as they are learning to talk. Sometimes adults 'guess' what a toddler has said to them.

It is quite common for parents to be able to understand their child's early attempts at talking when other people cannot. If you are talking to parents about progress in communicating be careful about general principles of talking to parents – you are a student! However conversations about a child's general communication skills can be positive in terms of how much more vocal they are – they are trying to communicate and practising language, even if it is difficult to understand!

Parents will have been consulted regarding any intervention programmes and specialist help via speech and language therapists. If parents would like their child to use sign language, carers will also need to learn basic signs to support the child. As with all other matters involving parents you should pass on information about a child's communication skills or otherwise to your supervisor. It is perfectly acceptable to pass onto parents that their child has said a new word today but never to tell them, as a student, of any concerns.

Think about it

Imagine asking for some carrots in a shop and being given some flour instead. Imagine that happening again – feeling angry and frustrated?
That is exactly how young children feel when they cannot make themselves understood. It is vital you can see when you have got it wrong and try other methods of understanding.

Assessment activities

Assessment Activity 14

You need to describe the sequence in which communication develops from birth to three years as well as how and why babies communicate from birth and the pre-verbal stage.

continued ▶

Assessment Activity 15

You should describe the importance of using recognised language formats and non-verbal forms, such as Makaton, when this is appropriate.

Assessment Activity 16

Why is it important to recognise and reward communication efforts in babies and young children to encourage language development?

Assessment Activity 17

Describe:

- a range of different communication methods
- responding to pre-verbal speech
- identifying needs from the communication of babies and young children
- other methods of communication when meaning is not clear
- recognising and responding to behavioural reactions to communication failures
- talking positively to parents about children's progress with communication.

Having completed these activities you are now ready to meet Pass criterion 6 (P6), which requires you to describe the different methods used with babies and young children under three years.

Assessment Activity 18

You can now go on to meet Merit criterion 4 (M4), which requires you to explain (describe in detail) how to interpret needs and respond to children and young babies.

Assessment Activity 19

Moving on to Distinction criterion 2 (D2), this requires you to evaluate (describe how worthwhile or not) the range of methods used in communication with babies and children under three to ensure that understanding is taking place.

8 Providing support for children with disabilities or special educational needs

Introduction

It is likely that in any placement you may work in, or in future work settings, you will work with children with some type of special need. This may be a disability or learning difficulty or a combination of both. It is arguable that the majority of people have some type of special need and that every child should have attention paid to their individual needs. Some children, however, present a greater challenge to those who care for them in terms of ensuring that they can take part in the full range of activities and experiences available in the child care setting. Their families also need support.

This unit will help you to gain the knowledge and understanding to help you to support children with disabilities or special educational needs.

In this unit you will learn:

1 how to support a child with disabilities or special educational needs

2 how to help the child to take part in activities and experiences

3 how to support the child and family according to the procedures of the setting.

8.1 Know how to support a child with disabilities or special educational needs

This section covers:

- disabilities and care needs
- information and care needs
- interactions
- legislation and Codes of Practice.

Disabilities and care needs

Did you know?

In the United Kingdom in 2002/2003 1.4 million pupils were identified as having special educational needs.

Many people have a special need of some kind. If you are short-sighted and use spectacles you have a minor disability that can easily be dealt with. Special needs range from a mild disability to significant physical disabilities and/or learning difficulties. It is important that you approach the task of meeting specific needs in the right way, which is to look at every child's individual needs and celebrate the diversity. It is society's responsibility to provide an environment and facilities that everyone can access, and to ensure that no one is excluded because of some physical or intellectual feature. All children have the right to access a broad and balanced curriculum.

The Special Educational Needs Code of Practice states that children with special educational needs should normally have their needs met within mainstream schools or early years settings.

All children need to be treated as individuals, with attention paid to all specific needs. Disability and special educational needs encompass a wide range of differing needs.

Knowing about the exact cause of disability or special educational needs does not really matter to people involved in the support of a child. As a child care worker you will be more concerned with how a child's development is affected and the support needed to help him or her towards the maximum independence. There may be specific physical needs that a child has or certain characteristics of some syndromes or conditions. The assessment that a child has should detail the areas of development and learning that require additional support that should lead to a plan for that child.

There are some approximate groupings of disability and special needs that show some indication of the needs that may be supported but this does not exclude the importance of considering every child individually.

■ Physical disability may cause problems with co-ordination and/or mobility, for example cerebral palsy.

■ Chronic (long-term) diseases and terminal illnesses include conditions such as **cystic fibrosis** or serious heart defects. There may be medical care requirements including medication and other treatments.

■ Learning difficulties (both learning disabilities and specific learning difficulties) may be moderate to severe or specific, such as **dyslexia**. May require additional support for learning in the classroom.

■ Loss of sensory abilities includes the impairment of vision or hearing. Will require special adaptations and alternative communication methods.

■ Emotional and behavioural difficulties include mental illnesses or hyperactivity and attention deficit disorder. May need support with medication and attention to planning and support.

Some children may have needs that fall into two or more categories. A child who has cerebral palsy may have a physical impairment, communication difficulties and also be a gifted child. A child who has a long-term illness may also be affected by dyslexia. A child with Down's syndrome may have a long-term heart condition and learning difficulties.

Information and care needs

The causes of disability and special educational needs fall into several categories that roughly cover prenatal (before birth) and post natal (after birth). However, for many children with learning difficulties and disabilities, there is no clear cause, for example **autism**.

Cause	Example	Possible effects
Before birth		
Inherited or genetic, for example chromosome abnormality	Down's syndrome	Heart problems
	Haemophilia	Low intelligence
	Brittle bone disease	Bleeding easily into joints, soft tissues
	Cystic fibrosis	Bones break easily, causing deformities to limbs
	Achondroplasia	Lack of vital enzymes in digestive and respiratory system, causing problems with breathing and digestion
		Very short arms and legs, resulting in small stature
Drugs taken during pregnancy	Thalidomide	Missing and shortened limbs
	Alcohol	Foetal alcohol syndrome
	Heroin	Addicted baby may be small for its age
	Nicotine	Small for dates, chest problems, for example chest infection

Cause	Example	Possible effects
Environmental: local to mother, for example vitamin deficiency General, for example radiation, pollution (often difficult to specify cause)	Spina bifida Early childhood cancers Toxocaris (from dog and cat faeces)	Lower limb paralysis, hydrocephalus Variable Blindness
Illness of mother in pregnancy	Rubella	Heart malformations, blindness and deafness
During and after birth		
Birth injury	Lack of oxygen to brain, trauma to limbs or head from forceps	Cerebral palsy – gross motor skill and sensory delay, poor fine motor skills Learning difficulties/disabilities Weakness of arm or leg
Illness of child	Meningitis Polio Otitis media	Learning difficulties/disabilities Paralysis Deafness or hearing impairment
Accidents and injuries	Home or motor accidents	Brain injury, paralysis Delayed development, physical injury or disability

■ *Causes of disabilities and learning difficulties*

Parents are often the best source of information about a child's needs and any conditions a setting needs to know about. If you are working with a child with a disability or special educational needs in your placement talk to your supervisor about the information that is known about the child. If there is a particular syndrome or condition affecting the child, then there are several sources of information available for you to research. These include Contact a Family which has an extremely good reference section covering many different conditions. You can find out more about Contact a Family by visiting their website, www. cafamily.org.uk.

Most major syndromes and conditions have their own associations and websites. The resource section on page 327 has a number of details, for example the British Deaf Association, Cystic Fibrosis Trust and British Dyslexia Association.

Following plans and procedures

Many children with specific needs will have an individual education plan (IEP). These plans have usually been developed by a number of professionals who are working with the child and may include targets for a number of areas of development. This is a short-term plan that focuses on aspects of a child's development. It is a useful tool because activities are chosen specifically to support the child.

Think about it

Choose a condition or syndrome that you have heard about or that affects a child you know. Find the association for that condition and have a look at the material available on its website.

It is usual for individual learning plans to be drawn up in consultation with parents. In many cases, it is the person who works closely with the child who puts the plan together, although in some settings this can be done by the person who co-ordinates special educational needs.

The plan usually consists of three or four targets for the child's development and also contains some activities and strategies that are to be used with the child. The plan is then reviewed using information gained from observations and from parents.

It is important to ensure that a child's plan is followed. Make sure that you talk to your supervisor in placement to ensure you are aware of any plans affecting children you work with.

Name: Omar   DOB: 26 March 2001

Area/s for development: Hand eye coordination

Start date: Jan 10th 2006

Review date: March 25th 2006

Early years key worker: Yasmin Ahktar

Targets to be achieved	Criteria for achievement	Resources/ techniques	Group strategies	Support/ assistant	Outcomes
1. To manipulate objects into place.	1. To complete a 12 piece puzzle.	1. Range of puzzles – 6, 8 and 12 pieces.	1. Have range of puzzles out in free play time.	1. Demonstrate how to complete part of puzzle – support and encourage.	
2. Independent hand-washing	2. To wash and dry own hands.	2. Water, soap and towel.	2. Focus on hand washing after pre-lunch toilet visits.	2. Encourage Omar to wash own hands – help to achieve and praise when successful.	

Parent's contribution:

Work with Omar on puzzles and other manipulative activities at home. Encourage progress to hand washing skills.

Parent's signature:

Practitioner's signature:

■ *Example of a child's individual education plan*

If you know a child has an individual plan, ask if you can read through it and think how you could use it to adapt or plan activities. Some settings show how the main curriculum plan is adapted to meet the needs of individual children. Others record the adaptations onto their activity plans. Using a plan to adapt an activity to suit the needs of the child will make sure that activities are used to help a child make progress and will avoid a child becoming frustrated because he or she cannot manage an activity.

Best practice in your work placement

How to meet children's individual needs

- Find out from colleagues about a child's individual needs.
- Use observations to help you work out how best to help a child.
- Ask your supervisor if you can develop an activity to work towards the child's plan.

- Make sure that your work supports a child's individual plan.
- Adapt activities in order to meet children's individual needs.

Case study

The importance of reading children's individual plans

Omar is five years old. His individual education plan for this term focuses on improving his hand-to-eye co-ordination. Jess is new in this placement in a primary school. A small group of children have been painting and are moving onto story time. Omar is proudly showing her his hands but Jess notices that he still has lots of paint on his hands although he is supposed to have washed

them. She tells him that he must go and wash them again as he has not done a very good job.

1 Why is it important to find out about children's individual needs?
2 How might Jess have responded differently with Omar if she had read his IEP?
3 Why was Jess's response to Omar not good practice?

It is important to be sure you know if you should be recording and reporting a child's progress in an activity you are carrying out with them. Even as a student your observation of success or not is important to pass onto the person responsible for a child's plan. The outcomes are recorded as a result of everyone's contribution. It is important to check this out and pass on your findings, however trivial you may consider them.

Overcoming communication difficulties

Children have communication difficulties for a number of reasons. They may be due to:

- sensory issues – hearing, speech, vision
- cognitive – difficulty understanding.

Imagine not being able to tell someone what you want or being able to understand what is happening. It is the same for children, as difficulties in communicating their needs or in not being able to understand what is happening, can make children feel frustrated and isolated.

In the next section you will be thinking about different ways of communicating with a child with communication difficulties. Make sure you have found out how every child you work with communicates best if this is a feature of their development. Ask your supervisor or the child's key worker.

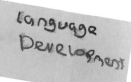
Language Development

Interactions

There are several ways a child may be helped with their communication. The best method will depend on the reason for the difficulty. Technology has opened up communication to children for whom it was very slow and tiring to get their messages across to people. Have a look at the chart below.

Method	Features	Comments
Language partner	Extra time with an adult to boost and develop language and communication skills. Should be fun for the child and can be done alone or with a small group	
Hearing aids	For children with permanent hearing loss	
Visual systems Picture Representations and picture exchanges	Pictures of objects, seen in most nurseries and primary schools Exchanges used by child taking picture of something they want to do, for example, a cup; the adult asks if they want a drink and the child then responds	Helps children to understand the meaning of words, and with exchanges about how communication is a shared and two way process
Voice simulation	An electronic system – by pressing a picture or typing a word a voice is produced to 'say' the word. Can be used to hold conversations	Good for people who have difficulty articulating language, for example with some forms of cerebral palsy
Sign representations, for example Makaton	Not a language in itself but a tool to help language. For example, a child who wants a drink cups the hands as if holding a beaker. The adult responds by saying 'Did you want a drink?'	Can be useful for children with cognitive disability
British Sign Language (BSL)	A complete language used instead of speech	BSL is often a first language for a deaf person, their 'home' language. English or Urdu, for example, could be their second language

■ *Ways to help children with their communication*

As with any work with children the key is to be sure that the form of communication is the best for the child. Communication is a fundamental right for everyone. A method of communication can only

Think about it

Find out if staff in your placement have skills in alternative languages or support systems. How many are used?

be the best for a child if everyone around them can also use it. Adults working with children with communication difficulties need to be fluent in the supportive or alternative forms that are used by the children.

A child learning to use an alternative form of communication needs as much reinforcement, praise and encouragement as a child who is learning to speak. Remember that a child using an alternative form of communication will not have the amount of reinforcement and example as a child hearing everyday speech does. It may have been relatively late in their communication development before the best method was identified.

As always, you need to check how much a child can understand and adjust your communication with them accordingly. Remember, in some cases a child may understand far more than they can communicate back to you.

Case study

Communication

Ella aged ten has cerebral palsy. She uses an electronic wheelchair to get about and has a voice synthesiser for communicating. Ella is a very bright girl and has full hearing and cognitive skills. She is pretty fast at using her synthesiser but it is not as fast as she would like it to be and she gets very frustrated when people break off conversations with her or worse still speak very slowly and as though she were only five years old.

Why do you think some people do not communicate appropriately with Ella?

Think about these points for good practice in alternative forms of communication – not all points are relevant for all communication difficulties. Which do you think would apply to Ella?

Best practice in your work placement

- Check that you have the child's attention before speaking.
- Make eye contact with the child.
- Acknowledge the child's communication positively.
- Do not correct the child's speech if they are using speech.
- Speak clearly and adjust your language to suit the child's age and ability.
- Do not speak extra loudly.
- Do not put your hand over your face.

- Be expressive with your speech and body language.
- If a child is lip reading make sure that you face into the light so that your face can be clearly seen.
- Identify the topic of conversation early on, for example point at what you are talking about.
- Use props, pictures and visual aids to support your speech as appropriate.
- Learn as many of the signs and methods used for communication as you can. Take a course if possible.

■ *A relaxed situation will help children who are affected by stammering*

Stammering is a communication difficulty that can affect a child's confidence badly. It affects the fluency in children's speech and so is also known as dysfluency. Many children between the ages of two and three years stammer as their speech is developing but this is usually temporary. For some children, however, stammering becomes more permanent. When they are relaxed, a child affected by stammering can often speak more fluently. Situations that cause the child to feel nervous, excited or tense are likely to cause stammering.

A child who stammers can be helped by:

■ avoiding situations when all the focus is on the child, for example circle times

■ making sure that the child feels that you have plenty of time for them, sit down and make eye contact

■ reducing the speed at which you talk to help the child to relax and speak more slowly

■ avoiding asking direct questions

■ never finishing off the child's sentence to 'help' or letting other children interrupt.

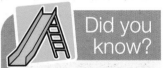

Did you know?

Pictures can be an excellent way to communicate with all young children. They are also a good way for parents to see what is happening. A series of pictures showing the routine of the setting can be used create a 'visual timetable' that shows the routine, for example pictures of children arriving and taking their coats off, snack time and home time.

Legislation and Codes of Practice

There are a number of laws and codes of practice that have placed the rights of adults and children with a disability or special educational need in the important place they should be which is alongside all other people. It is important that you are aware of the legislation that forms the basis of equal opportunities practice, but legislation is not enough. What is important is how you work with children to ensure that those from all backgrounds are recognised and their cultural needs met. You are a role model for the children you work with, so you have a responsibility to act in a non-discriminatory way and to promote equal opportunities. Sometimes this is not easy; you may observe practices and actions that are discriminatory, but never feel that it is acceptable to do so yourself. You should have the courage to challenge or at the very least report to a supervisor any such action.

The Disability Discrimination Act 1995

The Disability Discrimination Act (DDA) 1995 is designed to prevent discrimination against people with disabilities. The DDA 1995 covers access and provision for disabled people in the following areas:

- employment
- access to goods, facilities and services
- letting or selling land or property
- education
- public transport vehicles.

The Special Educational Needs and Disability Act (SENDA 2001)

The Special Educational Needs and Disability Act (SENDA) 2001 strengthens the rights of parents and children to access mainstream education. It also extends the DDA 1995 to educational settings. In England and Wales this Act is particularly important as it is enforced by the Special Educational Needs (SEN) Code of Practice 2001.

The Disability Rights Commission

This Commission was set up by the Disability Rights Commission Act 1999. The Commission has the power to conduct formal investigations and to serve non-discrimination notices and take other actions to prevent discrimination against people with a disability. If parents felt their child was being treated unfairly, they could take the case to the commission for investigation.

Think about it

Read your placement's policy for children who have additional needs.
Who is responsible in your setting for co-ordinating the policy?

Human Rights Act

This Act came into effect in October 2000. Under this Act, children's rights were further strengthened. The main features are the right to education and also the prohibition of discrimination. This Act has helped to shape further legislation. For example, all children now have the right to attend a mainstream school. Children who are sent to 'special schools' when their parents want them to attend mainstream school could argue that they are being discriminated against.

Models of disability

Laws and policies reflect society's views and attitudes. As a result of campaigning by organisations, the rights of children who have disabilities or special educational needs have been improved.

For many years disabled people have had to fight for their rights because of the attitude of many people that disabled people were 'different' from other people and did not have the same rights. Although this is not how most people now think, there are still some cases which occur where people have been denied their rights purely because they are disabled.

Over recent years society has moved forwards towards a more **social model of disability** that recognises the rights to make choices and be independent. It also challenges society to become more inclusive so that disabled people are not seen as being 'problems that need sorting out' or 'victims that need pity'. The social model recognises that any problems of disability are actually created by society. If someone is a wheelchair user, problems are caused not by the wheelchair but by the fact that some buildings do not have ramps and that buses are difficult to access. The solutions to problems of disability are therefore in society's hands, and involve changing the attitudes of the able-bodied.

Attitudes like this stem from a **medical model** of disability. The medical model of disability is an oppressive way of thinking about people. Disability is seen as something that must, whenever possible, be cured and treats people with impairments as victims and patients. It focuses on the disability the person has, rather than his or her abilities and can label a person as someone who is 'wheelchair bound' rather than someone who uses a wheelchair.

Think about it

Can you think of examples in the papers or on TV where a person has been refused something you take for granted, just because they are disabled? For example, a group of blind people were not being allowed on a plane to their holidays because they were allegedly a health and safety risk.

Case study

Discrimination

Joseph and David are 16 and have been friends since they were four years old. They both went to the same primary school and used to play football together. Even now they spend a lot of their spare time together as they are both keen fans of the same football team. At secondary school they are competing with each other to get the most GCSEs. Two years ago Joseph fell out of a tree they were both climbing and broke his back. As a result, Joseph is now a wheelchair user. Going to football matches with David has become very difficult. Although the ground has space for his chair it is not in the same place as they used to have their seats and the toilets can be difficult for Joseph to get to. Last night they went out to watch a basketball match at the local

sports centre where Joseph had to sit in a 'special' place for disabled people and he felt very uncomfortable. The main spectator area was up a flight of stairs. One of Joseph's teachers was surprised to hear that he is planning to go to university 'now' as she wonders how he will cope.

1 Why is Joseph being treated differently to David?
2 What should be done to stop this discrimination for Joseph?
3 How would you feel in Joseph's situation and in David's?
4 What view of disability do many of the people around Joseph have?

Did you know?

In 2004 the government launched a strategy to remove barriers to achievement for people with special educational needs and disability. All agencies involved are expected to work together to ensure that children and young people with disabilities or special educational needs are supported to access all their rights and entitlements to a full life.

Source: The government's teachernet website

Principles and issues

There are a number of key principles and issues that are important to the whole idea of the social model of disability. It is important that you understand them and become familiar with their principles if you want to work in children's development and learning.

Inclusion

Inclusion means looking for ways of helping children to join in who would traditionally have been excluded from settings or activities. Instead of expecting children to fit in with what you are doing, it means looking at what you are doing and checking that it meets with all children's needs. Staff have to be ready to adapt activities, change routines and sometimes even alter the layout of the setting so that children can join in. Inclusion is something to think about for all children if they have been at risk of 'exclusion' for any reason, for example age, race, gender, disability.

The policy of inclusion is a controversial one for some parents. In some areas, parents have opposed the closure of special schools as they are unsure whether providing mainstream education will best suit the needs of their children. On the other hand, other parents have fought hard to get their children into mainstream education.

Inclusion is important because it is fair. It means:

- that all children have the same chances to play and learn

- that children do not have to be segregated from others just because they are not 'the same'

- that groups of children learn that all people are different, all are special and yet all have some similar needs.

■ *Inclusion allows all children to have the same chances to play and learn*

Integration

Integration refers to how children with disabilities or special educational needs are included in mainstream settings.

Special educational needs (SEN) is used to describe children who need more help than others in order to learn or to access the curriculum. Some parents dislike their children being labelled or categorised as they feel that this will disadvantage them as others may treat their children less favourably.

The term **disabled** is used when a person with impairment faces restrictions as a result of their impairment. It is a difficult term as it can lead to labelling. A child with a hearing loss is not disabled when doing a jigsaw puzzle, but might be disabled if he or she cannot lip-read the person reading a story. The danger with any term is that people tend to jump to conclusions about what a person can and cannot do.

Using language to describe disability

Some language used about disability is offensive. It reflects attitudes that date back to when the medical model of disability influenced thinking, when disability was seen as the problem rather than the way society integrates people.

Ideas on appropriate language can change so you should make sure you keep up to date. Remember that it might not be the word itself that is offensive but the way it is used. For example, 'handicap' refers to the disadvantage that the person has compared to other people but the term 'handicapped' was frequently used in the past to describe the person. This is no longer acceptable. Some people regard the term 'disabled' in the same way.

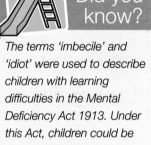

Did you know?

The terms 'imbecile' and 'idiot' were used to describe children with learning difficulties in the Mental Deficiency Act 1913. Under this Act, children could be permanently removed from their families. This is why these terms are considered to be offensive.

Terms to avoid	Terms that are preferred
Handicapped person	Disabled person
Invalid	Disabled person
Wheelchair bound	Wheelchair user
Sufferer, victim of, crippled by, afflicted	Person who has…
Spastic	Person with cerebral palsy
Mongoloid, mongol	Person with **Down's syndrome**
Mental handicap	Learning difficulty
Congenital	Genetically impaired
Disabled toilet	Accessible toilet

■ *Terms used to discuss disability*

Labelling

Words and terminology can also be a label. Labels help to reinforce stereotypes and, in turn, prejudices. If a child has a label people can then start to assume certain characteristics to him or her.

No one likes to be viewed only according to what you look like, cannot do or need. When you talk about children, you should always check that you are not labelling them according to their needs. There are some important pointers to consider:

- children and adults should not be labelled for their disability or need

- attention should not be drawn to a child's disability, difference or condition unless it is relevant

- listen carefully to the language that a child's parents use

- check with support organisations the terms that are currently being used.

Case study

Children with a disability

Tomar, aged seven, was born prematurely after a pregnancy of 30 weeks. As a result of problems during his delivery, Tomar has cerebral palsy. He uses a wheelchair to move around and a voice synthesiser to communicate. Although he cannot play sports, Tomar loves watching football, and enjoys playing games related to football. Tomar and his friends spend a lot of time together playing games at weekends. School swimming sessions are his favourite time. With the support of a personal assistant, Tomar attends a mainstream primary school and is looking forward to moving to senior school with his friends.

Lorna, aged six, was also born with severe cerebral palsy and relies on her wheelchair to move around. Her parents were never encouraged to hope that Lorna could attend a mainstream school. She attends a special school with children who all live a long way from Lorna. Lorna's parents are not happy to let her visit the one friend she has nearby as they worry she will not cope without them. Although Lorna loves shopping, her parents do not take her very often as it is hard work, and they find it difficult to cope with people staring at her. They think that Lorna will eventually live in a residential unit with care assistants looking after her.

Compare these two children, both with similar physical difficulties, and think about why they have different lifestyles.

Assessment activities

Assessment Activity 1

Describe a range of different disabilities or special educational needs that can affect children. You should include the following:

- Down's syndrome
- Autism
- Asperger's syndrome
- Spina bifida
- Haemophilia
- Cystic fibrosis.

Describe the care needs of children with these disabilities and what a child's individual plan consists of.

When you have completed this activity you are ready to cover Pass criterion 1 (P1), which requires you to outline (briefly describe) a number of disabilities or special educational needs that affect children and relevant care needs.

Assessment Activity 2

You can then consider Merit criterion 1 (M1), which requires you to explain (describe in detail) how the care needs of a child with a disability or special educational need can be met.

Assessment Activity 3

Draw up a list of the current legislation such as the Disability Discrimination Act 1995 and the relevant regulations and Codes of Practice affecting provision for children who are disabled or have a special educational need. You should include here how to refer concerns about a child according to the procedures of a child care setting.

You can now meet Pass criterion 2 (P2), which requires you to identify current legislation and relevant codes of practice affecting provision for children who are disabled or have a special educational need.

Assessment Activity 4

Write notes about how to communicate effectively with children who are disabled or have a special educational need. Ensure you include the following:

- verbal and non-verbal communication
- giving praise and reward for a child's efforts and achievements
- sensitivity to a child's age, needs and abilities

- having realistic expectations
- not labelling or stereotyping children
- alternative communication through the use of all the senses.

You are now able to meet Pass criterion 3 (P3), which requires you to identify ways of interacting effectively with children who are disabled or have a special need.

continued ▶

Assessment Activity 5

You can also now go on to explain (describe in detail what, how and why) the value of different methods of communication when interacting with a child with a disability or special educational need.

This will enable you to meet Merit criterion 2 (M2), which requires you to explain the value of different methods of communication when interacting with a child with a disability or special educational need.

8.2 Understand how to help the child to take part in activities and experiences

This section covers:

■ methods.

Methods

Observations

You have seen in Unit 1 that observations are a vital tool in work with all children. Have a look back at the detail about observations in Unit 1 to remind yourself of the different types. Observing and keeping records are just as essential in supporting children with additional needs. As well as looking at children's progress, observations also help to identify any barriers to children's progress and activities. They can help to work out how best to adapt activities for particular children. Observations can also provide information for other professionals involved in a child's individual plan.

Barriers to participation in activities

There are many potential barriers to children taking part in activities just because they have a disability or special educational need of some sort. It is important to understand what these are and then think about how they might affect particular children.

Think about it

Imagine being deaf and five years old and sitting in a circle with a group of children listening to a story. You can see the adult's lips moving and the other children laughing or looking interested but you cannot understand what they are enjoying.

Type of barrier	Impact	Ways to overcome
Communication, for example hearing, speech or visual loss, learning disabilities, mental health	Loss of communication and understanding	Hearing aids, voice synthesisers, alternative forms of communication
Physical, for example narrow doors, steps Toys that are too small Tables at the wrong height	Unable to get into buildings, rooms, access equipment and activities	Building adjustments, ramps Adjustable tables Large-scale equipment
Attitudes of adults, for example not offering an activity believing a child cannot do it Lack of thought as to how to change the activity in order that the child can still have a go Believe that it is up to children to 'fit in' rather than for activities to be changed	Loss of self-confidence Devaluing of child Denied opportunities	Training Planning Codes of conduct
Lack of specialist equipment or adaptations, for example inferior quality or wrong wheelchair Basic synthesiser instead of sophisticated version	Limitations in access, communication etc.	Referral to appropriate agencies, support groups to access correct equipment

■ *Barriers to children taking part in activities*

Think about it

Think about a child that you work with in your placement. Make a list of the potential barriers to the child's participation in the setting. Then, for each item on the list, explain how your placement aims to remove the barriers.

Removing barriers to children's participation

Inclusion means making sure that all children can have access to the same opportunities. This sounds easy, but in practice it means identifying possible hurdles or barriers that children face. Barriers due to attitudes are the hardest to deal with as many people have long held views that can be difficult to change.

Codes of practice can help people to behave in the appropriate way, but cannot affect outside views of people that may affect a child in everyday life.

Many aids and pieces of equipment are used to support children who have physical needs. These are usually recommended or provided by the services that are supporting the child and the family. It is important to learn how and when to use any piece of equipment. You should consult with parents or the professionals who have recommended the equipment and of course follow manufacturers' instructions. In some cases, children themselves will be able to talk through or demonstrate the equipment!

All child care workers have a responsibility to promote the rights of all children; especially those who may find themselves discriminated against in some way. It is important for child care workers to ensure that a child is not discriminated against in terms of the opportunity to reach his or her full potential. Look at these three examples.

- Jodi has hearing difficulties and as a result her speech has been delayed. She experiences communication difficulties unless

■ *Playing with hand puppets helps with communication*

alternative methods of communication are considered. When her group at nursery has story time, the nursery nurse always makes sure that Jodi sits at the front and that the story has a lot of visual appeal, using puppets, pictures and miming.

■ Samir has cerebral palsy, which means he has difficulty in controlling his movements without shaking. Playing in the home corner was difficult because it was a small area and Samir tended to knock things over. His teacher has relocated the home corner so that it is in a bigger area and Samir can now play safely in it.

■ Wheelchair users may have difficulties in playing outside with other children, unless ways are found to overcome obstacles. Rajeet has difficulty getting into the playground as access is up two small steps. However, he can move very quickly once in the playground in his lightweight wheelchair. With the help of one of the staff, Rajeet's friends have invented a new form of football that allows him to use his arms instead of his feet.

There are many other ways to overcome difficulties. It is essential to structure activities and opportunities for the entire group of children in your care, taking needs into account. All children can benefit when activities are adapted, such as making story time a wider experience and learning new ways of playing traditional games.

Adapting equipment for children with special needs

Sometimes special equipment may be needed to allow children with special needs to practise and develop all their skills:

■ a child who has poor fine motor skills and difficulty with fine hand and eye co-ordination may benefit from the use of thicker pencils and other tools

■ children with delays in developing gross motor skills (large body movements such as walking or running), or sensory problems (vision, hearing, etc.) may enjoy large-scale toys such as ball pools and soft foam cushions

■ a child with a visual impairment may be able to read large-print books, books written in Braille or Moon and will enjoy listening to stories recorded on tape.

Some centres are equipped with multi-sensory rooms that provide opportunities for children with a wide range of specific needs. These rooms feature a range of lights, sounds, smells and touch sensations that stimulate (or in some cases soothe) the senses. Any activity, game or toy designed to develop an aspect of a child's skill should aim to allow the child to use the skills that already exist and encourage him or her to extend them. For example, when a child reaches the stage of being able to turn the pages of a book, make sure the child has books with thick pages, showing pictures of interesting objects.

Sometimes there is no need to adapt equipment, but you may need to change your methods of promoting an activity. A child who has difficulty sitting still for long will struggle to take part in a modelling activity lasting 15 minutes. Think about how you can adapt the activity; you could sit with the child and keep up the encouragement or ask to look at his or her progress at frequent intervals. You could give the child some responsibility for drawing all the children's efforts together for a display. This may help to prevent the child's behaviour becoming unacceptable.

Encouraging positive behaviour

Imagine never being the object of positive attention, but only of negative attention, in other words constantly being shouted at, told off and punished. This is not ideal attention, but it is attention and for some children it is better than none. For many children with behaviour problems this is the cycle they have got into. From their first entry into nursery some children become known as the 'naughty one', and their reputation sticks. I am sure this sounds familiar to you. A child who does not 'fit' into the mould of accepted behaviour for some reason, for example with special learning needs, is even more at risk of being labelled.

■ Children whose behaviour does not 'fit' into expected patterns are often 'excluded' by both adults and other children. They may be told by other children that they cannot join in the game or an adult may sit them at a different table during an activity. Excluding children in this way only creates further difficulties.

■ Unwanted behaviour may be a signal to a child's unmet needs. Children who show attention seeking behaviours are saying that they need more attention. Children who bite and are aggressive to other

Think about it

You are in charge of a group of eight energetic five-year-olds; five girls and three boys. Samir is slower than the others in walking due to a condition affecting his muscles. Paul doesn't like rough games and is reluctant to join in groups. Lucy likes any game that is noisy and rough, but she broke her arm last week and has it in plaster. The weather has been wet and windy all morning and now the sun has started to shine. The class teacher asks you to take this group outside and organise some exercise for them in the grounds of the school for half an hour.

How would you plan your half-hour to include all of the children? What play and exercise would you provide, and what would the benefits be for the children?

children are telling you that they do not have the skills or understanding to play with them.

- Many unwanted behaviours, especially aggressive acts, are signs of frustration. A child might bite another because the child cannot tell the other child that he or she wants that toy too. In the same way, a child may deliberately throw all the pieces of a puzzle on to the floor because the child knows he or she cannot do it.

- A child who is not enjoying a situation or is bored may look for ways of changing it. In the same way a child who cannot see anything that they want to do may go and disrupt another child's game.

- Some children find it hard to remember the rules. They may know that they have to wait in one situation but will not do so in another similar situation. Some children's cognitive level may mean that they do not understand the need to wait and share or have no understanding about possessions.

- Changes in the child's life can often affect their behaviour. Examples include a new baby in the family, moving house, parents separating or rowing, access visits by absent parents, a poor night's sleep, illness or a new teacher or class. Any change in routine can upset a child. A child with a disability may have lots of changes in routines if she has medical or health needs.

Remember, all children are naturally curious and enthusiastic! Children learn by trying things out, but some adults may view this as naughty. Child care workers need to know what a child understands at different ages.

For example, a newly mobile baby learns by experimenting. For months they have only been able to observe the world around them. That fascinating black box on the table has a slot in it that the baby's mother puts another box into. How natural to see if the sandwich left on a plate while the baby's mother answers the door also fits into the video recorder! Obviously there are serious accident risks here as well, as the same curiosity can be extended to pulling that curly wire leading to the kettle or iron.

Children will generally behave positively if treated positively. This means praising and encouraging the behaviour that you want and giving children attention when they are behaving 'well'. The more children understand the reasons for wanting them to do things and they are shown attention and respect, the more they will want to please. It is far preferable to be told you are doing well and someone is proud of you than to be told off and told you are useless.

■ Show children how to behave by example. They learn by copying, and this applies to behaviour just as much as anything else.

■ Keep rules simple and minimal and let older children help to make the rules.

■ Be positive – tell children what you want them to do, not what you do not want.

■ For children who find it hard to play with other children, show them how to do it.

■ Set routines so that children know what is expected of them and when, and they will feel secure.

■ Praise and encourage children.

■ Listen to what the children have to say.

■ Consider whether activities are causing frustration and are not matched to the child's abilities and needs. Look out for multi-sensory activities or ones where the child is active.

■ Only make demands that are reasonable for children's ages and situation. Remember that when children are ill or tired their needs change.

■ Do not shout or use physical force. Physical force is illegal for a child care worker and harmful from parents. Shouting achieves nothing other than having to shout louder next time.

■ Use diversion tactics with very young children. Distract them with a new activity or interest. Negotiate and explain the reasons to older children.

■ Remember to laugh whenever possible – it often helps to defuse a situation.

■ Plan ahead so that children are busy and have sufficient adult attention so that they do not need to use inappropriate behaviour.

Case study

Scribbling on the wall

Harry wandered into the room and saw the big fat crayons on the table. He went over to pick up the red one. He looked around for a second and then started to scribble on the wall. At that moment, Harry's mother came into the room.

1 Was Harry being 'naughty'?

2 If you knew Harry had special educational needs, would your opinion be the same?

3 How would you deal with the situation?

Assessment activities

Assessment Activity 6

Ben has spina bifida and he has just started nursery. Find out ways in which you can help Ben to take part in activities and experiences. These should include the following:

- sensitive observation to identify any barriers to participation in activities
- offering alternatives if required
- adapting activities, experiences, environment, for example furniture, in consultation with others, in order to enable Ben to take part
- safe use of any specialist aids and equipment if these are needed
- encouraging Ben to take part in a positive manner.

You are now ready to meet Pass criterion 4 (P4), which requires you to outline ways to help children to take part in activities and experiences.

Assessment Activity 7

You can now go on to explain (describe in detail) how a child with a disability or special educational need can be helped to take part in activities and experiences. This will enable you to meet Merit criterion 3 (M3).

Assessment Activity 8

Following Activity 7, you can evaluate (describe how worthwhile or not) ways of helping a child with a disability or special educational need to take part in activities and experiences. This will enable you to meet Distinction criterion 1 (D1).

8.3 Understand how to support the child and family according to the procedures of the setting

This section covers:

- partnership
- support.

Partnership

Children belong to their families. They spend the majority of their time with their families and these are the people who are likely to be the most familiar with a child's individual needs. Remember this important fact about any child and that working in partnership with families should be an automatic process.

Parents have usually learned how best to help their child and will have developed strategies that support the child. Many parents will also have researched extensively in order to work out how to help their child, especially where the child has a medical or physical disability. They may have contacted support organisations, seen other professionals and met other families with similar circumstances.

Parent partnership services

In most areas, services are being established to help parents get support and information. They can be called a variety of names. In England, the local education authority is required to provide these services. The aim of these services is to provide a link between the settings that care and educate children and the parents. They can help parents get their views across and step in if communication between parents and settings is difficult.

The Special Educational Needs Code of Practice 2001

The Special Educational Needs (SEN) Code of Practice 2001, which is used in England, outlines seven key principles when working with children. Many of these are based on partnership working with families. These principles are based on good practice and are worth reading even if you do not work in England. Staff in settings working with children with special educational needs work to this Code.

1 Acknowledge and draw on parental knowledge and expertise in relation to their child.

   This principle recognises that parents will usually be able to share some valuable advice, thoughts and strategies with practitioners.

2   Focus on the children's strengths as well as areas of additional need.

This principle is about remembering that children are 'whole people' and are not problems that need curing or sorting out. Think about the language you are using and also about how it might sound if it was said to you.

3   Recognise the personal and emotional investment of parents and be aware of their feelings.

Parents love their children unconditionally and see them as valuable. They may be very protective of their child and may not be in full agreement about some aspects of plans for them.

4   Ensure that parents understand procedures, are aware of how to access support in preparing their contribution and are given documents to be discussed well before the meeting.

Meeting with parents and working through individual learning plans is an essential part of supporting children. This principle is about making parents feel at ease and ensuring that they can properly contribute to a meeting.

5   Respect the validity of differing perspectives and seek constructive ways of reconciling different viewpoints.

This principle is about understanding that parents are entitled to their own opinions about what is best for their child.

6   Respect the differing needs that parents themselves may have, such as a disability or communication and linguistic barriers.

Some parents may have particular needs that may prevent them from contributing. Inclusion means thinking about parents' needs and looking for ways of meeting them. This might mean translating documents, encouraging parents to bring along a friend or putting up a travel cot so that a baby can be brought along to a meeting.

7   Recognise the need for flexibility in the timing and structure of meetings.

This principle reminds you that parents may have jobs, difficulty with transport or other commitments. Partnership with parents means looking for times that everyone finds convenient, not just you.

Think about it

Ask your supervisor how your placement works to the Code of Practice.
What sort of polices and procedures are based on it?

The impact of having a child with additional needs within a family

All parents find pleasure and challenges from having children. Being a parent can be fun, challenging and loving as well as stressful and tiring. Parents who have disabled children or children with additional needs are no different, but they may have some additional challenges.

Just as every child is different, the impact of having a disabled child or a child with additional needs is different for every family. There are some common factors that parents may experience and that have been the subject of studies.

Can you think of reasons why parents of a disabled child have to spend more money? Think about household costs, food, transport and clothing.

Financial

Research has shown some significant facts about the finances of families with a disabled child. Mothers and fathers of disabled children are less likely to work and when they do their earnings are likely to be lower than parents without a disabled child. The causes for this may include problems of suitable child care, visits to hospitals, therapists or sometimes illness.

Parents of a disabled child spend on average twice as much on comparable categories of expenditure as parents whose children do not have a disability despite the fact that parents of disabled children have incomes well below the national average.

Effect on the family

Some families can feel isolated. They may not get invitations out for a variety of reasons, they may not have transport or the place where they are going might not be equipped for their child. Some parents also find that other people are not able to accept and cope with their child. This can also affect other children in the family.

Finding time can be the hardest thing for some parents. While most children are demanding in terms of time when they are small, they gradually become independent. For some parents, supervising their child and meeting his or her needs can be constant. This means that they may not have time to talk, play and relax with their other children or partner.

Family breakdown is much more common among families with a disabled child. As a result, many parents are lone parents which puts greater strain on the sole carer.

Worry about the future

All parents worry about their children. For some parents, their worries are financial or they have concerns about the next steps for their children, especially after their death. Other parents try not to look too far into the future and take each day as it comes.

Positive impacts

It is also important to stress that many families find that there are positive impacts that make having a child who has additional needs extremely special. Some families find that they develop strong networks of friends, some of whom have children with similar needs to their own. Often the child's other siblings learn about caring and gain in maturity and confidence. Finally, some families find that their child brings them great fulfilment and helps them to appreciate things that other parents may not notice.

Support

Involving family members

Supporting any child should be a shared experience between all involved partners. Most child care settings welcome parents to support and help their child. When a child has a disability, workers should be seeking advice from parents about the most effective way to support them. Changes in plans, activities and support need all partners to work together. You should observe this in your placement and see staff planning activities to include parents wherever possible.

Feedback to the child and parents

Feedback to the child and parents is important. Children who are given frequent positive feedback on their activities and behaviour will want to carry on receiving praise and encouragement. Praising children, or in some cases giving them something tangible such as a sticker, is effective. This also helps children to learn how to gain adult attention appropriately.

Recording children's progress

Some children with special educational needs may not be able to communicate effectively with their parents about what they have been doing. If a specialist transport service is used to support the child, parents may not be coming into the setting very often. It is important to make sure that parents are kept in close touch with the daily routine and achievements of their child.

There are many ways this contact can be encouraged:

- daily record book
- photographs using digital cameras
- encouraging use of child's own method of communication, such as picture representation etc.

Your placement will have a procedure for ensuring the most effective means of contact for each child. Make sure that you record progress where appropriate or pass on information to the person who will do it.

Think about it

Find out the procedure for keeping parents in contact with their child's activity at your placement.

Specialist local and national support groups

As a student in placement, your main source of support will be your supervisor or tutor. However, in the future when you are working in a child care or learning environment you may need to seek support yourself. There are many sources of support and information for the families and workers with children with additional needs including:

- early years teams
- local support groups
- national support groups
- health professionals
- social services
- educational psychologists
- SEN teachers
- internet
- toy libraries.

Think about it

Find out what facilities are available in your local area for children who have special educational needs.

National support organisations

National organisations, such as Epilepsy Action provide a range of services. They not only provide support for children and their families, but also produce information for the general public. Some organisations provide helplines and leaflets and also run training courses for professionals. Many organisations aim to raise public awareness and may campaign for better services and rights for children. National organisations will often have a website where you can access information. A very useful starting point is the Contact a Family website that has links to many specialist organisations. These can be found at www.cafamily.org.uk.

Local support groups

Local support groups are often organised by parents who find it helpful to meet with others and share experiences, information and advice. You should be able to find out about what is available in your local area from the library, education department or more easily from parents.

Professional support

A child with a disability or special need may have a number of different professionals involved with their support. Requirements under 'Every child matters' are putting more importance on all agencies working together. There has been this expectation for a long time but local authorities are now going to be judged on how well this is happening. It is very easy to see the benefits of joint working for one child as they may be using services from:

- health
- social services
- education.

■ *Local support groups can be helpful for parents*

Professionals from these services may be able to give additional information, strategies or advice to help a setting and parents work more effectively with the children. In some cases, they may also need a setting to assist them by working in particular ways with children.

The table below outlines the roles of some of the principal services that are usually available.

Service	Role
Speech and language team	Speech and language teams include speech therapists. They assess, diagnose and work out a programme of exercises to help children's communication and speech.
Sensory impairment team	Many education services have a team dedicated to helping children with a visual or hearing impairment. They may visit homes and settings to advise on how best to help the child and how to use equipment effectively.
Health visiting service	Health visitors are trained to promote health across all age ranges in the local community. Health visitors can provide advice for parents about care and development.
Occupational therapy service	**Occupational therapists** support by assessing for the equipment and adaptations that will help to maximise physical movements and development. In many areas there are specialised occupational therapists who work with children.
Physiotherapists	Physiotherapists work directly with children and their parents to provide exercises and movements that will help the child to strengthen an area of the body or reduce the impact of a medical condition.
Social services	Social services support children and their families by providing funding and support to meet children's needs. Children who are defined as 'in need' because their needs are complex and severe are likely to have a **social worker** assigned to them. Respite care, a service which allows parents some time off, is usually organised by social services.
Early years services	Advice and support can also be gained from early years services that are connected to the education department of the borough council. Early years teams usually have experienced practitioners who may visit and advise a setting.
Educational psychologists	Educational psychologists are professionals who have been trained to assess children's development and learning. They identify children's needs and help parents and professionals meet them. Parents with concerns about children's learning or behaviour can refer children to educational psychologists, as can professionals with parents' consent. Educational psychologists often watch a child in the setting in order to build a picture of how the child is coping, as well as seeing the child separately. They are then able to give advice and suggest a programme to assist the child.
Toy libraries	Toy libraries lend large and small toys and equipment to families and also to organisations. They usually stock equipment that meets the needs of children with sensory impairments.

Think about it

Think of a child in your setting who has additional needs. Make a list of possible sources of support and information about the child's particular needs.

Contact details for organisations that can provide helpful advice on working with children with additional needs are provided in the Useful contacts section on page 327.

Assessment activities

Assessment Activity 9

Write notes about partnership with parents. You should include the importance of parental and family knowledge of the child and the effects upon a family of having a child with a disability or special educational need. Planning for a child's individual requirements with both colleagues and parents should also be covered.

You can now meet Pass criterion 5 (P5), which requires you to describe the impact (that is, the effect) a child with a disability or special need might have on a family.

Assessment Activity 10

You also need to write notes about how to support the child and the family.

Your notes should include:

- helping family members to take part in activities
- giving feedback to the child, the family and to other adults about the child's progress
- recording progress of the child according to procedures

- seeking help from others when information and support is needed, for example professional support
- finding out abut specialist local and national support and information for children and families.

You can now meet Pass criterion 6 (P6), which requires you to outline the ways in which support can be given to the child and the family.

Assessment Activity 11

You can now go on to explain (describe in detail) how working partnerships with parents can help to support the child and the family. This enables you to meet Merit criterion 4 (M4).

Assessment Activity 12

You can now evaluate (describe how worthwhile) ways of supporting the family of a child with a disability or special educational need. This enables you to meet Distinction criterion 2 (D2).

Useful contacts

ADD/ADHD Family Support Group
1a The High Street
Dilton Marsh
Westbury Wilts
BA13 4DL

Association for Spina Bifida and Hydrocephalus
42 Park Road
Peterborough
PE1 2UQ
01733 555988

www.asbah.org

British Dyslexia Association
98 London Road
Reading
RG1 5AU
0118 966 827

www.bdadyslexia.org.uk

British Dyspraxia Foundation
8 West Alley
Hitchin
Herts
SG5 1EG
01462 454986

www.dyspraxiafoundation.org.uk

Coeliac UK
PO Box 220
High Wycombe
Bucks
HP11 2HY
01494 437278

www.coeliac.co.uk

Cystic Fibrosis Trust
11 London Road
Bromley
BR1 1BY
020 8464 7211

www.cftrust.org.uk

Diabetes UK
10 Parkway
London
NW1 7AA
020 7424 1000

www.diabetes.org.uk

Disability Rights Commission
DRC Helpline FREEPOST MID0216
Stratford upon Avon
CV37 9BR
08457 622 633

www.drc-gb.org

Down's Syndrome Association
155 Mitcham Road
London
SW17 9PG
020 8682 4001

www.downs-syndrome.org.uk

Duchenne Family Support Group
37a Highbury New Park
Islington
London
N15 2EN

Hyperactive Children's Support Group
71 Whyke Lane
Chichester
PO19 7PD
01803 725182

www.hacsg.org.uk

National Asthma Campaign
Providence House
Providence Place
London
N1 0NT
020 7226 2260

www.asthma.org.uk

National Autistic Society
393 City Road
London
EC1V 1NG

The National Deaf Children's Society
15 Dufferin Street
London
EC1Y 8UR
020 7490 8656

www.ndcs.org.uk

**National Federation of Families with
Visually Impaired Children**
c/o Queen Alexandra College
49 Court Oak Road
Birmingham
B17 9TG

National Toy and Leisure Libraries
68 Churchway
London
NW1 1LT
020 7387 9592

www.natll.org.uk

SENSE
11–13 Clifton Terrace
Finsbury Park
London
N4 3SR
020 7272 7774

www.sense.org.uk

SCOPE
6 Market Road
London
N7 9PW
0800 800 333

www.scope.org.uk

Sickle Cell Society
54 Station Road
Harlesden
London
NW10 4UA
020 8961 7795

www.sicklecellsociety.org

Glossary

Abuse: deliberate injury or harm to another person, particularly vulnerable people e.g. children, older people and people with disabilities. The abuse can be physical, emotional, sexual or neglect.

Adaptations: changes made to the arrangement or design of a building, piece of equipment or an activity ensuring it is inclusive.

Adolescence: the period of development leading to adulthood – starts at puberty. A period of rapid physical growth and development.

Adoption: the legal transfer of a child from their birth family to another family.

Anorexia nervosa: an eating disorder in which severe and potentially dangerous weight loss occurs. Approximately 50 percent of all patients need hospital treatment, with between 5–10 percent dying as result of the condition.

Antibodies: proteins produced by the body in response to foreign substances such as bacteria and viruses (also called antigens). Antibodies circulate in the blood and 'attack' any specific antigens.

APGAR: a scoring system used to assess a newborn baby. Breathing, heart rate, colour of the skin (especially hands and feet), muscle tone and response to stimuli are measured at one minute and again at five minutes after the birth.

Asthma: a constriction or narrowing of the airways that causes wheezing and coughing – often due to an allergen, exercise, pollution or emotion.

Attachment: the very early relationship of a baby with his or her primary carers. Also known as bonding.

Attention Deficit Hyperactivity Disorder (ADHD): a condition in children which affects their behaviour. They are unable to concentrate, sit still for periods of time, are easily distracted and have short attention spans.

Autism: a condition that disrupts the development of a person's communication and social skills, resulting in difficulties in making sense of the world. Some of the common features include difficulties in coping with change, communication and social relationships and lack of creative pretend play in children. Some people with autism can show high levels of skills in some aspects of life such as numeracy. The condition has no known cause or cure.

Bacteria: very small micro-organisms. Some types of bacteria are essential to maintain good health, but others are harmful and cause disease.

Balanced diet: a diet that contains all essential nutrients, in the right amounts, for good health and development.

BCG: a vaccination used to protect against tuberculosis.

Bedtime rituals: are regular behaviours or activities that children enjoy at bedtimes. These can be useful in settling a child to sleep e.g. a bedtime story or saying goodnight to favourite toys. In some children the activity can be very long and delay bedtime settling.

Behaviour: the way people act and conduct themselves in certain situations. Behaviour is often identified as 'good' or 'bad' depending on the situation and the expectations of those involved. For children appropriate behaviour is linked to their age and stage of development.

Behaviour policies and procedures: these set out what sort of behaviour is expected of the children, and what will happen if they do not behave in the accepted or appropriate way

Bilingual: this refers to children, or adults, who can fluently speak two languages.

Birth to Three Matters: Government directed framework to promote a child's development from birth to three years. Should provide the basis for planning care and development activities with this age group

Body language: a way of communicating thoughts, feelings and attitudes without words e.g. turning away from someone to show that you do not want to speak to them.

Bonding: *see attachment*

Brittle-bone disease: an inherited condition in which the bones are very easily broken. A baby suffering from this condition may be born with broken limbs, and can fracture bones through normal handling.

Bulimia: an eating disorder in which the sufferer constantly over eats and then self induces vomiting. This often occurs in secret and can have the same long-term effects as anorexia.

Bullying: threatening, intimidating and harassing behaviour by one person towards another. It can involve name calling, aggression, demands for money or acts of violence

Caesarean section (c-section): the delivery of a baby by a surgical operation. The baby is removed through a cut in the mother's abdomen into her uterus. The procedure is used if the baby is in distress in labour or for other medical reasons.

Carbohydrates: are the main energy source in the diet – contained in sugar, pasta, potatoes or rice.

Carpet time: a time when children, usually in primary school – particularly Foundation Stages – sit down and share their news. It is used to encourage communication and sharing of worries.

Centile chart: are charts used to record a child's weight and height as compared with standard growth rates of other children.

Cerebral Palsy: a condition caused by damage to the developing brain during pregnancy, birth or early post natal. Movements, posture and communication are affected in varying degrees.

Child protection: a term used to describe the guidelines produced to promote and safeguard the safety of children. It covers child protection conferences, assessment orders, the Child Protection Register and Children in Need.

Childminder: offers care for children in his or her own home. Registered by OFSTED, all childminders are trained and regularly inspected to ensure they are maintaining high standards of care and education.

Children and Young Peoples Plan: the document produced from April 2006 by local authorities in England to show their plan to work with other relevant agencies to meet the five outcomes of Every Child Matters (qu) for children and young people in their area.

Circle time: *see carpet time*

Cold cooking: cooking with children that does not require heat – by use of a hob or oven.

Colostrum: the fluid produced by the breast during pregnancy and the first days after delivery. It contains low levels of fat and sugar and high levels of antibodies to provide the ideal first food for a newborn.

Commission for Racial Equality (CRE): commission set up following the Race Relations Act (1976) with the aim of working towards the elimination of discrimination, monitoring the act and taking legal action against breaches of the act.

Confidentiality: the respect for the privacy of any information about a child, parent or other client – a founding principle of care. It is supported by the Data Protection Act (1998).

Convulsions: a reaction of the brain to certain stimuli, resulting in uncontrollable shaking, rigid limbs and sometime short-term loss of consciousness. In babies and young children convulsions are a common response to a very high temperature. It is also a feature of epilepsy.

Culture: refers to shared rituals and practices that give a particular group – society or family, a sense of identity.

Cystic fibrosis: a hereditary condition that causes problems with the absorption of fats and nutrients from food as well as chronic lung infections.

Disability: a long-term condition affecting a person's physical or mental ability to carry out normal activities of daily living.

Disability Rights Commission (DRC): an independent body established to help eliminate discrimination against people with disabilities and to promote equality of opportunity.

Discrimination: a term used to describe situations in which a person, or group of people, are not treated as fairly as others based on judgements of gender, sexual orientation, lifestyle, religion or culture.

Diversity: recognising and valuing differences between individuals and groups of people.

Desirable Learning Outcomes (DLOs): the minimum curriculum requirements for children aged four years, covering early literacy, numeracy and a range of personal and social skills.

Down's syndrome: a congenital condition that results in delayed development, characteristic facial features and often heart problems.

Dysentery: a bacterial infection of the digestive tract resulting in severe vomiting, diarrhoea and pain.

Dyslexia: a specific learning difficulty affecting literacy and/or numeracy.

Early Learning Goals: targets given in the Foundation Stage curriculum for children to reach by the end of their reception year.

Emergency Protection Order: a court order that gives a social worker the power to remove a child, who is thought to be in danger, from their parents or primary carers. The order lasts for up to 8 days and gives parental responsibility to the social services.

Emotional development: the development of a child's identity, self image and the development of relationships with others.

Equal Opportunities Commission (EOC): an organisation set up to enforce laws relating to sex discrimination, promote equality of opportunity between men and women and propose reviews and amendments to legislation.

Equal opportunities policy: policies and related procedures that ensure equal and fair access to employment, services regardless of gender, sexuality, race, religion, class and age.

Every Child Matters: the government's response to ensuring that all services supporting children and young people work together to the best effect. Local authorities must work closely with health, education and training, social services and the voluntary sector to meet children's needs and show how this is happening in their 'Children and Young Peoples Plan'. The plan is written to cover five outcomes affecting a child's life; Being Healthy, Staying Safe, Enjoying and Achieving, Making a Positive Contribution, Economic Well Being. Services for children and young people must also ensure they are meeting the outcomes.

Fats: needed for energy, absorption of vitamins: A, D, B and K, to protect organs in the body and provide insulation, are an essential component of a balanced diet.

Fibre: fibrous material found in many vegetables, fruit, wheat and oat products — essential to stimulate the bowel, by providing bulk to the faeces.

Fine motor development: movements of the hand and wrists.

Foster care: the care of a child by appointed foster carers.

Gastroenteritis: (see dysentery).

Genetics: the study of the factors relating to inheritance.

Gluten: a protein found in some cereals, especially wheat. It can cause an allergic response in some people resulting in digestive problems.

Gross motor development: development of movements that involve the use of a whole limb such as sitting, standing or walking.

Haemophilia: an inherited gender-linked condition resulting in an inability for blood to clot. Cuts and bruises can be potentially life threatening and suffers require transfusions of the missing clotting factor to stop the bleeding.

Halal: a particular way of killing animals for consumption as prescribed by the Muslim faith.

Harassment: any unwelcome conduct, verbal or physical, which has the intent or effect of creating an offensive environment or situation.

Health visitors: registered nurses who have undertaken further training in preventative health. Usually based at a GP's surgery, health centre and Sure Start schemes, health visitors monitor and promote the health of babies and young children and older clients. They also work closely with other child agencies in child abuse cases.

Holding therapy: a method to manage a child's outburst of temper. The child is calmly but firmly held by an adult until the child is calmed, followed by a cuddle to reassure the child.

Immunisation: the activation of an artificial immune response by giving someone a very mild or dead form of a disease-causing bacteria or virus. The body is then stimulated to produce antibodies which will protect the body from a live version of the disease.

Incubator: a special crib that controls the temperature and oxygen content around a baby who is very ill or premature.

Independence: the ability to control all ones' own activities and lifestyle without support from someone else. Children gradually move towards independence as they become able to feed, wash and dress themselves and start to make their own decisions.

Infection: a condition caused by contact with a disease-causing organism, such as bacteria, virus or fungus, leading to signs and symptoms of the illness.

Inspection: examination by experienced trained professionals of the practices and services in a particular setting. Early years settings are inspected by OFSTED inspectors who ensure that children in the setting are well cared for and receiving appropriate educational input.

Letdown reflex: the response of a woman's breasts to suckling at the start of a breast feed, or sometimes when her baby starts to cry. Milk production in the alveoli starts and travels 'down' into the milk ducts.

Meningitis: inflammation of the meninges in the lining of the brain caused by bacteria or viruses. It is most common in children under five years and can be fatal or cause serious disability.

Milestones of development: skills that are looked for as children develop, usually linked to age.

MMR: a vaccination to prevent against Measles, Mumps and Rubella.

Nanny: a person employed to care for a child in that child's home. There are no requirements of registration or training for nannies that only care for the children of one or two families.

National Children's Bureau: a charity that promotes the interests of children and young people.

National Curriculum: government standards ensuring all children are taught the same basic curriculum. There are four key age-related stages, each with tests (SATs) to ensure all requirements of that stage have been met.

National Society for the Prevention of Cruelty to Children (NSPCC): a voluntary organisation with powers to act in the care of children and their families. It employs qualified social workers and works closely with the statutory social services and the police.

Natural immunity: the bodies' natural response to illness or disease.

Non-accidental injury: the act of deliberately causing physical harm, can include burns, fractures, bruises, head injuries and poisoning.

Nutrients: the vital components of food that provide the necessary requirements for a healthy functioning body.

Observations: watching a child, or group of children, with the aim of commenting on an aspect of his or her development or behaviour.

Occupational Therapist (OT): a professional working with children and adults with particular needs that requires specialist equipment or support.

OFSTED: the organisation which inspects, monitors and reports on the performance of schools, nurseries and childminders.

Orthoptist: a professional specialising in the treatment of visual defects, prescribing eye exercises and monitoring the progress of the condition.

Otitis media: an infection of the middle ear. Common in young children as the Eustachian tube – tube from the ear to the throat – is often very narrow and easily blocked by mucous.

Post-natal depression: a psychological disorder affecting a new mother in the weeks after her delivery. It involves feelings of worthlessness, sadness, anxiety and being overwhelmed by motherhood. Severity ranges from a relatively mild form (baby blues) treated at home, to severe psychosis needing hospital treatment

Prejudice: making negative judgements about other people based on stereotypes or assumptions

Protein: nutrient in food that helps with the growth and repair of cells. Found in meat, beans, nuts, dairy produce and fish

Puberty: the period between childhood and adolescence. A rapid increase in hormone production results in the development of secondary sexual characteristics such as breasts pubic hair, and the onset of menstruation.

Racism: negative attitudes and behaviour towards people from another racial group. Racism can be both obvious and subtle using behaviour, words or practices which advantage or disadvantage people because of their skin colour, culture, language or ethnic origin.

Reasonable adjustments: changes that have to be made to enable a person with a disability access to a service or facility.

Salmonella: a bacterial infection resulting in severe gastroenteritis.

Sexism: discrimination or unfair treatment on the grounds of someone's gender.

Social workers: qualified professional who work with individuals and families with arrange of problems. They operate in the voluntary and statutory service.

Socialisation: lifelong process starting at birth, of learning about yourself and how you fit into the wider world. There are three types: Primary socialisation – within the family; secondary socialisation – formed with friends and peers; tertiary – relationships with other groups in society.

Special Needs Co-ordinators (SENCO): the person in a setting who co-ordinates and oversees the setting's Special Needs Education policy.

Standard Attainment Tests (SATs): tests that measure the achievement of children at the end of each key stage of the National Curriculum.

Statutory services: health and social care services provided as a requirement by the law of the country.

Sudden Infant Death Syndrome (SIDS): the sudden, unexplained death of an infant between three and twelve months, also known as cot death.

Sure Start: a multi-agency (health, social services and education) programme to improve the start in life available to children from deprived areas.

Turn taking: an obvious pause in 'conversation' when a baby intently watches his or her carer talking to them, the baby will then respond with facial responses and vocalisations.

United Nations Convention on the Rights of the Child: the statement by the United Nations setting out the rights of all children and young people throughout the world.

Vaccination: *see immunisation*

Vitamins: essential for general health required in small quantities and available in a range of foods. Some are fat soluble – Vitamins A, D, B and K – the rest are water soluble.

Weaning: the process by which a child transfers from a purely milk diet to that of a normal family diet. This process takes place over a number of months through various stages of sloppy and mashed foods.

Index